The Sky Detective takes you on an amazing journey through the years before and during revolutionary Iran through the eyes of a young girl. A seeker of knowledge from a young age, she confronts the limits of the world she is given to transcend societal rules and limitations to find her true calling. I loved watching this book evolve, and celebrate how it enlightens us all to follow our dreams."— **Linda Joy Myers, President of the National Association of Memoir Writers, and award winning author of Don't Call Me Mother—A Daughter's Journey from Abandonment to Forgiveness.**

How a girl's memoir, growing up in a chaotic time of a revolution, takes you softly into the realm of innocent beauty is the miracle of "The Sky Detective." — **Parviz Sayyad, Highly Famed Actor and Director of Iranian Cinema**

A compelling debut memoir by an accomplished geophysical scientist that offers a vivid look at life in Tehran between 1973 and 1982, before and after the Iranian Revolution...Filled with details of day-to-day life, this volume offers a unique perspective on a country and a people that remain shrouded in mystery for most Westerners. An authentic firsthand account of troubled times in a tumultuous country. — **Kirkus Reviews**

An accomplished, award-winning American atmospheric scientist recounts her coming of age against the backdrop of the Iranian revolution in this engaging and deeply perceptive memoir...In crisp, compelling prose, Tabazadeh peppers her account with memories of school and other childhood preoccupations, even as the country undergoes major political upheaval...Readers of all stripes will appreciate a front seat to the proceedings in The Sky Detective. — **Blueink Reviews (starred review)**

D0367054

An Iranian scientist, whose accomplishments include a presidential award and working for NASA, shares her enticing story...Her childhood story as she tells it is solidly crafted. The writing is strong, the pace engaging...Over the years, Tabazadeh learns many lessons that are punctuated with both tinges of sadness and humor...Those who gravitate toward true-life coming-of-age tales will enjoy this book. Those who know little about Iran during this time period will appreciate the blend of history with the author's experiences. Most of all, though, those who come to care for the girl will want to know more about the woman. — *Clarion Foreword Reviews (four out of five stars)*

The Sky Detective:

A Memoir

AZADEH TABAZADEH

THE SKY DETECTIVE: A MEMOIR

Copyright © 2015 Azadeh Tabazadeh.

All rights reserved. No part of this book may be used or reproduced by any means, graphic, electronic, or mechanical, including photocopying, recording, taping or by any information storage retrieval system without the written permission of the author except in the case of brief quotations embodied in critical articles and reviews.

iUniverse books may be ordered through booksellers or by contacting:

iUniverse
1663 Liberty Drive
Bloomington, IN 47403
www.iuniverse.com
1-800-Authors (1-800-288-4677)

Because of the dynamic nature of the Internet, any web addresses or links contained in this book may have changed since publication and may no longer be valid. The views expressed in this work are solely those of the author and do not necessarily reflect the views of the publisher, and the publisher hereby disclaims any responsibility for them.

Any people depicted in stock imagery provided by Thinkstock are models, and such images are being used for illustrative purposes only. Certain stock imagery © Thinkstock.

ISBN: 978-1-4917-6060-4 (sc)
ISBN: 978-1-4917-6062-8 (hc)
ISBN: 978-1-4917-6061-1 (e)

Library of Congress Control Number: 2015902183

Print information available on the last page.

iUniverse rev. date: 09/21/2015

In memory of Najmieh

For Modjtaba and Azar,
with love

Contents

Author's Note..ix

The Science Prize... 1

The Chemistry Kit... 6

Meeting Najmieh.. 18

An Unusual Present.. 27

A Road Trip to Shomal...................................... 32

A Memorable Encounter..................................... 41

Khanoom Ashrafi 53

The Summer of Hell 72

Black Friday: The Aftermath............................... 91

Revolution Madness 107

Under the Ayatollah's Spell 123

The Hostage Crisis.. 132

The Iraq War 140

Grandma's Last Wish 151

The Escape 168

Escapades in Madrid.. 203

The Sky Detective 229

Acknowledgments 233

Author's Note

This book is a recollection of my memories as I recall them. I have changed names to protect the identities of individuals still living in Iran. My sister and brother, Afshan and Afshin, have similar names, so I have changed my brother's name, Afshin, to Jahan to avoid confusion between the two. I have also left out or glossed over some people, whom I love dearly, to focus the story on events and interactions that have shaped my life.

This sky where we live is no place to lose your wings, so love, love, love.

—Hafiz, the famous poet of Persia

⟡ The Science Prize

My stomach knots as I glance at an audience of more than seven thousand people gathered in the grand ballroom at the Marriott in San Francisco. This year, I've been selected by the American Geophysical Union to receive a prestigious science medal. Thank God I'm not alone up here on the stage. Men in dark suits or tuxedoes are seated to my left and right, waiting for their turns to speak.

The notes for my speech are crumpled inside a vintage beaded gold purse I purchased at an antique shop last week to match a navy-blue-and-gold St. John suit that I had bought earlier for this occasion. My husband will likely raise an eyebrow when he sees our credit card bill next month, but for now, he appears cheerful, chatting with my parents in the front row—Baba in a dark tailored suit and Mamman in a flowing lavender silk dress that she wore to our wedding eight years earlier.

A few days after my parents learned of this award, they sent me a large bouquet of flowers. Hidden in between the stems and the leaves, I saw a note written in Baba's meticulous handwriting: *To our lovely, amazing daughter. You have made us all proud to be Iranian.* His words brought tears of pride to my eyes as I remembered my adolescent

1

years when life seemed like a burden unworthy of the wait to become an adult.

Back then, every morning, I reluctantly dressed in a dark cloak and a long headscarf and headed for school, came home, and waited with my family for Iraqi planes to once again bomb Tehran—bombs that kept us all hidden in our dark, damp basement until dawn. Through those dark hours, I often thought, *What on earth am I here for?*

As I look up from the stage, the glint of Baba's gold Rolex watch catches my eye. He purchased it two years earlier to attend a ceremony at the White House, an occasion he often brags about. I took him along with me as my guest of honor to receive a presidential award, a half-million-dollar grant from President Clinton's office to continue my research on polar stratospheric clouds—a special class of clouds that naturally form over the poles but can interact with chemicals humans release to produce a hole in Earth's ozone layer. This layer, located in the lower stratosphere, absorbs most of the harmful UV radiation that is incident upon our planet. Even minute amounts of ozone degradation within this layer translate into copious amounts of UV radiation reaching Earth's surface, posing a threat to the survival of all living organisms.

Baba, touched by the president's generosity, vowed to vote democratic in the next election, but then he changed his mind. He voted for Bush instead of Gore, and that broke my heart, since Al Gore has always been the most recognized and outspoken advocate for environmental research, my area of specialty. My father, I believe, will never cast a vote for a Democrat, for in his mind, President Carter is the reason Iran became the "Islamic Republic of Iran" in 1979.

The moment I've dreaded is almost here. My heart beats fast as I hear, "It is my great pleasure to join in recognizing Dr. Azadeh Tabazadeh's talent, accomplishments, and promise as memorialized in the Macelwane Medal. Azadeh is noted ..." Once again, an honor that I am grateful and humbled to receive comes at a cost of facing my worst fear. I'd rather kiss a snake than take center stage in front of all these people.

Minutes later, I'm standing behind the podium, head down, rummaging through my tiny gold purse to retrieve my crinkly notes inside. The microphone is on, so the audience can hear me scrambling behind the scenes to get ready for my talk. With notes in hand, I take a deep breath, thank a few colleagues, and begin.

> Once my daughter, Dionna, asked me, "What do you do at your work?"
>
> "I am a scientist," I told her.
>
> "What's that?"
>
> "I study the clouds, rainbows, and many other interesting things that you often like to paint."
>
> "Well, I also like to paint dinosaurs, and I don't think I want to be a scientist. I want to be a bone collector when I'm all grown up."
>
> Luckily, what she meant was to take all of her friends to a desert to dig for dinosaur bones. She also tried hard to convince me not to worry too much about the clouds, because they are always there in the sky for everyone to see, whereas dinosaur bones are hiding in the sand waiting for "little" people to find them.
>
> At last, I told her, "If you work really hard, someday you will be the most famous grown-up bone collector on Earth."

I pause for a moment to look at the audience: row upon row of faces glowing under crisp chandelier lights. Laughter fills the air as I tell the story of the chemistry kit that my uncle gave me as a present when I was eight—a kit that got me hooked on science early on but also caused my mother to snap at me from time to time.

Before closing, I look directly at my parents' gaze. This may be my last opportunity to thank them in front of such a large crowd.

Nineteen years ago, a few years after the Islamic Revolution in Iran, it was just a dream for a young woman to even think of pursuing a career in science ... It is because of my parents' unselfish sacrifices that I am living today the life of my dreams ...

Drenched in sweat and slightly shaking, I walk back to my seat with my hands wrapped around a small mahogany box presented to me after my talk.

Inside the box, a large silver medal is inscribed with my name, the date, and a citation that reads: FOR SIGNIFICANT CONTRIBUTIONS TO THE GEOPHYSICAL SCIENCES BY A YOUNG SCIENTIST OF OUTSTANDING ABILITY.

The words instantly boost my ego and soothe my nerves. I can finally breathe a sigh of relief and even laugh in my head at the sight of my name—Azadeh Tabazadeh—listed on *Wikipedia* among a sea of Richards, Davids, Johns, and Michaels, the previous recipients of this award. I know it will happen sooner or later; a curious web browser will click on my name, expecting to see a picture of a nerdy-looking guy from a strange country with a name that's either difficult to pronounce or impossible to place on the map. Instead, a photograph of me—an unveiled woman from an estranged but now well-known country—fills the screen. The browser may pause for a moment and puzzle over my appearance.

A short trip to a shopping mall is not the reason that I appear Westernized in that photograph. In 1982, my brother, my cousin, and I, all teenagers at the time, fled Iran by crossing a vast barren desert to reach the borders of Pakistan and beyond. For thousands of miles, the scorching sun burned our faces raw as we traveled by foot, on crowded mopeds, and in the back of rusty pickup trucks, putting our lives in the hands of Pakistani smugglers who were now trafficking people, instead of drugs, out of Iran. My life has changed a great deal since then, but the world, it seems, has remained the same—countries at war or in the midst of bloody revolutions with no political resolution in sight.

A week after the award ceremony, I set out to buy a chemistry kit for my daughter, Dionna, at a Toys "R" Us near my work at NASA in Moffett Field, California, hoping that the gift may entice her to pursue science and stay away from world politics of any kind.

In the store, I find the section where the science kits are stacked, but nothing interesting catches my eye. The professional-looking kit of the 1970s, which I got as a kid, has now become just another cartoonish-looking box lost in the land of Toys "R" Us.

Disappointed, I leave the store empty handed, wondering how many little girls will miss the opportunity I was given at age eight to find myself.

✺ The Chemistry Kit

Tehran, March 1973

I wake up to the sound of loud laughter, grab my robe, and rush down the stairs. At the bottom of the staircase, a medium-sized, black leather suitcase leans against the railing. It resembles the valise that Dr. Vahedian, our family physician, carries during house visits, but this one, I assume, belongs to my uncle Mahmood. He left Iran last year to study abroad and is now back for a short visit to celebrate *No Rooz*, New Year, with our family on March 21, which is exactly ten days away.

Uncle's thundering voice echoes from the kitchen, "A breakfast is incomplete without a few slices of *jambon*. Is there a grocery store nearby that sells jambon? I can't wait to butter a piece of fresh lavash and make a fat jambon sandwich."

"*La ilaha illallah,*" Grandma warns him. "Mahmood, God will punish you in hell if you eat jambon. Pigs are filthy animals. They eat their own waste. Muslims don't eat jambon. Don't you know that?"

"La ilaha illallah" is Grandma's favorite phrase. It sounds much better in Arabic than in Farsi—there is no God but Allah—but what does it really mean, anyway? Isn't Allah the same thing as God?

"God. What God?" Uncle asks Grandma. "There is no God. Who said you couldn't eat shit if it tasted good? Your mighty Allah! Tell me, Mother, why is your Allah so incredibly nosy? Why should

6

He care if I eat jambon or not? Aren't there more urgent matters in this world for this Allah of yours to intervene?"

"What's jambon?" my brother, Jahan, asks, rolling his curls around his index finger as I walk into the kitchen.

Grandma sighs and shakes her head as agate prayer beads pass between her fingers. "La ilaha illallah. Son, stop your nonsense. Bite your tongue."

"Well, well, well, *salaam*, little lady," Uncle says and stands up, giving me a warm hug and a couple of whiskery kisses that tickle my cheeks. "You're up early today. You haven't changed a bit since the last time I saw you."

The ends of Uncle's thick, black mustache are curved steeply upward, and he often twists the tips with his fingers when he listens or talks. Baba calls Uncle *Stalin* instead of Mahmood, for his face bears a strong resemblance to Joseph Stalin—Uncle's beloved Russian hero—a personality hated by almost all Iranians. Baba looks somewhat like Uncle, but he is a head shorter and a lot skinnier, and his mustache is perfectly trimmed.

"Salaam, Uncle Mahmood," I say, smiling.

"Child, hurry up. Eat your breakfast. We're going out soon to buy jambon for Grandma."

"What's jambon?" I ask again, since no one answered Jahan's question a few minutes earlier.

"La ilaha illallah. That's enough, Mahmood. Don't teach my grandchildren bad habits," Grandma says and turns to look straight into my eyes. "If you eat jambon, you'll burn in hell, and that's all you need to know."

Uncle springs to his feet and scoops Grandma off the chair as she pulls down her baggy floral-print dress to cover her skinny bare legs. "Mother, I'm not putting you down until you tell me what 'la ilaha illallah' means in Farsi."

"La ilaha illallah. Put me down, Mahmood!" Grandma cries out.

Uncle chuckles and sits Grandma back on the chair, her thin hair standing up in disarray.

"Mother, why do you keep uttering phrases in Arabic that you don't understand?" Uncle asks, shaking his head.

"Uncle, is that your suitcase in the hallway?" I interrupt.

"No. That's your suitcase."

"Mine? What's in it?" I ask, looking up with my mouth open.

"Eat your breakfast first, and then you can open your present," Mamman says as she tucks a strand of red color-treated hair behind her ear.

Mamman and Grandma are both short and slender, but they look nothing alike. Mamman's eyes are large and hazel and are set inside a pair of arched brows, whereas Grandma's are dark and piercing and sit right under a patch of short and thin brows. People say I have Mamman's eyes and brows, Baba's pointy nose and curly hair, and my aunt Akram's full lips. I also think I have Grandma's square chin, though no one has ever told me so.

"But I'm not hungry at all," I say, twisting the end of my frizzy ponytail. "I'll wait for lunch. Can I open it now, please?"

"That's fine," Mamman agrees.

I dash out, eager to find out what can possibly be inside that suitcase for me. In the hallway, I sit down next to the suitcase, unlatch the two locks on the top, and pull the two compartments apart. On one side, there is a folded piece of white fabric, a pair of funny-looking glasses, a pair of gloves, a magazine, glass beakers, a wooden clamp, and a small glass alcohol lamp that looks like a perfume bottle topped with a braided cotton wick protruding through an aluminum cap. Intrigued, I rub it a few times, wishing for a genie to pop out like the one that smokes out of a brass lamp in *Aladdin and the Magic Lamp*.

The opposite side of the suitcase resembles a miniature bookshelf with four separate shelves, each housing brown sealed bottles filled with colorful powders.

"What kind of a toy is this?" I ask, holding my breath.

"It's a chemistry kit," Uncle says, standing over me.

"What's chemistry?"

"Chemistry is a field in sciences ..."

I can already tell this is a one-of-a-kind toy that no other kid in Iran has ever seen before. "How do I play with this toy?"

"You follow the instructions in the manual to make colorful, shiny crystals. It says right there," Uncle says, pointing to the foreign alphabet on the cover.

I sigh. "But, Uncle, I can't read German."

With one brow raised, Uncle fiddles with his mustache and mumbles, "Um, let's think. Gosh, I guess I've got to translate all this into Farsi for you."

"Great! Can we start now? Please?"

"Sure. Why not? Go on, child—hurry. Grab a notebook and pencil."

I run to my bedroom and return in record time with a notebook in one hand and a sharp pencil in the other. Cuddling next to Uncle on the sofa, I write down "Experiment I: Growing Blue Crystals." After a good fifteen minutes, the description of the first experiment is translated word for word into Farsi.

"Well, why don't you go on up to your room and start the experiment?" Uncle says as he clasps his hands above his head and lets out a heavy sigh.

I latch the suitcase and drag it up the stairs to my bedroom, eager to see which vial contains copper sulfate, the salt called for in Experiment I to make blue crystals. The manual slips out as I unlatch the suitcase. On its cover a young boy is dressed in a white coat, goggles, and gloves. I follow along and put on the full costume, grab a glass beaker, and run to the bathroom.

While glancing at my notes, I place the beaker containing twenty-five milliliters of hot water on my desk. My eyes move back and forth across the suitcase shelves looking for the vial labeled copper sulfate. As I twist its top open, my nostrils fill with that awful scent of rotten eggs. With my nose plugged, I reach to scoop out a tablespoon of what's inside. A grayish-looking powder emerges, making it harder to escape its overwhelming smell. I dump the powder inside the beaker and stir, waiting for the solution to become cloudy.

Hours pass as I sit in my room and watch the gradual growth of a deep-blue crystal on a thick piece of roughened string, ignoring Mamman's calls for lunch and Uncle's shouts to go out and buy jambon for Grandma.

Halfway through the experiment, my cheerful three-year-old sister, Afshan, opens the door and pops in, rambling, "Do you want to play with my new German doll? She's really big. She's very pretty. Her name is Mummy. She also talks. See?" She approaches my desk as her doll begins to speak German.

When I turn my goggled face, she turns and runs away, her screams and the doll's foreign voice ringing in the background.

Hours later, I carefully empty the solution into the bathroom sink to retrieve the crystal. Thank God it doesn't stink nearly as bad as the smelly powder used to make it.

I place the crystal in my hand, close my fingers, and rush down the stairs. No one except for Uncle seems to care much about the blue shiny crystal sparkling in the palm of my hand.

"Excellent, child, excellent. Did you record all your observations as I told you?"

"Yes, Uncle. I wrote down everything I saw!" I exclaim.

"Are you ready for the next experiment?"

"Yes, I'm ready," I say and rush back to my room to fetch the manual, notebook, and pencil.

"Experiment II: Glowing Crystals," Uncle dictates, and I write it down.

As soon as the translation is done, I run back to my room— this time to grow a crystal that supposedly glows in the dark. The procedure for Experiment II is identical to Experiment I, except that I need to use alum instead of copper sulfate, plus ten drops of neon fluorescent ink.

I pour a few spoons of alum salt into a warm mixture of water and fluorescent ink. Instantly, a colorless, ice-like crystal appears and grows quickly. Curious, I turn off the light. *Wow, what's in this thing that makes it glow like a night-light?*

By the time I finish Experiment II, everyone in the house is fast asleep. I crawl into bed exhausted but inspired. I now have an answer if someone asks me, "What do you want to be when you grow up?"

"I'll be a chemist," I'll tell them. A sense of accomplishment falls over me as I watch my newly constructed crystal glow in the dark just like a bright, shining star.

In my dream that night, the crystal on my shelf grows larger and becomes brighter, transforming into a glowing crystal ball like the one in my book *Snow White*. People from all over the world travel far and stand in long lines for a chance to meet me, for I can gaze into my crystal ball to tell them of their pasts and foresee their futures with a certainty that no one else can match.

The next morning, I wake up remembering my dream. It feels good to be important and have others rely on me. Maybe someday I'll be someone famous, someone who can make things or do things that no one else can. *Is there such a thing as a crystal ball? If not, maybe I can invent one.*

In the kitchen, I find Uncle alone, stuffing a large buttered piece of lavash with jambon, cucumber bits, and tomato slices. As he rolls the bread, he offers me a bite.

My mouth waters for a taste, but I say, "No, thanks. Grandma will be very upset if I eat this."

"Don't tell me you believe all this religious mumbo jumbo. You know, if you think about it hard, it's really all very silly!"

"Uncle, why don't you believe in God? I believe in God."

"Have you seen Him lately?"

"Who?"

"God. We are talking about God, child."

"No, I haven't seen God yet," I say, feeling confused.

"Then why do you believe in something you haven't seen yet?" Uncle says and shrugs.

No one else I know dares to talk about God like Uncle does. He shouldn't talk this way. "Well, everyone else believes in God."

"So everyone else has seen this God of yours, except for you. How come?"

"I don't know if anyone has ever seen God. He lives too far away for anyone to see Him."

"Well, if He lives that far away, then I can eat my jambon in peace." He then takes a large bite of his sandwich. A few pieces of bread and cucumber seeds cling to his bushy mustache as he chews on.

"No, you can't, Uncle. You have to be careful," I say, thinking of the angels who are sitting on his shoulders and listening to us.

"Why?" he asks, helping himself to a second bite of his sandwich.

"Well, the angels on your shoulders will tell God if you do something good or bad."

"If memory serves me well, I think the one sitting on my right shoulder debriefs God on all the good deeds I've done, and the one on the left side does the opposite."

"Yes, that's the way it goes," I say, gasping in disbelief as Uncle raises his right arm over his left shoulder and slaps it hard with the palm of his hand.

"There, I just killed the angel who tells God I'm a bad boy."

He shouldn't have done that. My hand touches my own shoulder as I stare into his eyes. "You can't kill an angel like that. Don't you know that angels live forever?" I say, fearing that God would likely punish Uncle by sending him to burn in hell.

"Poor child. Don't believe Grandma's fairy tales about God, prophets, and angels. Hopefully, as you grow older, you'll wise up. Next time, ask Grandma what she's actually telling God when she prays."

"I have already asked her. She taught me the words of *namaz*. I pray with her all the time. She doesn't know what the prayers mean in Farsi, because they're in Arabic."

"Bravo child, bravo. So Grandma, and now you, pray to this God in a language that you both don't speak or understand. Intriguing indeed, very intriguing! Now, let's talk about more important things. How did your experiment go last night?"

Glad to be given a chance to switch topics, I quickly reply, "Very well. The crystal I made glows at night, just like the manual said. You should come and see it when it gets dark."

"Child, if you enjoy making crystals, then you can't believe in God."

"Why not?"

"Well, that's a long story. You'll get it when you're older. If you believe in science, then there is no God."

I walk away, perplexed, not understanding why I can't believe in God and enjoy growing crystals at the same time.

In the hallway, I run into Mamman.

"Wait a second, Azadeh," she says, and I turn around. "You need to stop wearing your goggles in the house. Your sister is afraid of you."

"Fine," I say nonchalantly.

After a few days of dismissing Mamman's warnings, she steps on my goggles, breaking them beyond repair. Later, she tells me it was an accident, but I know she did it on purpose so poor Afshan won't cry anymore. What I don't understand is why it's okay for me to cry, not Afshan.

Always the peacemaker, Baba tries to remedy the situation by allowing me to wear his reading glasses instead. I can't see well with them on, and Baba gets annoyed wiping the lenses after I'm done, but I still prefer to wear them while working with my chemicals.

After that, my little sister Afshan giggles when she finds me busy with work, instead of running to Mamman screaming at the top of her lungs. Sometimes she even puts on the lab coat, gloves, and Baba's glasses before posing in front of the full-length mirror at the end of the hall. As I watch her, I wonder whether she can see her reflection smiling with the world around her blurred and magnified.

๑ ๑ ๑

No Rooz, the start of spring, is now minutes away. Everyone in the house, except for Grandma, is gathered around the ceremonial *haftseen* table—composed of *haft* symbolic dishes, each one beginning with the Farsi letter *Seen*, thereby completing the word haftseen. The number haft has been sacred in Iran since the time of ancient Persia, and the seven dishes—lentil sprouts (*sabzeh*), dried oleaster fruit (*senjed*), garlic (*sear*), apple (*seab*), sumac fruit (*somaq*), and vinegar (*serkeh*)—symbolize the seven angelic heralds of life, prosperity, love, health, joy, beauty, and patience. Other items include a large mirror at the center of the table, lit candles, painted eggs, live goldfish in a bowl, Iranian sweets, a pot of blooming hyacinth, and a copy of the Koran.

Seconds before the clock strikes, Grandma walks into the dining room, chanting and shaking a flaming brazier of *esphand*, wild rue, a sacred herb whose smoldering fumes are believed to ward off evil spirits. Black smoke quickly fills the room, giving off a disgusting, acrid smell, making my throat itch and my eyes burn.

"Mother, the fumes are going to kill us all before purifying the air and chasing out all those evil spirits." Uncle chuckles, lets out a few fake coughs, and chuckles again.

"Hush up, Mahmood," Grandma replies with eyebrows furrowed.

My brother, my sister, and I then proceed to collect crisp *toman* bills, tucked inside the pages of the Koran for each child by the adults in the family the night before No Rooz.

The ceremony continues with a traditional No Rooz feast: basmati rice mixed with dill, fried whitefish, and a traditional vegetable omelet with raisins and walnuts. Uncle must love whitefish a lot; his plate is heaped with a mountain of rice topped with three large slices of crispy fried fish. I wish I could pass on my only slice to him, but I can't, because Grandma always notices if someone is not eating the food that she has worked tirelessly preparing. Thank God that I don't have to endure the raw taste of sea on my mouth for another 365 days.

After the feast, I cuddle next to my sleepy uncle on the couch as he dictates, "Fill the alcohol lamp ... up to the red line ... with ethyl alcohol ..."

My heart swells when I hear the word *lamp*. Finally, I get a chance to play with this thing. This time, Uncle escorts me to my room to help me set up.

"Where is the alcohol?" I ask as I take out the lamp from its casing.

"Good question," Uncle says, playing with his mustache. "The manual said you can buy the alcohol from any drugstore, but I bet we can use a bottle from your father's liquor cabinet for now. Show me where he keeps his alcohol."

We walk down the stairs and into the dining room. I open the door underneath the tall china cabinet and point to the alcoholic beverages stored on two large shelves.

"Oh, gosh! *Wow*, that's a lot of alcohol for a Muslim family. Shame, shame, shame," he says, tapping his index fingers. "Alcohol consumption is a dreadful sin in Islam. Let's take this half-full whiskey bottle."

He grabs the bottle, twists its top open, and takes a few gulps as we climb the stairs back to my room. A few sweeps of his arm clear my desk before he gestures in my direction.

"Put the lamp right here, child."

The alcohol lamp, filled up to the red line, sits atop a puddle of whiskey on my desk. Uncle lifts it to dry its bottom with rolls of tissue paper, wipes the table clean, and tosses the soaked tissue in the straw wastebasket behind him. He then lights the lamp, blows out the match, and throws it in the basket.

Shortly thereafter, snapping and cracking sounds make us turn our heads.

"Oh, shit!" Uncle shouts as he grabs my pillow and shoves it deep inside the basket.

The flame draws down and goes out, leaving behind a burning smoke that fills the room, graying the air, making it hard for me to think of what I ought to be doing next. While rubbing my eyes, I see Uncle across the room struggling to open the window with my favorite blanket hung over his shoulder. A stream of cold air rushes in as Uncle waves the blanket back and forth.

Minutes later, the door bursts open and bangs against the wall. "What's going on here?" Mamman asks, staring at me.

"Nothing. Relax. We just put out a little fire, Azar. It's not her fault," Uncle says as Mamman's pupils grow and shrink like a flashing traffic light.

"I don't want you *ever* to play with this kit again! Understood?" Mamman shouts and purses her lips tight.

"Come on, sis," Uncle says as his glasses slide down to the tip of his nose. "Look, I just singed my mustache fighting this damn fire. It won't happen again. I'll promise you. I've already told her not to use the alcohol lamp unsupervised."

"A lamp? Where is this lamp?" Mamman asks, surveying the room. Uncle blows out the lamp and hands it to her. She brings it close to her nose and sniffs a few times. "What's in this thing, Azadeh?"

"Whiskey," I say quietly and swallow.

"You put whiskey in this lamp without first asking your father or me? You're grounded for the rest of the holiday." Mamman's brows remain tightly knitted as she snatches the lamp and the whiskey bottle and storms off.

"She hates me. Baba would never do this to me," I say, tears prickling my eyes.

"I'm not so sure about that, child." Uncle nods and pushes his glasses up his nose. "Listen, your mother is just trying to protect you."

"I don't need her protection," I sniffle. "I love that lamp. I want it back. That's my favorite toy. I haven't even had a chance to play with it yet."

Uncle tries to console me, but I can't stop crying, wondering what Mamman is doing or might have already done to my precious lamp.

That evening, shortly after Baba returns from visiting his parents, I'm summoned to the kitchen.

"Tell your father what you have done," Mamman demands.

"I swear I didn't do anything wrong. It was an accident," I say matter-of-factly.

"Well then, *I'm* going to tell him."

I fold my arms across my chest and watch my parents argue back and forth. Mamman's voice rises each time as Baba's calm voice follows and trails off. In the end, Baba persuades Mamman to allow me to use a burning candle in place of the alcohol lamp.

After dinner, Baba tells Uncle, "Stalin, let's go and move this controversial laboratory onto the veranda before Azar loses her mind."

"Yes, sir, Mr. Engineer." Uncle salutes Baba. "Your wish is my command."

As Uncle and I get busy setting up the experiment that we started earlier in my room, he pats me on my shoulder and says, "Improvise, child. That's what makes you become a leader later in life."

Meeting Najmieh

The loud buzzer goes off. Mamman asks me to go and open the gate, and I know it's her waiting out there.

Outside, the air feels hot and humid. I fiddle with the lock, almost burning my fingertips, before it clicks open. As the heavy, ornate iron gates slowly swing away, I see a young girl staring down at her shoes. Next to her, an elderly man is holding a walking stick in one hand and a small suitcase in the other.

I introduce myself and smile. The girl looks up, brushes her floral silk headscarf aside, and quietly says, "Salaam, *khanoom*, my name is Najmieh."

Hello, miss! No one has ever addressed me as a miss before.

"I'm Najmieh's father!" the old man shouts, revealing a mouthful of gold teeth.

Najmieh looks just like my porcelain doll: large, almond-shaped hazel eyes, rosy cheeks, pale skin, and light-brown wavy hair. A raisin-shaped mole just above her upper lip on the left-hand side adds extra charm and character to her face. She has on a tight, yellow cotton long-sleeved shirt over a black dress and bright-green, baggy satin pants, typical wear for women villagers from the northern provinces of Iran. Her feet are squeezed into a pair of black, closed-toe cotton shoes with her heels sticking out from the back, dirty and cracked.

It's hard to understand why Najmieh is shorter than I am, as

Mamman told me yesterday that she is eleven, and I am only eight. I know people say I'm too tall for my age, but I'm still a head shorter than Homa, our neighbor's daughter, who is also eleven.

Following greetings, Najmieh and her father walk behind me through the fragrant jasmine garden, up a set of stone steps to the main balcony, down the carpeted hallway, through the living room, and into the kitchen, where Mamman is sitting at the breakfast table with her hands clasped together. Next to her is a tall glass cup filled to the brim with steaming hot tea.

"Salaam, *agha*," Mamman says and extends her hand before turning in my direction. "Azadeh, you can go out and play."

"Salaam, khanoom!" the old man shouts. "Najmieh will make an excellent servant, obedient and hardworking. You have my word."

As I head out, I glance at Najmieh examining her hands and wonder if she's thinking about me like I'm thinking about her. I hope we can soon become playmates like my brother, Jahan, and Ali, our servant before Najmieh. A few weeks ago, Baba took Ali to his office to work and live there. I miss having him around, but I'd rather have a girl live with us instead. I'm amazed at how strikingly different Najmieh and Ali look. Unlike her, Ali had dark skin and nearly black eyes.

I once asked Baba, "Why is Ali so dark?"

"He's probably mostly Arab," he said. "He comes from Bandar Abbas, a large port city on the Persian Gulf. Most natives of this area have dark complexions because of many years of interracial marriages with Arabs on the other side of the Persian Gulf."

Based on what Baba said about Ali, I would guess Najmieh's fair skin has to come from the Russians, since her family lives near the Caspian Sea, next to the Russian border. It's interesting that people who come from the two ends of Iran look almost nothing alike. I wonder if my olive skin is a result of being partly Arab and partly Russian, since Tehran is in between the south and the north.

Not long after I leave the kitchen, I hear Najmieh's father shouting good-bye. I walk to the doorstep and stand behind Mamman and

Najmieh. She is now staring at her father with her hand up in the air, waving rapidly from side to side. I don't understand why her father isn't turning his head to look at her and wave good-bye, like my parents always do to let me know everything is fine. As he disappears behind the gates, Najmieh's hand stands frozen in the air, and her ears and face are shining red. Her quiet weeping makes my heart sink through the floor, but I don't know what to do or say to make it easier on her.

"Azadeh, why don't you show Najmieh the house?" Mamman says, patting Najmieh on the shoulder.

"Okay, Mamman. Let's go, Najmieh," I say, reaching out to grab her arm.

We walk from room to room and eventually end up in my bedroom upstairs. Najmieh speaks Farsi with a Rashti accent, and at times it's difficult to understand her dialogue. She comes from a small village close to Rasht, a major city in Shomal, the entire northern region of Iran.

As we sit on the floor next to the nightstand, I pull out the bottom drawer and say, "Najmieh, look at all these crystals." I pick up a purple crystal and hand it to her. "I made them just a few months ago."

"How did you make them?" she asks as she brings the crystal close to her face.

"Well, my uncle Mahmood helped me a little bit, but not much. I did most of the work myself. It was a lot of fun making all these crystals. Maybe we can make some together, if you like. I still have some powders left."

"I know how to make crystals too," she says nonchalantly.

"You do? Do you have a chemistry kit?"

"What's that?"

"Wait a second. I'll show you."

I run to my closet, returning with my black leather suitcase. I open the latches on the top and tell Najmieh all about what's inside and what I did with each item to make all the shiny, colorful crystals.

Najmieh notices a large, empty spot in the suitcase, points, and asks, "What was there?"

"My alcohol lamp." I sigh, feeling as hollow as the empty slot it came in.

"Where is it?"

"I don't know. My mother took it away."

"Why?"

"Because she didn't like it," I say, not wanting to tell her the truth.

"Lunch is ready, Azadeh!" Mamman shouts from downstairs.

"You have to show me how to make crystals your way," I tell Najmieh as we get up to leave.

"It's pretty easy. We can start after lunch if you like."

"No, not today. I'll tell you when the time is right," I say, knowing that Mamman would likely deem the steps involved to be dangerous, thereby not allowing us to make crystals Najmieh's way.

The whole family is seated around the kitchen table when Najmieh and I walk in. We each take a seat, and Mamman fills our plates with salad, basmati rice mixed with lentils and raisins, and a couple of chicken drumsticks.

We're almost finished when Mamman asks, "Najmieh, you know how to wash dishes, don't you?"

"Yes, khanoom. I know how to do it very well. I'll start right away."

As I leave the kitchen, I pause and glance at Najmieh. She stands on a stool with her hands under the running faucet and her back facing me. I sigh and wish she could just come and play with me.

A few hours later, Najmieh walks into my room. I am sitting on my bed with a book in my lap. "Come in, Najmieh. Sit here," I say, patting the bed next to me.

She plops onto my bed. "You have *so* many books, Azadeh khanoom," she says, looking at my crowded bookshelves.

"Would you like to borrow this one to read? I have already read it a few times. It's one of my favorites. It's about two dogs, a rich one and a poor one that in the end become friends."

"Is the pretty one the rich one?" she asks, pointing to Lady on the cover of *Lady and the Tramp: The Story of Two Dogs*.

"Yes. Her name is Lady."

"Azadeh khanoom, I don't know how to read, but I wish I could."

"But you are eleven years old, Najmieh. You should know how to read."

"Azadeh khanoom, no one in my village knows how to read." She sighs.

"Well, then, I can teach you if you want. Would you like that?"

"Yes. Yes, very much," she exclaims. "But what about your mother? I don't want to get into trouble."

"What about her? She doesn't care about these things," I assure her.

We start right then. I draw the Farsi alphabet on a piece of binder paper and ask her to copy each character twenty times. She's an excellent pupil and learns the alphabet in a few days.

After a month, Najmieh reads like a kindergartener, slowly and impatiently, skipping words here and there, the ones she can't figure how to pronounce yet. Over time, her reading continues to improve, but I usually read books to her because it takes her forever to finish a page. Her favorite book is *The Tales of Mullah Nasruddin*, written by Mullah Nasruddin himself, a well-known philosopher and wise man who lived during the Middle Ages in Iran.

Najmieh, I think, adores the tales because she can see herself as a typical character in most of them, a peasant who has better common sense than the powerful sultan, the ruler of her land. Every single time, as I get close to reading the end of a tale, she always fidgets around with a gloat in her eyes and a proud smile on her face, as if *she* is the one who is about to outsmart the sultan.

۞ ۞ ۞

Months later, early in the morning, my parents leave for Europe, putting Grandma in charge of the house. They will be gone for three whole weeks, which gives Najmieh and me plenty of time to make crystals her way.

After lunch, I see Grandma walking into the family room with a pillow and blanket tucked under her arm—a sure sign that she's all ready for her long afternoon nap.

Just before she lies down on the couch, I pop in and say, "Grandma, is it okay if I make crystals with Najmieh in the kitchen?"

"What kind of crystals?" she asks, fluffing up her pillow.

"Just sugar crystals, Grandma. It's not a big deal."

"Well, that's okay, but don't break anything."

"I won't, Grandma. I promise."

I turn on the TV for her and sit down on the armchair next to the couch. She drops a few *nabats*, crystallized sugar candies, into a cup of warm water and stirs.

"Nabat, my dear, can do wonders for an unruly stomach," she says and gulps the sugar water.

Days of Our Lives, a popular American soap opera, is on. Before long, she is fast asleep, snoring loudly. I tiptoe out of the room, close the door, and head for the kitchen.

Najmieh is standing on a chair next to a large pot of water boiling on the stove. I bring another chair and run to the basement to fetch a two-kilogram bag of sugar.

"Pour the sugar in very slowly, one spoon at a time," Najmieh instructs.

I do as she says while she stirs the pot. Soon all the sugar is gone, but Najmieh is still stirring.

"We need a lot more sugar, Azadeh khanoom. I used way too much water," she says, shaking her head.

"No problem, Najmieh. I'll go get some more."

I run back to the basement and return with a second bag of sugar, spooning it in slowly as she stirs the pot.

Suddenly, Najmieh puts her hand in my face. "Stop. We have enough sugar now."

My hand freezes in the air as she turns off the flame and bends over. I bring my face next to hers to inspect the inside of the pot, but the fog from the boiling water makes me squeeze my eyes shut.

"Perfect. The water is just clouding up," she says, fanning the steam.

We each grab one handle of the pot and head for the veranda, where fifteen crystalline vases are set up for our experiment. With a soup server, I transfer eight scoops of hot sugar water into each vase, as Najmieh follows behind to place a pencil across the opening of each one.

A few days earlier, Najmieh and I had tied a piece of rough string around each pencil. To roughen the strings, we ground each piece, back and forth, between our teeth until its surface was no longer smooth. Najmieh said if we skipped that step all the dissolved sugar would turn into slush.

Fifteen strings now dangle deep inside fifteen crystalline vases filled with warm sugar water. We cover each vase with a washcloth and leave the veranda.

Once in the kitchen, Najmieh tells me in a quiet voice, "It takes about a month for the crystals to grow large."

My jaw drops as I turn to face her. "But, Najmieh, why didn't you tell me all this before we started? We can't possibly wait that long."

"Why not?"

"Because Mamman will be crazy mad if she sees her precious vases out on the veranda, Najmieh!" I shout.

"But you said your grandma said it's okay to make crystals."

"Yes, she did, but I didn't explain what we were going to do exactly."

"Why not?" she asks, her eyes widening.

"Because she didn't ask, Najmieh!" I shout again, not understanding why she is asking me so many obvious questions.

"Sorry, Azadeh khanoom. What are we going to do now?"

"Nothing," I say in a calm voice. "Grandma never goes out on the veranda."

"What if she does?"

"I'll think of something to *say* if she does. I can't concentrate and figure things out if you keep talking, Najmieh," I say, glaring at her.

Najmieh glances around to avoid my stare, likely realizing what she has done wrong and feeling bad about it.

"Azadeh khanoom, I don't want to cause any trouble. I've got to get back to work. It's time to prepare afternoon tea for your grandma and cook dinner for tonight."

"I know, Najmieh. One last thing before you go—don't let Afshan set one foot on the veranda. She likes to play hide-and-seek out there."

"Very well, khanoom. I'll keep her out."

§   §   §

The three weeks Mamman is gone pass like a flash. She is due back tomorrow, which makes today cleanup day. Najmieh and I are waiting for Grandma to go to the family room with her pillow and blanket before heading to the veranda.

We have been out on the veranda every day to check the growth of our crystals, but today is the *final* day. Unfortunately, eight vases display nothing but slush at the bottom, probably because their strings weren't roughened enough to seed crystals. However, what's inside the remaining vases makes up for all that gunk—seven Barbie-sized crystals float and sparkle, reflecting dots of rainbow colors that scatter and dance around us.

"*Wow*, we did it, Najmieh," I say and pat her on the back. "You really are *very* smart."

"You think so?" she says, her mouth curled into a doubtful frown.

"I know so, Najmieh. No one else knows how to make crystals without a kit, not even my uncle Mahmood."

A cheerful gaze lights up her face, assuring me that she now believes in herself. We carefully pull out each crystal by its dangling string and set it aside on a towel to dry in the sun. Then we clean up quickly, putting each vase exactly in its claimed spot back inside Mamman's tall china cabinet—all before Grandma wakes up from her afternoon nap.

The next evening, I hear Mamman telling Grandma she's ready to drive her home. I run to the door and say, "Grandma, can you please come with me? I want to show you something."

"What, sweetie?"

We walk hand in hand up the stairs and into my room. "Grandma, I want to give you these," I say, handing her the two best-looking crystals out of the bunch. "You can eat them, if you like. One for you and one for Grandpa."

"Dear, I know I can eat them. That's nabat on a string."

Grandma is right. That is nabat, crystallized sugar. I always eat them as little candies. I can't believe we were making nabat this whole time. I bet Najmieh knew what we were doing all along. Thank God she's not here to witness what just happened—a lightbulb moment I'd rather forget.

"Where did you get them?"

"Grandma, I made them just for you," I blurt out. "I know nabat is your favorite candy." *Never mind that I just realized this was nabat*, I whisper to myself, like a foolish sultan would admit to himself at the end of a Nasruddin tale.

An Unusual Present

One night, Najmieh and I are up late watching TV as we unwrap a mountain of decorations for the next day's party. Jahan and I always celebrate our birthdays together, although he is exactly one year and ten days older than I am. Rumor has it that he cried so much on his first day of first grade that Mamman decided to hold him back a grade, so that's why we are both in fourth grade in spite of our age difference.

As I place a string of colorful paper stars on the coffee table, I look up at Najmieh unfolding a bright-orange paper lantern and ask, "So, Najmieh, when is *your* birthday?"

"I don't know," she says and shrugs.

"What do you mean you don't know?"

"I just don't know," she says and looks down. "It's not important."

What is she talking about? One's birthday is hugely important. "Well, then, ask your mother when you see her next time. I am sure she can tell you when you were born."

"I will if I ever see her again." She sighs, holding back tears.

"You'll see her soon. Why not?"

"Azadeh khanoom, how can I see my mother? She lives so far away," she says, sniffling and rubbing her eyes.

Feeling angry at myself for making her sad, I say, "Don't cry, Najmieh. We go vacationing in Shomal a lot, sometimes even twice

27

a year. I'm sure you can see your mother then. Mamman said your parents live in a small village very close to our villa in Shomal."

Just the thought of seeing her mother makes her teary eyes shine crystal clear. Her face beams with joy as she thanks me for the promise to visit her mother. My heart feels heavy as I catch sight of Najmieh leave with a smile on her face. I wouldn't be smiling like that if I knew my parents had given me away to work and make money for them.

The next day, I wake up early and look out the window. Large snowflakes are coming down hard, covering the ground and trees in fluffy white. February is always dead cold in Tehran, and from the size of the flakes, I can tell a snowstorm is gearing up for a major landing before the day's end.

I rush down the stairs and find Afshan and Najmieh busy hanging decorations for the party. I skip breakfast and join them. We hang all the decorations and tie colorful balloons to dining chairs arranged against the wall.

As I watch the catering crew assemble a large barbecue on the veranda, I think of Uncle Mahmood and all the fun experiments we set up together at that very spot. I'm sure if he were here, he would have given me another awesome present for my birthday, nothing like the usual—a Barbie this, a Barbie that. I don't even like Barbie and her stuff. Her clothes are always too tight, and I can never put them on her without Najmieh helping me. I only like to play with my Barbies when Najmieh dresses them up, puts them in a classroom, and does all the homework I assign inside the small booklets that we made together for each Barbie by cutting and pasting sheets of binder paper.

The doorbell rings at about two o'clock, and within fifteen minutes, the house is filled with children, chitchat, and unruliness. Girls shimmer in colorful party dresses, standing next to boys who appear somewhat uncomfortable in slacks and crisp collared shirts.

Najmieh is all dressed up too in a silky yellow-and-black polka-dot outfit, one of Mamman's old garments. To me, she looks too grown-up, but I suppose she likes it, since her eyes lit up like a candle when Mamman gave her the clothes to wear earlier in the morning. I have on my all-time favorite outfit—a short, sleeveless, red leather dress with delicate gold chains hanging loosely around my waist over a white puffy collar shirt, white fishnet stockings, and black dress shoes.

As kids arrive one after another, presents pile onto the white oval dining table, stretched from one end of the dining room to the other. There is no need to guess which presents are mine; a flowery pink wrapping gives each one away. I bet *Explorers on the Moon*, a comic book in *The Adventures of Tintin* series, which just came out, is probably somewhere in Jahan's pile. I can't wait to read it, but now I have to wait for Jahan to read and reread it a few times before I get my chance. It's not fair that his presents are almost always better than mine. I'd rather get adventure books, Legos, and puzzles instead of princess books, Barbies, and bead kits to make jewelry that I never end up making.

At three o'clock, a man's voice comes out of a loudspeaker. "The puppet show will start in five minutes."

Instantly, all the strident voices throughout the house subside into a soft murmur. Children run quickly from all different directions into the living room to claim that perfect spot on a large cream-and-blue Nain rug facing the fancy maroon puppet stage.

"You're about to witness *Shāhnāmeh*'s best-known epic," the narrator announces as dark-red velvet curtains move from the center to each side.

The kids all yell at unison, "The story of Rostam and Sohrab!"

In this tale, Rostam, *Shāhnāmeh*'s legendary hero, unknowingly murders his only son, Sonrab, during a bloody battle. I know all this because memorizing and interpreting poems from *Shāhnāmeh: The Epic of the Persian Kings*—which tells the mythical and historical story of Persia from the creation of the world until the seventh century when Arabs invaded Iran—is a part of our school curriculum.

Throughout the play, frequent cheers and occasional gasps fill the room, although each of us knows how the story goes. I wish the narrator had instead acted out the tale of Gurdāfarīd, a brave heroine in *Shāhnāmeh* who dresses in armor to face Sohrab in battle, since the male warrior in her province is too afraid to fight against him. I love stories where women behave just like men, bold and courageous, but those are rare. In fairy tales like *Cinderella*, *Snow White*, or *Sleeping Beauty*, women are not doing much other than cleaning, cooking, or sleeping until a handsome prince shows up and takes them away.

Hours later, the kids gather again to watch the second play, a comedy sketch called *Samad Goes to School*. The script is adapted directly from a movie with the same title that premiered last year. Samad is a well-known comedy character portrayed by a famous actor of Iranian cinema, Parviz Sayyad. Sayyad created and played the role of a naive but street-smart country boy named Samad in a popular sitcom TV series called *Sarkar Ostovar*. Ostovar, an educated native of Tehran, accepts the post of sheriff of an illiterate village in northern Iran, where Samad and his family live. To the annoyance and embarrassment of Sarkar Ostovar, Samad becomes instrumental in solving all the crimes committed in his county.

I turn my head and see Najmieh walk in and sit all the way in the back of the living room. Moments later, her hands go behind her ears. She's listening hard, and I know why: Samad speaks Farsi with the same Rashti accent as she does. Time after time, Samad outsmarts Sarkar Ostovar, bringing laughter to the room, especially to Najmieh, since she truly is the Samad in this room among a sea of educated Tehranians.

As I watch Najmieh take pride in her heritage, I think about her place in this crowd. Like Samad, Najmieh can be very bright, but she doesn't go to school to prove that she's smart by getting good marks on her report cards. I wonder what kind of a student she would be if she did go to school just like my brother and I did.

At about nine o'clock, the doorbell rings for the last time. That has to be for Ramin, Jahan's best friend, since everyone else is now gone. As I open the door, a strong wind springs up and howls around the house. Chilly air whistles and swishes in, cooling my face before I see her—a cute Yorkie puppy with a large green bow tied on the top of her head.

"This is the best present *ever!*" I squeal, hugging Mamman's waist. Jahan and I have been begging Mamman for weeks to adopt one of Ramin's puppies before someone else did.

"You are the best Mamman *ever!*" Jahan exclaims.

"You did it, Azar," Ramin's mother says in a funny German accent as she gently puts the dog down. "We call her Peggy, but you can change her name if you like."

My siblings and I spend the next hour playing with Peggy until Baba says it's time for bed. Mamman allows Najmieh and me to sleep on a mattress on the kitchen floor with Peggy. She curls up between our pillows, next to our heads. She surely doesn't smell like a dog. Her scent is very refreshing, like a strong shampoo, maybe even some kind of laundry detergent.

I am surprised that Mamman gave us such an unusual present this year, one that will surely but sadly keep Grandma away. I don't get why dogs are singled out in the Koran as having a *najes* tongue, since my cats do the same exact thing with their tongues as Peggy does, licking themselves all over—I mean *all* over.

I fall asleep listening to Peggy's heart ticking fast next to my ear. In my dream, Grandma steps into our house dressed in a skintight black dress and a white fur coat with her hair parted in the middle, black on the right side and white on the left, just like Cruella de Vil—the villain in the *One Hundred and One Dalmatians* who aspires to make fur coats out of dog pelts. When she sees Peggy roaming around, she tosses her fur coat over her shoulder and storms off, as I wake up feeling wetness on my face. Peggy is standing over me, licking my eyes and forehead.

The next morning, I wave through the rear window of my school bus as Najmieh waves back, holding Peggy's paw in her hand. Sometimes I wonder why things are the way they are. Najmieh should be on this bus, going to school with the rest of us.

A Road Trip to Shomal

Najmieh bursts into my room, panting. "Azadeh khanoom, your mother is an angel."

"What are you talking about, Najmieh?"

"Khanoom just told me that she'll take me to my village next week when we are in Shomal," she says and exhales loudly.

"*Wow*, that's great news, Najmieh," I say, feeling my heart expanding. "I have been telling you that she would. Our villa on the Caspian shore is not too far from where your parents live."

"I can't wait to see my mother, Azadeh khanoom. It has been a whole year since I saw her last."

We spend the next hour giggling and discussing what outfit she should wear to the occasion. In spite of my friendly objections, she has her heart set on wearing the yellow-and-black polka-dot silk dress that she wore to my birthday party six months earlier. That dress, I think, is too formal and much too hot for a summer outing in Shomal, but in the end, I halfheartedly agree with her.

ⅅ ⅅ ⅅ

The night before our trip, I find Jahan in the kitchen arguing with Mamman. "I want Najmieh to stay home. I don't want her to come with us."

I don't understand why Jahan can't get over the fact that Peggy has chosen Najmieh as her best friend instead of him. To me, it makes perfect sense; Najmieh is with her all the time while we are out at school or having fun with our friends and neighbors.

"Please, Mamman, I want Najmieh to go on this trip. Afshan wants her to come too," I say, contradicting Jahan for the zillionth time.

"That's a lie. She's only four. She doesn't know what she wants," Jahan says.

"I know what I want," Afshan protests, putting her hands on her hips.

"No, you don't. Your sister is putting words in your fish mouth," Jahan tells her, puckering and moving his lips.

Afshan whimpers, "Can't you *see?* I'm a little person, not a *fish.*"

Mamman's brows turn into a frown as she puts her teacup down. "Najmieh is coming along, and that's it!" she shouts. "I have had it with you two arguing about this. I need her to help me with the household chores."

"I hate you both!" Jahan shouts with his nostrils flaring.

Peggy whines as Jahan picks her off the ground and runs out of the kitchen. Minutes later, Peggy is back, standing on Najmieh's lap, wagging her tail.

"Good for you, Peggy. Welcome back to the girls' club," I say, patting her on the head.

The next morning, I wake up to find Baba standing over Najmieh and me. To beat the summer heat, we often sleep on the rooftop inside a small mosquito tent with Peggy and a few stray black-and-white neighborhood cats, stargazing into the wee hours of the night. We think we can tell which star is which by the way it winks. The ones in front of our eyes twinkle a lot, but as we look farther and farther up, the twinkling becomes sparse and nearly stops at the very top.

"Azadeh, how many times have I told you not to let street cats sleep on your hair?" Baba asks, shaking his head.

"It's okay, Baba. Charlie is the cleanest one. He's always licking himself," I say, lifting myself off the mattress.

Charlie is up too, meowing loudly. I named him Charlie, for he has a small black mustache under his nose just like Charlie Chaplin.

"He has fleas, and now you have fleas in your hair."

"Don't worry, Baba. I'm not the type of person who gets fleas."

"Whatever, Azadeh," Baba says and sighs in frustration. "Get up. Start getting ready for the trip. You too, Najmieh. Get up. Khanoom wants you to make all the beds and clean the dishes before you go."

"Very well, agha. I'll do it right away," Najmieh says, getting up quickly.

"Baba, can you come with us too? Please?" I ask.

"No, I can't. I have a lot of work to do, Azadeh."

"You are always working, Baba."

"Maybe I'll drive down for a few days next week."

"No, you won't." I sigh, knowing that he won't show up. He never does.

Shortly thereafter, I'm sitting on the steps of the veranda, feeding my stray cats some chicken leftovers from the night before on a large piece of old newspaper. On the cover, a picture of the shah and President Nixon catches my eye. The headline reads ONGOING OPEC NEGOTIATIONS.

A few months earlier, I overheard Baba tell his friend, "The Americans will get rid of the shah if he keeps insisting on raising the price of oil. You know, I think Iran will be better off with him gone."

Before that, I didn't know that the Americans could get rid of the shah and that Baba thought he wasn't good for Iran. *Who will take his place if he loses the throne?* His son is only a few years older than I am, so he can't possibly rule Iran. I guess another dynasty could take over the Pahlavis, the same way the shah's father unseated the last Qajar shah, the dynasty before the Pahlavis. I have to admit that history is by far my least favorite subject in school. Unlike science, most facts concerning history escape my mind the minute I'm done taking a test to show that I've mastered the material.

৯ ৯ ৯

After thirty minutes in the car, we leave the outskirts of Tehran while traveling north on the Karaj Highway that runs parallel to the shallow, noisy Karaj River. Fruit orchards snake up the river along the slopes of the Alborz mountain range that stands between Tehran and the Caspian Sea.

I look out the window and stare at the large buses traveling in the opposite direction, wondering how many village girls like Najmieh are on their way to start a new life in Tehran with an affluent family like ours. Are they crying on the bus, telling their fathers to please take them home, or are they hiding their feelings and sitting quietly, like Najmieh is right now? If my father ever dares to give me away like Najmieh's father did the year before, I will cry and cry until he stops the bus and takes me home where I belong.

An hour later, the Karaj Highway merges into the narrow, two-lane Chalous Road, nicknamed "the Death Road." Every year, I see at least a few major accidents on this road—a car flipped over there, another one crushed on the side of the road, or the worst ever, a car in flames at the bottom of a cliff. The No Passing traffic signs mean absolutely nothing to most drivers on this road. Time after time, cars whiz by us, even if we're stuck in the middle of a steep, blind curve.

If Baba were the driver, he too would be passing every single car on the road, but that's not the case with Mamman. She is now holding the steering wheel tightly and shifting gears as we climb higher and higher into the mountains. Occasionally, an anxious driver hoping to shave minutes off his trip appears first behind and then beside us. While I stare at the driver, Mamman peers straight ahead, not paying much attention to what the guy next to us is fuming about. Meanwhile, he's honking, throwing his hands up into the air, and glaring at Mamman with that I-knew-it-had-to-be-a-woman kind of a look. Mamman often pulls to the side of the road, allowing for a train of impatient drivers to pass us. When she parks too close to the edge of a cliff, my heart skips a beat, for usually there are no guardrails to stop us from diving to our dismal fates. Every single time, I close my eyes, let fear wash over me, and pray. *God, please return us back to the road in one piece.*

I know Mamman is kind of an unusual woman, a sort of a legend of her era. Unlike most women in Iran, she drives, is blunt, and has no reservations expressing her views in situations where most women would rather not.

A few weeks earlier, I watched with pride as Mamman told Jafar-Khan, her brother-in-law, that he had no business telling her not to drive. I don't like Jafar-Khan, either; he's always pushing and bossing my aunt around as if her opinion carries no value. I know my aunt wishes to be more like Mamman, standing up for herself, but she never does. She should listen to what Mamman often tells me: *Azadeh, you can be who you want to be. Don't ever let a man tell you what you can or cannot do.* That's why I'll never let someone like Jafar-Khan tell me what do with my life.

As we approach the summit of the Alborz mountain range, Mamman slows down and parks on the side of the road. We walk a few hundred feet and settle under a shady tree to picnic by a rushing stream. The strong smell of eggs, feta cheese, and mortadella wafts from the containers as soon as the lids are pulled back. Minutes later, everyone is busy making his or her own favorite lavash sandwich.

Before I take the last bite of my egg sandwich, I ask Mamman, "Can I go to look over the cliff with Najmieh?"

Mamman stretches her legs on the blanket and pours herself a cup of hot tea, filling the air with the sweet aroma of cardamom, and says, "Yes, but don't get too close to the edge."

At the top of the cliff, I look up at the sky, all blue and cloudless. Down below, both sides of the Alborz mountain range are before us. On the south side, a brown smoggy haze dulls the entire city of Tehran. I bet if cars didn't spew all that black smoke from their tailpipes, there wouldn't be all this junk in the air, making the sky murky and gray next to the ground. On the north side, a blanket of green stretches all the way to the blue of the sea for as far as my eyes can see. From up here, I'd rather live on Najmieh's side, where the air looks crystal clear all the way from the ground to the top of the atmosphere.

"You were born somewhere very close to that sea, right there," I tell Najmieh, pointing to the Caspian Sea.

"I know, but I have never been to the sea."

"Why not?"

"I don't know, but my mother once told me that the sea is only for rich tourists, not people like us."

Her mother is wrong. The sea belongs to everyone, the rich and the poor. "Well, this time, you'll see it. You're now a tourist. You're with us, right?"

"Right. I guess I am," she says, smiling.

"Girls, hurry up! Get back in the car! We are ready to go!" Mamman shouts.

As we cross the summit and descend toward the Caspian Sea, the hillside turns green, and the air feels heavy and cool, filling my nostrils with the familiar scents of Shomal—damp earth, musky wood, and the distant smell of rice fields.

After swishing in and out of long tunnels for hours, we reach the lush foothills of the Alborz mountain range on the northern side. Najmieh calls my name, and I look out the window in her direction.

"I used to work in those fields with my mother and sisters." She points to a vast field of rice paddies where women and children, dressed in traditional, colorful garments and straw hats, are hard at work.

The villagers are up to their knees, sometimes their hips, in water, so I ask, "Didn't you get cold standing in water like that?"

"That part was fine. My legs felt warm after a while, but I hated those leeches."

"What are leeches?"

"They are like giant earthworms, but they are all white and much bigger and fatter than earthworms, especially after they bite your leg and drink your blood."

"They drink your blood? How?" The thought of fat earthworms attacking Najmieh's bare legs makes me shudder, reminding me of a horror movie I saw at my cousin's house the summer before. A man was thrown into a swimming pool infested with piranhas, and instantly, his flesh turned into bones.

"They stick to your legs like glue and suck your blood."

"Ouch, Najmieh." I squint my eyes to shake off the scary thought. "How did you get rid of them?"

"My mother would scrape them off my legs with a sharp knife. Sometime my legs would bleed, swell, and itch really bad."

She rolls up her pants, and unlike my calf, hers is covered with tiny scars.

"Do they still hurt?" I bend over and rub her calf.

"No. But I'm sure glad I'm not out there."

"Me too. I'm glad you're right here with me," I say and turn to look out the window.

Many girls my age are working in the fields, standing in deep murky waters; some even look shorter than the paddies. I can't believe I've never noticed them before, for we've traveled this road many times before. Now I know what Najmieh did all day long before she came to live with us. I don't understand how her mother, whose job it is to protect her, can walk her right in the middle of dangerous waters like that. Sadly, just like her father, her mother seems not to care for her that much, either.

The dashboard clock just flashed five o'clock. Except for a bathroom break, we have driven nonstop for almost three hours. Jahan asks Mamman if we can stop at Pahlavi Beach for a quick swim and snacks before heading to our villa.

"That sounds great, Jahan," Mamman says. "We just passed Rasht. Pahlavi Beach is only minutes away."

"I was born in a small village very close to Rasht," Najmieh tells me. "On most Fridays and holidays, I walked from my home to Rasht with my older sisters."

"What did you do with them in Rasht?" I ask, thinking that she probably went clothes shopping with her sisters in a big city like Rasht.

"We sold straw hats, bamboo carpets, and baskets to tourists."

"Did you make a lot of money selling those things?"

"Sometimes we did. Some tourists would give us more money than the price my father said we could sell the items for."

"What did you do with the extra money?"

"Most of it I gave to my mother, but sometimes I bought *koloocheh* for myself." Koloocheh is a round, soft, walnut-filled cookie, a delicacy of northern Iran.

"Koloocheh is one of my favorite cookies," I say, licking my lips. "I'm sure we can buy some at the beach."

At Pahlavi Beach, Mamman gives Najmieh some money to buy koloochehs, roasted beets, and sodas from a kiosk nearby. When she returns, Jahan, Afshan, Mamman, and I are dressed in swim trunks. Mamman asks Najmieh to watch Afshan, as she takes Jahan and me into the sea.

While standing neck deep in water, I glance at Najmieh on the shore. She's twirling Afshan around with her pants rolled up above her knees, most likely enjoying the feel of the waves lapping at her feet. It's hard to believe this is Najmieh' first visit to the beach. I bet I can teach her how to swim, like I taught Grandma a few summers earlier.

I kick my legs up and lie flat on my back, wishing that Grandma were here floating next to me. Too bad she didn't come with us this year like she normally does, although a car ride with her and Peggy would have been a nightmare.

Maybe next year Najmieh and Peggy can stay home so Grandma can join us instead. I love swimming with her in the sea, her in her black *chador*, me in my tiny little purple bikini. Sometimes her chador would wash all the way to the shore, and I'm usually the one who swims back to retrieve it for her before she emerges out of water, stumbling ashore, looking like a wet, heavy crow.

On the shore, I sit on a bamboo rug near Afshan and Najmieh, biting on a koloocheh and sipping soda. As I lift handfuls of sand and let it pour through my fingers, Afshan dumps bucket after bucket of sand over Najmieh's still body while Peggy barks and takes quick breaks to lick Najmieh's face. Najmieh is almost completely buried when her body starts to slowly rise above the ground, stirring up sand and sending it everywhere, over my head and into my eyes.

When Afshan looks up and sees Najmieh, she drops her bucket, screaming. As she runs with her head turned, she bumps into Mamman.

"Najmieh is going to get you, Afshan," Mamman says, picking her off the ground and running into the sea.

As Najmieh shakes the sand off her clothes, the cheerful expression on her face turns sullen. She sits next to me on the bamboo rug, drumming her fingers.

"What's wrong, Najmieh?" I ask. "You look sad."

"Azadeh khanoom, can I tell you a big secret?"

"Sure. I won't tell anyone, Najmieh. I promise."

"Before I left my village to come and live with your family"—she sniffles a few times—"my father was talking about placing my mother in a motel in Rasht to work as a dishwasher." She breaks out crying.

Watching her weep makes my insides clench. I pat her on the shoulder and sigh in frustration. *Why can't her life be as simple as mine?*

"Should I tell your mother?" she asks, wiping her nose on her sleeve.

"No, Najmieh. That's not a good idea. Let's hope your father changed his mind."

Digging my nails into the sand, I look up at the sky, sunny with patchy clouds. A sparkling rainbow is stretched over the entire Caspian Sea. Inside its arch, seagulls glide and dip in and out of the water, catching fish. If feels as if we are the seagulls and Najmieh is the fish; something is wrong with the way her life is lived.

🌀 A Memorable Encounter

Branches slam against the windshield as we reach the end of a narrow road that opens into a private beachfront community on the Caspian shore. Mamman stops the car behind the gate, and a security guard runs over.

"Salaam, Khanoom *Mohandes*," he greets Mamman.

There we go again! Someone calling Mamman *Khanoom Mohandes* because Baba is an engineer. Hopefully, someday I'll be a real *Khanoom Daneshmand*. I don't want to be called a daneshmand only because my husband happens to be a scientist.

After passing a row of mostly elegant whitewashed villas, I see ours, a deep-sky-blue stucco structure accented with bright-red trim. Baba says the glossy red fence with matching doors and windowpanes nicely complements the unique color of our villa, but the kids in our neighborhood often tease my brother and me. *So you two live in that blue house with the red picket fence? Dear God, who picked those colors? You? Did your bikes come with the house, blue and red?*

I guess Baba wasn't thinking of us when he purchased this property. Mamman is not too crazy about the colors, either. She says Baba didn't really know it was blue with a touch of red until after he had purchased it; but that's just the way Baba is, always buying expensive toys and clothes for us and lots of pricey, one-of-a-kind jewelry for Mamman. We often like his taste, but sometimes we

41

just have to pretend to like his lavish presents because otherwise his feelings would get hurt.

The smell of old wood and salty air seeps out as the shiny, red wooden door creaks open. Mamman asks Najmieh and me to go around and open all the windows to air out the house. We start right there in the living room/kitchen area and end up in the small bedroom that I share with my little sister, Afshan.

"I think you're going to sleep here with Afshan and me, Najmieh."

"Are you sure?"

"Yes. You can't sleep in Mamman's room or Jahan's room. Also, there are no curtains in the living room, and it gets way too bright in the mornings to sleep there," I say as I look out the window and space out.

Once again, that tree fascinates me. Birds, thousands of them, are flocking to it like they did the year before and the year before that. I don't know why, but black starlings seem to love that tree. Every evening at dusk, they dive above and around it in sheets for a few minutes. Then, suddenly, they race toward it to claim their very own spot on a sturdy branch. I don't know why they do this, and nobody else seems to know, either.

"Najmieh, do you see the birds swarming around that tree?" I ask as they whistle and trill while landing in it.

"Yes, I see them. Little birds do that here, but not in Tehran."

"What do you mean?" I ask.

The tree is now filled with birds. A few stragglers still fly about, looking for spots to land.

"Birds in Shomal like to sleep together at night," Najmieh says, looking as if she knows what she's talking about.

"Why?" I shrug, still staring at the tree as loud calls and chirps subside into a soft chatter. No more stragglers in sight. Every inch of the tree is now covered with tiny black birds.

"Because owls and hawks will eat them if they're alone."

That makes perfect sense. There is safety in numbers, right! Grandma didn't know why the birds flock to that tree when I asked her the previous summer. Also, I thought owls ate seeds and fruits like parrots did, not birds.

"Why do they like only that tree, Najmieh? There are lots of trees out there. Why only that one?"

"I don't know, but my mother once told me that little birds like to sleep and make their nests on smelly trees."

"Oh, I see. I think your mother is right."

I'd better stop talking, or she might think I'm totally stupid. Never mind that I am the one who goes to school every day, not her. I'll go out there tomorrow morning to smell the tree. The birds might get angry and attack me if I disturb them right now like in that scary movie by Alfred Hitchcock, *The Birds*.

Minutes later, the entire roost is fast asleep—no more chirps, no more peeps. My ears fill with the sounds of a warm summer night in Shomal—crickets buzzing, beetles hissing, frogs calling, and owls hooting every once in a while.

I wake up the next morning to the sound of thousands of wings whirring. No need to walk to the window and watch the flight, for I have seen it countless times. The sky is just fading into dawn, but the moon is still there, reemerging after the birds are gone. Gazing at the white lace curtains swaying in a gentle breeze, I feel myself drifting back into a peaceful sleep.

Before breakfast, I go outside to smell the tree. White droppings carpet the ground underneath it, but I can't tell if the strong aroma is due to bird poop or the tree itself. With my nose pressed against the thin, pale trunk, I take a few deep sniffs. My nostrils burn the same way they do when I have a cough drop in my mouth. It smells like that white cream, the one that old people rub all over themselves to soothe their stiff muscles. I wonder why the birds are attracted to this unpleasant scent, but I'm not going to ask Najmieh any more questions. Let's move on to something that I know something about like math or science—anything but the birds and the trees.

That evening, Najmieh and I stop at the nearby petting zoo. This year, the main attraction is Mr. Spock, a chimp named after the *Star*

Trek character. Except for his massive protruding ears and the cute, tight, shiny, blue *Star Trek* shirt, he doesn't look much like Mr. Spock. But he's so adorable, alert, and seemingly happy that we are watching him. He scratches his head and makes funny noises while mirroring Najmieh by moving his head left to right as she does.

Suddenly, Jahan appears from nowhere, squirting Mr. Spock's face with his water gun. He grabs the bars and jumps up and down screaming while Jahan points and laughs at him. I tell Jahan to cut it out, but as always he ignores me. Frustrated, I leave with Najmieh to find the zoo attendant and tell on him.

Shortly thereafter, Jahan's loud screams make Najmieh and me rush back to him. Jahan is pinned against Mr. Spock's sturdy cage, and the chimp's long, thin fingers are wrapped around his curly hair. Jahan struggles to free himself, but Mr. Spock is not in a mood to budge, grunting and showing all his teeth as he bangs Jahan's head against the bars.

Fear turns my legs into a pair of tree trunks that I can barely walk on. The next thing I know, Najmieh is on the opposite side of Mr. Spock's cage, shaking the bars with every ounce of her might. As Mr. Spock leaps for Najmieh, Jahan falls to the ground. My shaky hands reach out to drag his lifeless body away from Mr. Spock's grab.

"Jahan, please say something, anything! Please, wake up!" I cry out, curled next to him on the ground.

Najmieh is now standing over me, squirting water into Jahan's face with his water gun, the same one that got him into trouble with Mr. Spock. I look up for the attendant, but all I can see is a kaleidoscope of tightly packed faces chattering nonstop, likely wondering, as I am, if Jahan is dead or alive.

After what seems like eternity, Jahan opens his eyes. "What happened? Is my head bleeding?"

A deep breath escapes my lips as I debate whether to hug Jahan and tell him that I'm glad he's alive. "No, it's not bleeding, but you have a huge bump on your forehead. You shouldn't have gotten Mr. Spock so mad at you," I say, pulling my hand away.

Jahan sits up and looks around until his eyes meet Najmieh's. "Thank you for saving me from that hairy beast, Najmieh."

"Jahan agha, that's my job. I'm glad you're okay," she says, stretching her arm in his direction.

Mr. Spock is now sitting on a red stool in the middle of his cage, deep in thought, likely proud of himself for delivering a good dose of well-deserved hard petting at the petting zoo. As for me, I am no longer interested in asking the attendant to let me pet Mr. Spock. I'll just keep on respecting him from a distance.

Jahan is so lucky that Najmieh came along on this trip. Otherwise, he might be dead right now; I wouldn't have been able to think so fast and act so quickly to save his butt. I don't get why Baba says going to school makes people smart. Najmieh hasn't set foot inside a classroom, and yet she seems to be smarter than Jahan and me.

§ § §

A week later, as we are having breakfast on the patio of our villa, Mamman says, "Kids, no beach today. We are leaving soon to visit Uncle Ahmad in Rasht before heading to Najmieh's village."

"I will clear the table right away, khanoom," Najmieh says, standing up quickly.

As I watch her nervously load the tray with cups and dishes, I pray to God to make her wish come true. I want nothing more than to see Najmieh and her mother reunite later this afternoon.

An hour later, we are on our way to Uncle Ahmad's house. As we approach a main square in Rasht, I turn to look at Najmieh sitting across from me in the backseat. She's staring out the window, biting her nails.

To distract her, I ask, "Najmieh, do you know anything about that building over there?" I point to a historic building in the periphery of the square.

"No, I don't, Azadeh khanoom."

"It's a very famous building, and Rasht is very well known for it."

45

"Why is it famous?" she asks, taking her finger out of her mouth.

"It's one of Iran's first municipality buildings. The Russians designed and helped to construct it in the early 1900s." Actually, I didn't know anything about this building, either, until the year before, when Uncle Ahmad, who reads history books day and night, filled me in.

"Who are the Russians?"

"Well, there are many countries in this world, Najmieh," I say and clear my throat. "Russia borders Iran in the north ..."

With her mouth half-open, Najmieh listens intently as I tell her about the history and geography of the area. She often interrupts to ask what this word or that word means, and I patiently take my time to proudly answer her questions.

"We're almost there, kids," Mamman tells us.

"Is Gisela making goulash today?" Jahan asks.

Gisela is my uncle's round and smiley German wife. She makes delicious Hungarian goulash, a tomato paste stew with chunky pieces of meat and green bell peppers. I like goulash too, but I'd rather save room for dessert.

"Yes, that's what she said last night on the phone," Mamman says, pulling into the driveway.

"I hope she's making her strawberry cream cake," I say, licking my lips.

I love everything Gisela bakes. Her cakes and pastries taste much better than anything you can buy from the fanciest bakeries in Tehran.

Uncle Ahmad opens the door to greet us. Just like a Hollywood movie star, he is tall, dark, and handsome. Baba says he could be Marlon Brando's twin, but Mamman thinks he looks more like Paul Newman with brown instead of blue eyes.

"Welcome, welcome," Uncle says, putting his arms around Jahan and me. Then he lifts Afshan off the ground, cuddling her in his arm. "Do you know who I am?"

"Yes, I know who you are," Afshan giggles. "You're Bardia's father."

"Bardia! Bardia, Afshan is here!" Uncle shouts, putting Afshan on the ground.

Bardia appears quickly, grabs Afshan's hand, and peels her away. He is a few months younger than Afshan, but he's already a head taller than she is, and unlike the rest of us, he is fair skinned like his mother, Gisela.

The whole house smells like paprika, the main spice used in making goulash. I sniff a few times to see if I can smell something sweet, but I can't. I'll be so disappointed if Gisela didn't bake a cake for today.

Gisela appears, smiling and wiping her hands on her white apron. "Salaam to you all. Welcome, welcome, my dear family."

Mamman, at five foot one and under a hundred pounds, looks almost childlike hugging Gisela's waist, even with her platform shoes and her hair puffed up high.

"I have made your *favorite* cake, Azadeh," Gisela says, stroking my hair.

"Strawberry cream cake?" I hold my breath.

"No, I thought strawberry-filled *chocolate* cake was your favorite."

"Oh, I'm sure I'll love that one too. It sounds even better than plain strawberry cream cake."

After lunch, a dessert plate with a huge piece of cake is suddenly staring at me. The smell of sweet chocolate fills my nostrils as I prepare to take my first bite. I lick my lips and chew. Strawberry-filled chocolate cake is now my favorite dessert.

An hour later, we leave Uncle's house with two souvenirs: five large slices of strawberry-filled chocolate cake and my cousin Bardia. He'll stay with us for a week to keep Afshan company.

The car quickly fills with noise. Najmieh is in the passenger seat, giving Mamman directions to her village. The backseat is crowded with four kids and a dog. Afshan is sitting on my lap, talking nonstop to Bardia. "I'll show you Mr. Spock, Bardia. You know that monkey I've been telling you about, the one who wears clothes like people do ..."

"That's it, khanoom! My village is right there!" Najmieh exclaims, pointing to a lush settlement ahead. I cross my fingers and pray for her mother to be there.

Mamman turns left onto an unpaved road. Now I can see the entire village in a glance. It's the size of a soccer field, enclosed by acres and acres of rice paddies. Some paddies are green, standing tall in high water; others are yellowed, bending low on muddy grounds, but most are dry, sheaved, and stacked on the side of the field. I bet Najmieh knows why some are green, some are yellowed, and some are cut.

It's late in the day, and nobody is working in the fields. Only a handful of women are walking toward the village, each carrying two large loads of dry rice balanced skillfully on the tips of a shoulder stick. As we pass each woman, Najmieh turns her head for a closer look; her mother could be hidden in between bundles of dried-up grass.

Mamman parks the car in front of the village chief's driveway. His Spanish-style villa stands out among a sea of rundown, small, white-painted mud houses topped with stacks of straw. The scene reminds me of *The Three Little Pigs*. Only the chief's house would remain standing in the aftermath of a major storm, just like the sturdy brick house of the third little pig that withstood all the huffs and puffs of the Big Bad Wolf.

Many women and young girls sit outside in front of their homes. Next to each group, a large piece of linen fabric lies covered by a layer of rice grains about a few inches thick. Young girls scoop rice into large sieves and wait for their mothers to toss the grains high up into the air. I quicken my pace to catch up with Najmieh.

"What are they doing with the rice?" I ask.

"They are separating the grains from the other stuff," she says.

"What stuff? The yellow, crinkly straws?"

"Azadeh khanoom, look over there," she says, pointing to a mud house ahead. "That's my mother sitting there." She takes off running, shouting, "*Mamman jan!*"

The woman drops her sieve, stands up, and embraces Najmieh,

kissing every inch of her face, sobbing hard. Mamman strokes my hair as we shed silent tears. If I could make a moment last forever, it would be this one, without a doubt.

Najmieh's mother looks even older than Grandma. When she smiles, I can only see a few scattered teeth in her mouth. Her leathery skin is grooved and wrinkled, but her eyes express so much warmth and kindness, just like her sweet daughter Najmieh. Only her cotton shoes are solid red. Sunflower, pink pansy, and twin cherry prints each add more color to her brown scarf, turquoise dress, and green, baggy satin pants. Nothing really goes together, but in a way, it all seems to work.

She pushes Najmieh back as the creaky wooden door flings open, and the stern voice of her husband roars behind it.

"Najmieh, what are you doing here? What have you done?"

Then he turns in Mamman's direction and starts speaking in a gentle, polite voice.

"Khanoom, I'm so sorry for whatever Najmieh has done."

"It's okay, agha. She hasn't done anything," Mamman says firmly. "We're just here on vacation and brought her over to see her family."

"How rude of her to ask you to take her all this way," he says, glaring at Najmieh.

"Are you listening?" Mamman says and repeats her words in a loud voice.

"Agha jan, I didn't say anything to khanoom. I swear," Najmieh says quietly.

"Shut your mouth," he commands her, and she shrinks back.

Peggy charges at him and growls, but her leash pulls her back. Mamman asks Jahan to take Peggy back to the car and tie her to a tree. If I were a dog and could act out my emotions, I would bite him in the shin. He should be hugging and kissing his daughter instead of shouting at her, making her feel embarrassed in front of us.

"Goli, why are you standing there like that?" Najmieh's father asks, frowning at his wife. "Can't you see khanoom is here? Hurry up! Go inside. Make some tea. Bring something out for us to eat."

"Very well, agha," she says and walks away, dragging Najmieh with her.

"Do you want to come?" Najmieh whispers in my ear.

I nod and follow.

Inside the tiny house, the walls are bright and bare, except for five or six metal hangers nailed in to hold a man's jacket and a few colorful garments. A few tribal rugs carpet the floor, but most of it is just dirt pressed over uneven ground. Najmieh's mother now stands next to a portable oil lamp, ready to light the burner; Najmieh is hugging her tight around her waist, her cheek pressed hard against her back. I can tell they love each other a lot and want to be together, just like Mamman and me.

A lit lantern on a panel above the window, a crescent-shaped hole in the wall covered with a sheet, illuminates the entire house. Two plywood beds are topped with pillows and folded, colorful blankets, but there are no mattresses. I never thought people could actually live this way, but maybe Najmieh prefers to be here with her mother instead of living with us in Tehran.

"What's your name, khanoom?" Najmieh's mother asks.

"Azadeh," I say, smiling.

"What a beautiful name," she says, turning to look at Najmieh. "Najmieh, do you know what her name means?"

"Yes, of course. Azadeh means 'freedom,'" Najmieh declares, smiling.

"But do you know what it really means?" she asks Najmieh again. "You and I ain't free like your khanoom is. You might dress like a city girl now, but you ain't free."

What she said is sadly true. Her husband controls their lives, but I don't understand why she has to listen to him; he doesn't even seem to work and make money like Baba does for our family, despite the fact that Mamman often disagrees with him.

Najmieh's mother pours three cups of tea and stacks them on a tray. Najmieh follows behind, carrying a thin silver tray topped with fresh walnuts and a gigantic pale-green plastic saltshaker.

As I step outside, my mouth drops; the platter that holds five pieces of Gisela's strawberry-filled chocolate cake is in Jahan's hands.

"Thank you, Jahan," Mamman says. "It was a great idea to give Najmieh's family a gift. Why don't you give it to Najmieh's mother to take inside?"

Mamman is not being fair. Gisela made that cake for me, not Jahan, and I don't want to give it away, especially to that grumpy old man who is now going to eat it all because he is too greedy to share it with his skinny wife.

"Thank you very much, agha. It smells wonderful," Najmieh's mother says as she puts down the tea tray and takes the cake platter from Jahan's hands.

We're sitting outside on a colorful tribal rug when Najmieh's mother returns with the empty cake platter in one hand and a lantern in the other. It's near dusk, and the daylight is almost gone. Birds are singing and chirping everywhere, landing in trees, just like they do every night outside our villa. The festivities go on and on until all the tea is drunk and every morsel of walnut flesh is salted and consumed.

Mamman hands Najmieh's father some money and stands up. He puts the cash in his pocket and thanks her as he pushes on his knees to get up.

"Goli, hurry up. Walk khanoom and the kids back to the car," he tells his wife curtly, his gold teeth glistening in the dark. "Najmieh, I want you to *never ever* ask khanoom to take you all this way again. Do I make myself clear?"

"Yes, agha jan. I won't," Najmieh says and turns bright red as her mother bends over to pick up the lantern from the middle of the rug.

Hand in hand, Najmieh and her mother lead the way. The rest of us trail behind the dim light, tripping over uneven ground.

From the backseat, I watch Najmieh and her mother embrace tightly before she crawls in with her head down, sniffling. She kneels on the seat and stares out the back window, waving good-bye as her mother's frame quickly blends into the darkness. Now only the yellow glow of the lantern stands witness to her presence until Mamman rounds the corner.

Najmieh turns her body and sits down, crying quietly into her hands. I wish I could reach out and hold her hand, but I can't; Afshan, Bardia, and Peggy are in between us. Watching her weep for her mother makes me feel ashamed of my longing for a piece of cake. Her troubles in life seem *so* much bigger than mine. I can get angry at Mamman for giving away a piece of cake, but I know she will never ever give me away like Najmieh's mother just did. She must feel awful now, unloved by her own parents. How can she keep on living knowing that her parents don't want her? I wouldn't be able to survive if I were her.

It feels strange that the two of us live together, play together, and often sleep together, and yet our worlds seem to be galaxies apart. *What are we? Friends?* I don't know what we are, but Captain Kirk and Mr. Spock in *Star Trek* are from different galaxies, and yet they seem to be friends, so I guess we can call ourselves something like that, as well.

# Khanoom Ashrafi

I wake up extra early and head for the basement to check on my kittens. Two weeks earlier, while we were still in Shomal, Baba discovered them inside a worn-out suitcase in the basement. They belong to Charlie, my favorite stray black-and-white cat. I was stunned when Baba told me over the phone that Charlie was a girl, since she not only has a Charlie Chaplin mustache, but she is also the most ferocious cat in our neighborhood.

It's funny how I would always name my cats thinking that I knew how to differentiate males from females based on the way they behaved. I guess I just assumed that cats were like people, but I'm starting to think that maybe the roles are reversed in the feline world. I know Baba is nice and he listens to Mamman, but most men, like Najmieh's father or my aunt's husband, for example, are bossy and controlling. I would say that we are a true cat family in every sense of the word. We now own four cats and six kittens, but more importantly Mamman seems to be the boss of our family, like Charlie is the queen of all cats.

I wish I could stay home and play with my kittens all day long, but I can't, since fifth grade starts exactly one hour from now. To my disappointment, three of the kittens still have pus in their eyes. Frustrated, I rush up the stairs and into the kitchen, where Najmieh is busy making breakfast for Jahan and me.

53

"Najmieh, do you know how to clean my kittens' eyes?"

"Yes, Azadeh khanoom. I've watched you clean them *many* times. I'll soak cotton balls in warm tea and wipe their eyes as soon as I'm done here. Go on. Get ready. The school bus will be here soon."

"Thank you," I say, feeling a pang of guilt gush through my veins. A nagging sense of disloyalty creeps over me every time I leave Najmieh behind to go to school, for I know if tables were turned, she would insist on taking me along with her.

On the school bus, Jessica tells me Khanoom Ashrafi, the fashion icon of our school, will be our fifth-grade teacher. I can't believe my good fortune this year—my best friend, Jessica, and I will be in the same class together, and we get to have Khanoom Ashrafi as our head teacher. Looking over at Jessica's blonde shiny curls that fall perfectly over her shoulders makes me feel a little jealous. I don't care that my hair is dark, but my unruly curls are impossible to manage, and I almost always have to wear my hair up in a frizzy ponytail.

As Jessica and I walk into the classroom, I pick up the pleasant scent of Khanoom Ashrafi's jasmine perfume. She is sitting behind the teacher's desk, smiling, looking flawless.

After all the students are seated, Khanoom Ashrafi stands up, giving us a full view of her perfectly matched outfit and flashy accessories. She has on a pair of brown bellbottom pants and a tight, long polyester bubblegum-pink shirt decorated with a gold chain of large hoops that hangs loosely around her waist. When she moves her head, blinding light shines and jingling sounds emanate from her gigantic spiral gold earrings that dangle just above her shoulders. The pink on her fingernails perfectly matches the color of her shirt and the bright lipstick that makes her lips appear much fuller than they are. I can't see her shoes, but they must be those trendy platform types that add at least four inches to her short stature. I remember seeing Googoosh, the Iranian pop star, in a similar outfit on a music variety show a few weeks earlier. After the program aired, the newspapers called Googoosh a life-size Persian Barbie in pink.

Jahan and I both think Khanoom Ashrafi and Najmieh could

pass for twins, and that's not just because of their identical boyish haircuts modeled after Googoosh's latest hairdo. They both have fair skin, light-brown hair, and large, almond-shaped hazel eyes. I bet if Najmieh had gone to school, someday she could have been somebody just like Khanoom Ashrafi—maybe even prettier and smarter.

Khanoom Ashrafi's voice breaks my thought. "I would like for each of you to stand up, introduce yourself, and say a few words about your favorite subject in school."

When it's my turn, I stand up and take a deep breath. "My name is Azadeh Tabazadeh. I know chemistry is not a subject of study in fifth grade, but chemistry is by far my favorite subject."

"Well, that's very interesting, Azadeh," my teacher says, nodding. "Chemistry is my favorite subject too."

My eyes almost pop out as I sit down. Khanoom Ashrafi might look like a pop star, but inside, she could be just like me. As Jessica rises to introduce herself, my mind wanders off.

I wish Khanoom Ashrafi would teach us some of the chemistry that she knows instead of all that boring history about the great dynasties of Iran—or, more correctly, the great dynasties of Persia. I did learn one useful piece of information in my history class the year before: Iran used to be called Persia up until just forty years earlier. The name was changed in 1935 because Reza Shah, the father of the current king, wanted the world to know that Iranians were Aryans, not Arabs. Later, Mamman told me Reza Shah feared Hitler and wanted him, not the world, to know that Iranians were of the Aryan race. I didn't quite get what Mamman was talking about, but the subject didn't interest me enough to pursue it further. All I know is that I am so tired of reading about the colossal empires of Persia, how they were always the best of the best, the cream of the crop, the greatest civilizations known to man, and the list goes on and on. If they were really all that great, then why did they topple one after another?

I have already forgotten the names of all the kings we had to memorize for our final history exam in fourth grade, but I still remember the names of all the salts—such as cobalt chloride, manganese nitrate, and copper sulfate—that I mixed up with warm water to make sparkly rosy red, pink, and blue crystals with Uncle Mahmood a whole year and a half before I took that boring history exam. Isn't it more fun to know, for example, that copper sulfate salt is a pale, grayish powder, but its crystal is the deepest blue you have ever seen, like the dark shores of the Caspian Sea? I bet no one else in our class knows that a salt and a crystal are made of the same chemical stuff, and yet they can look, feel, and even smell totally different. Salts usually stink and smell bitter, but their crystals have hardly any scent.

Uncle Mahmood once told me, "Did you know that the graphite inside your pencil and the rock on your mother's finger are chemically made of the same stuff?"

When I asked him to send me another chemistry kit from Germany to make diamond crystals from graphite, he laughed and ruffled my hair.

"Child, if I knew how to do that, I would be the richest man alive."

ᕼ   ᕼ   ᕼ

A month into school, and I love coming to class bright and early each morning to see Khanoom Ashrafi. She's the only teacher I know who can fill up an entire blackboard with equation after equation without even glancing at her notes. Someday, I want to be just like her: pretty and super smart. But today, things seem a little different; my teacher is not standing by the door greeting students as we walk in.

The chatter in the room grows louder and comes into an instant halt at the sight of Mr. Kabiri, the tall and always seemingly angry assistant principal. A frown wrinkles his long forehead as he shouts, "Be quiet, class! Khanoom Ashrafi called in sick. I'll be substituting for her today."

No one appears a bit excited about the news, especially me, since I know Mr. Kabiri doesn't like me.

The month before, Mamman almost got Mr. Kabiri fired

for slapping Jahan. Apparently, he had accidentally tripped on a misplaced carton of milk, causing its content to splash squarely onto Mr. Kabiri's private parts, ruining his one and only silky gray suit. Fuming, Mr. Kabiri had forcefully picked Jahan off the ground by his collar, slapping him hard several times. The news didn't surprise me much, because I thought Jahan had probably planned the whole thing to show off in front of his friends and get a few laughs, though Mr. Kabiri's overreaction probably scared him half to death.

After the incident, my mother was called in to further discipline Jahan, I suppose. She rushed to school and found my brother hunched over in the principal's office with red handprints on his face and bloody tissue paper stuffed up his nose. Jahan later told me Mamman screamed at Mr. Kabiri and threatened the principal until an agreement ensued: Mr. Kabiri would apologize to Jahan if Mamman agreed to replace his damaged suit with a brand-new one. I can only imagine that historic moment of apology—my skinny, five-foot mother looking taller than the ponderous six-foot-four Mr. Kabiri.

Since that day, Mr. Kabiri's dark, beady eyes are always on me, probably waiting for me to screw up so he can prove to everyone that I'm a bad kid just like Jahan.

I slide down in my seat to make myself small, hoping that Mr. Kabiri won't notice me. He sits behind the teacher's desk in his brand-new, chic, navy-blue suit—the one that Mamman bought him a few weeks earlier. Then he crosses his legs and stares at his clasped hands in front of him before looking up in my direction.

"Tabazadeh, come to the blackboard," he says, gesturing me over.

A flash of warmth spreads all the way from the back of my neck to my cheeks as I stand up, only to realize suddenly that I need to use the bathroom. With every step I take, the urge to go becomes more difficult to bear.

Instead of approaching the blackboard, I sorely walk over to the desk and whisper, "Mr. Kabiri, can I please use the restroom first? Please?"

"No. Go to the blackboard. *Now*," he says firmly as he uncrosses his legs and points to the blackboard.

Like a penguin, I waddle from his desk to the blackboard, keeping my thighs tightly pressed.

"Pick up a chalk, Tabazadeh."

As I raise my hand to write, anxiety turns terror into sweat on my skin. The next thing I know, urine is running down my bare legs and dripping over my black-soled uniform shoes. My face burns with shame as I hear voices cracking up and laughing at me. I freeze for a few long seconds before running out, bawling. *I'm never going back to school, never—not even if Mamman gets Mr. Kabiri fired over this.*

§ § §

An hour later, my kittens are crawling all over me. The basement feels just like me, inside and out, dark and stinky. My eyes are puffy and wet, but I've got no more tears left to shed.

"Azadeh khanoom, why are you home so early? Shouldn't you be at school?" Najmieh asks as she walks in.

"Why do you care, Najmieh? Why don't you go to school instead of me?"

"What's wrong, Azadeh khanoom? Why are you so upset?" She sits down next to me on the ground, stroking my hair. "Did something happen to you?"

"Yes, something terrible happened to me in class," I say, choking back tears.

"What?"

She looks at me, and I look down. Tears roll down my cheeks and hit the floor. My lips part a little, but I swallow my words. She probably knows something already; my socks are stinky and wet, and I can smell myself.

"You won't understand, Najmieh. You don't go to school."

"Just tell me, Azadeh khanoom. Maybe I can help," she says, wiping my tears.

"No, you can't help me, Najmieh. Nobody can help me. Nobody."

"It's okay, Azadeh khanoom. You'll be okay," Najmieh says, stroking my hair.

"Stop touching me, Najmieh! Get out! Just leave me alone!" I shout.

Najmieh reluctantly gets up and leaves. As the sound of her footsteps fade, a lightbulb clicks in my head: *I'll get on Gold and gallop away.* Tallah is a beautiful gold-and-black Turkmen horse at the stables where my brother and I take riding lessons. I quickly put on my riding uniform and scurry into the kitchen. While looking around, I trash my soiled clothes and shoes in the garbage can. If I start walking now, I'll be at the stables plenty early to ask to ride Tallah today.

On the way, I pull my riding hat down to conceal my eyes, purposely looking for clusters of crinkly leaves to stomp on. The creaking sound of leaves crushing under my feet is what I hope to hear, but instead, laughing voices fill my head, voices that sound louder now than they did this morning in class when they were laughing at me.

At the stables, I head straight to Tallah's stall. She is the smallest but the prettiest horse in the barn with her shimmering golden body, knee-high black socks, and dark, silky mane and tail. I forgot to bring her carrots today, but she's still rubbing her wet cushiony mouth against my cheek.

The groom once told me, "Horses only kiss people they like."

I kiss her forehead to show her that I like her too. While stroking her sturdy neck, I whisper in her ear, "I wish I were just like you, Tallah—so powerful, so confident, so sure of myself."

The gate screeches behind me. I turn my head and see the groom walking in. As usual, a stinky burning cigar hangs from the corner of his lips, making him sound as if he's talking underwater.

"Salaam, Azadeh khanoom. You're early for your lesson today."

"Salaam, Ahmad agha. I know I'm early. My mother just dropped me off. She told me to tell you that I can start early today," I say, quickly turning my face to rub Tallah's neck, for Grandma says a grown-up can always tell if a kid is lying by looking squarely into her eyes.

"That's fine. I assume you would like to ride Tallah again?"

He's now standing in front of me, blowing out gray smoke into Tallah's golden face.

"Yes. I would love to," I say, imagining myself riding faster and faster, flying off into the sky on Tallah's back. I wish she could soar the skies like Pegasus, the white-winged horse in one of my books who always rescues kids from troubles they're in.

The groom puts Tallah's saddle and bridle on and says, "Go ahead and ride for a while before your instructor shows up."

He gives me a leg up, and I settle into the saddle.

"Thank you," I say, and he clicks his tongue.

I take Tallah for a few gallops around the square before turning her head in the direction of the fence, hoping that she can clear it and take us to a new place—a place where no one knows a thing about me. Standing in my stirrups, I crouch forward for a fast gallop over the paling. But instead of jumping, Tallah bucks and kicks her hind legs, shooting me off like a bullet over the fence. I feel like I'm flying for a split second before everything goes black.

ဪ ဪ ဪ

Everything blares white. I blink a few times but can't tell if that's Baba's face inside a shining halo, staring at me. The blurry image clears a bit as I feel a hand squeezing mine.

"Baba, it's so bright. Where are we?"

"We are in the hospital, sweetie. Your right leg is broken in several places," he says, rubbing my forehead.

I look up and see my right leg hanging from a hook. A heavy white cast is wrapped around it, and all I can see are the tips of my toes.

"Baba, I can't feel my leg. I can't move my toes. What's wrong with my leg?"

"It's okay. Don't worry, sweetie. You have too much medicine in you. Once it wears off, you'll be able to move your toes," he says, smiling.

I doze off and wake up hours later in excruciating pain. A sharp, stinging pulse shoots up from deep inside my leg, traveling fast through every inch of my body. I dig my nails into my palms and scream for help. A nurse hustles in and pushes my frantic mother aside.

"This will take away your pain," she says, replacing the empty plastic bag that feeds my body through a tube and a thick needle in my wrist.

Moments later, the pain is gone. I close my eyes and fall asleep.

The next day, I start to feel much better. I can stay awake longer before falling asleep and wiggle my toes without much pain.

At noon, a nurse walks in and tells Mamman that she'll be back soon to disassemble my IV and bring me some lunch. Then she approaches my bed.

"Can you sit up, sweetie, and swallow these pills? They are the same ones that you took last night."

My lips pucker in disgust. I hold my nose and swallow one large pill, taking a few sips of water, followed by a second large pill and a hefty gulp to wash off the chalky, bitter aftertaste. My mouth smells a bit like one of the stinky salts in my chemistry kit, maybe copper sulfate, but this can't be copper sulfate, because it's white, not grayish blue. Like *Alice in Wonderland*, I've once again stepped into the mystical land of chemical wonders. I wish I could stay there forever and think about things that matter most to me, but I can't, because my mind is stuck in the past, constantly worrying about what happened in class.

Mamman grabs the glass of water from my hand and asks, "When you are ready, Azadeh, we have to talk about what you were doing at the stable. Who took you there?"

Her question stings like a bee, knotting my throat as I try to speak. Luckily, the nurse comes back and stands at the foot of my bed with a tray of food.

"Azadeh, I'm going out for a few hours to run some errands," Mamman says, picking up her purse.

Relief washes over me as she walks through the door.

§ § §

"Azadeh, do you need to go pee or poo?" Mamman asks as Baba lays me down on a hospital bed at home, which is set up at the corner of the family room so I don't have to climb up and down the stairs to use the bed in my room.

I don't know what to tell Mamman. I need to go, but not in front of her if I can help it. Najmieh puts a glass of water next to my bed, smiles, and gently scratches my shoulder.

I look up at her and smile. "I've got to go soon," I say alarmingly.

Mamman picks up a bucket and rushes over to my bed. "Najmieh, come here," she says, waving her over. "I want to show you how to help Azadeh."

Najmieh interrupts. "Khanoom, I think I know what to do."

Mamman leaves, and I go as soon as Najmieh places the bucket under my butt. She looks the other way and asks if I'm done when the sound of spraying fades into the background noise of raindrops drumming on the rooftop.

"Thank you, Najmieh."

"No problem, Azadeh khanoom. That's my job."

"That's not your job, Najmieh, but I appreciate your help."

Najmieh leaves with the waste as Mamman walks in with a big surprise that makes my heart swell: Grandma is now standing over my bed.

"But what about Peggy, Grandma?" I ask with my mouth open. She hasn't set foot in our house since we got Peggy as a birthday present last year.

Grandma bends over and gives me a warm hug. Then she pushes me back and stares into my eyes. "That dog, my dear, is the reason you have a broken leg. Dogs are demons in disguise. I'm afraid that beast has chased all the angels out of your house, making you all vulnerable to curses and evil eyes."

She shakes her head and turns to look straight into Mamman's eyes as if she has failed to protect her child by allowing Peggy to possess our house.

"Azadeh jan," Mamman says, "Grandma is here to help us find out who has put an evil eye on you."

"How are you going to do that, Grandma?" I ask as she sinks into a soft armchair besides my bed, cradling an egg in her palm.

She starts to draw small circles on the egg with a sharp black pen as Mamman recites the names of ten suspects, one circle for each name. After all the names are read, Grandma gently squeezes the egg while reciting the names over and over. The egg finally cracks after ten minutes or so at the mention of Fereshteh's name, a distant relative.

"I knew it. That woman is evil," Mamman says in a booming voice.

Confusion fills my head as I think of Fereshteh, since she doesn't even know Mr. Kabiri, the true villain who set the events in motion that led up to my embarrassing accident. Also, it's hard to imagine an angel, a *fereshteh*, with an evil eye. *What is an evil eye supposed to look like, anyway?*

I glance over at Grandma and gasp; her eyes are rolled so far back into her head that they are barely visible. That, I bet, is the look of an evil eye, but those, I would imagine, have to be Fereshteh's eyes. A chill slithers up my back as I beg God to spare my body from being invaded next.

With her eyes closed and her head rolling, Grandma stands up, swirling a flaming brazier of esphand, wild rue—a sacred herb whose smoldering fumes are believed to ward off the evil spirits—above my head while chanting under her breath. The acrid smoke quickly fills up the room, making my eyes water and my throat burn. The harsh smell that Grandma says will surely purify the air keeps me awake thinking that maybe Fereshteh's evil eye had hypnotized Mr. Kabiri to hurt me, like a snake charmer who mesmerizes a snake to do what he tells it to do. If Grandma has done everything right, then Fereshteh's spirit is now warded off, and Mr. Kabiri can hurt me no more.

§ § §

A week later, early in the afternoon, I hear jingling sounds and the click-clack of high-heeled shoes approaching my room.

As I turn my head, Mamman jumps in, smiling from ear to ear. "I've got a surprise for you."

I can now smell the scent of Khanoom Ashrafi's jasmine perfume. My heart skips a beat as my all-time favorite teacher click-clacks into the room.

"Salaam, Khanoom Ashrafi," I say, finger-combing my messy hair.

"Salaam, Azadeh jan. How is your leg?" she says, smiling.

As always, she looks beautiful, all dressed up like a Barbie doll in a striped pink-and-burgundy knit short dress with matching knee-high burgundy boots. Even with the snowstorm howling outside, her hair looks just perfect.

"My leg is fine. Thank you for coming all this way to see me," I say, wondering if she knows about my accident.

"I'll be coming to see you every day to make sure you finish elementary school this year so that you can graduate with the rest of your friends."

Mamman interrupts. "I'll pick up Khanoom Ashrafi after school every day to bring her here to teach you privately at home."

"Your wonderful mother loves you so much, Azadeh," Khanoom Ashrafi says. "She didn't even tell you that she's also driving me home after we're done."

"That's no trouble," Mamman says. "I'll send over some tea and sweets."

Mamman walks out, leaving me alone with my teacher. Khanoom Ashrafi click-clacks over to my bed, putting down a stack of paper on the side table.

"Shall we start, Azadeh?"

"Sure, but I haven't done any homework in a week."

"That's okay. You're a smart girl. You'll catch up in no time. Today, we'll work only on math, and I'll give you some poetry and history to read for tomorrow."

Before long, I'm completely entranced, yearning to learn everything my teacher knows, especially now that she thinks I'm smart.

A knock on the door makes Khanoom Ashrafi pause and look up. Najmieh walks in carrying a tray of steaming tea, sweets, and a plate of fruits.

"I like your haircut. It looks just like mine," Khanoom Ashrafi tells Najmieh, patting her hair.

Najmieh blushes. "Thank you. I like your haircut too. Khanoom takes me to a salon every few weeks for a quick trim."

As I stare at Khanoom Ashrafi and Najmieh side by side, I'm amazed by how much they look alike. That style of haircut, though, will never work on someone like me, for I don't have silky, smooth hair like they do—like I wish I did.

An hour passes without any further interruptions until Mamman knocks and steps in. "Khanoom Ashrafi, I am ready to take you home."

"Great. We're done for today," she says, standing up and loading her bag with papers and textbooks. "See you tomorrow, Azadeh."

As soon as they walk out, I start working on my math homework, sketching a trapezoid on paper and marking the angles and legs as stated in the problem set.

Najmieh walks in with a tray to clean up and peeks over. "What are you drawing, Azadeh khanoom?"

"A trapezoid."

"What's that?"

"It's a geometrical shape. It looks like a messed-up rectangle."

"What?"

"Sit next to me, Najmieh. I'll show you," I say, and she climbs into my bed. "I have to calculate how much it will cost to put a picket fence around a garden that's shaped like a trapezoid."

"How are you going to do that?" she asks excitedly.

As I work on the problem, I explain to Najmieh what circumference, area, angle, and leg mean. The cost of the fence comes out to be twelve hundred tomans, about one hundred and eighty American dollars in 1975.

"That's a lot of money, Azadeh khanoom. I have to work a whole year to earn that much."

"It is," I say hesitantly, thinking that it's really not that much, since I collect more than that each year during No Rooz, the Iranian New Year, by going from house to house with my siblings and parents to pay respect to the elders. The only thing that I have to do to claim the money is to kiss the Koran at each house and take the cash that's left inside its pages for me.

"Najmieh, can I ask you something?"

"What?"

"Do you like to go to school?"

"I do, very much. But I'm so far behind, Azadeh khanoom."

"I meant night school, Najmieh, where mainly adults go to learn how to read and write. My parents paid for Ali, our servant before you, to attend night school."

"They did?" she asks with hesitation in her voice. "But my father isn't going to let me go to school." She lets out a heavy sigh.

"I'll ask Mamman to ask your father and will let you know."

As I watch Najmieh leave with a tray of leftovers, I wonder how she gets by in this world without her mother's love paving her way. Right now, my mother is chauffeuring my teacher so I won't fall behind in school, and poor Najmieh doesn't even go to school.

That night, I ask Mamman, "Why don't you send Najmieh to night school like you did with Ali?"

"It's not safe for a young girl to walk the streets at night, Azadeh."

"Why can't you drive her and pick her up?"

"I don't have time, Azadeh."

"But you have plenty of time to pick up Khanoom Ashrafi from school, take her to our house, and then drive her back to her house?"

"Yes, because you are my daughter, and she is not," Mamman says in a loud voice. "Also, her father wouldn't hear of it."

"Why don't you ask him, Mamman?"

She sighs. "I've had a very long day, Azadeh. This conversation is over. You need to finish your homework and go to bed. I'll ask Najmieh to come in and help you change."

"Sorry, Mamman. I didn't mean to make you upset," I say as she walks through the door, ignoring the rest of my apology.

Moments later, Najmieh walks in and closes the door behind her. "Azadeh khanoom, I heard what your mother just said. Please don't trouble her on my account. She is right. My father is not going to let me go to school."

"Maybe he will, Najmieh," I say, enraged at the unfairness of the world that I live in. If I were Mamman, I would send Najmieh to school without asking her father. He has no more claims on her; he gave her up last year. Why should Mamman care about what her father thinks? How is he going to find out if Najmieh goes to school? He only shows up once a year to collect his check and disappear. Mamman shouldn't be paying him any money, as that money belongs to Najmieh, not him.

ﺵ ﺵ ﺵ

A few weeks later, my leg feels much better. I'm not supposed to walk without using crutches, but I do it, anyway. Crutches bruise my underarms, but walking with a cast doesn't hurt one bit, so I only pretend to use crutches when my parents are watching.

Mamman just kissed me and left to pick up Khanoom Ashrafi and four of my good friends for a cozy birthday celebration.

Ten minutes later, Najmieh bursts in. "Azadeh khanoom, they're here."

When I hear the click-clack of Khanoom Ashrafi's shoes and my friends' giggles coming down the hallway, I pick up a handheld mirror to make sure my hair is intact.

Soon screams fill the air, followed by long hugs, kisses, and chitchat. Jessica has a pretty party dress on that perfectly matches her blue eyes, but Bita, Neda, and Lily are still dressed in school uniforms, white shirts, and pleated plaid skirts.

Khanoom Ashrafi stands back, watching us with a kind expression on her face. I feel so blessed to have her as my teacher this year. It's only because of her that I'll pass fifth grade with all my friends.

Not long after, Mamman carries in a small cake and a box of colorful markers. My friends draw pictures on my cast and sign their names underneath their drawings. Khanoom Ashrafi draws a weird-looking hexagon connected by lines to English letters O and H.

"What is this, Khanoom Ashrafi?" I ask, looking up at her face.

"That's the chemical formula of aspirin, something that you've probably been taking a lot of in the past few months," she says, signing her artwork.

Wow, that looks like a pirate's secret treasure map. "How did you remember all that?" I ask, impressed by her seemingly endless knowledge of all subjects.

"It's easy. You can do it too if you want. Just open your present. I know you love chemistry."

I tear off the wrapping and read the book's title in my head: *Organic Chemistry.* "Do you know how to draw all these formulas?" I ask, flipping through the pages that display similar drawings to what she drew on my cast.

"Well, most of them, I think, *and* I am going to show you how to do it, as well."

My heart bursts with joy as I thank her for the present and the promise to help me understand this mysterious book.

That night, I try my best to comprehend the information in chapter 1, but I can't figure a single thing out. Meanwhile, the aspirin formula on my cast is tempting me to pick up a notepad and copy it down. I trace it on paper over and over until I can draw it without peeking, the same way my teacher drew it on my cast.

In the next few weeks, Khanoom Ashrafi teaches me a few chemistry concepts. I love the logic of naming organic compounds and drawing out their structures on paper. I now know the technical name for aspirin is 2-acetyloxybenzoic acid, and I also know why it's called that. It's easy; if you see the formal chemical name written out, then it's a piece of cake to draw its structure in a flash.

On the day of our last private lesson, Khanoom Ashrafi tells me, "Azadeh jan, I want you to do something important for me."

"What?" I ask.

"When you come back to school after No Rooz, I would like you to draw the full structure of an animal cell on the blackboard."

The thought of standing at the blackboard, where I had my embarrassing accident, knots my stomach, but I quickly say yes to please my teacher.

"That's great. I knew you would agree, but remember that you may very well refer to your notes while drawing and labeling the cell parts in class," Khanoom Ashrafi says, putting a few pens in her handbag. "Azadeh jan, before I go, I want to know if there is something on your mind … something that you may want to share with me."

Instantly, my heart beats fast, pumping tons of blood up and into my face, making my cheeks hot and my ears burn. "No, I can't think of anything," I say, swallowing, thinking that she is likely referring to my accident in her class.

"Well, I have something very important to tell you. Sometimes a grown-up can do something to a child that is extremely wrong. If that ever happens to you, you should never blame yourself because a grown-up has done something inappropriate. Do you understand what I'm trying to say?"

"I think I do," I say, sniffling and rubbing my eyes.

She bends over and whispers into my ear, "I want you to know that whatever happened to you in class was not your fault."

When she hugs me good-bye, I feel like a bird, light and free, as if her words have lifted the weight of shame from my shoulders.

During the No Rooz break, a growing pile of scratch paper floods my desk and wastebasket as I go through hundreds of sketches. A sigh of relief escapes my body the first time my memory allows me to draw a fully colored and labeled animal cell without peeking at my notes.

§ § §

The night before school starts, Najmieh walks into my room and slowly closes the door behind her. She's holding a couple of plastic bags in her hands.

"Azadeh khanoom," she says quietly, "I hope it's okay that I saved these items for you."

"What items?" I ask.

"Your uniform and your school shoes," she whispers.

I had completely forgotten about tossing them in the trash after my accident. Tears flood my eyes as I stare at Najmieh.

"Thank you, Najmieh. So, you know?"

She walks to my closet and starts to put away my school wear with her back facing me. "No, I don't know anything, Azadeh khanoom. I just thought you might need your clothes and shoes someday, so I took them out of the trash and cleaned them for you. I hope that's okay."

"Thank you, Najmieh," I say and walk over to the closet, wrapping my arms around her waist. "Thank you for always watching over me."

She turns, and we embrace. "That's my job, Azadeh khanoom," she says with her head on my shoulder.

"That's not your job, Najmieh." I sigh, angry at her parents *and* my parents for allowing her to live this way. At this age, going to school should be her one and *only* job. "Najmieh, I hope I've been a good friend to you as you have been to me."

"You are, Azadeh khanoom, I swear. You are the only friend I have."

"Well, then, quit calling me Azadeh khanoom."

"Very well, Azadeh. That sounds strange, doesn't it?"

"Just a little, Najmieh khanoom," I say, and we burst into laughter. Feelings of guilt wash over me as I watch Najmieh leave with a smile on her face—the same smile that often makes me wonder if she's truly happy or she wants me to think she's happy because her job is to keep me happy.

§ § §

The next morning, I put on my uniform and shoes, eat breakfast, and leave for school with Mamman. I'm not taking the bus today, for Khanoom Ashrafi has asked me to come to class early to start drawing the animal cell.

As the students trickle in, I keep my eyes focused on the board, labeling each part of the cell with a thick white arrow pointing to it—the nucleus, the ribosomes, the lysosomes—without looking at my notes, the same way my teacher would have done it herself.

"Get your colored pencils out and copy Azadeh's drawing," Khanoom Ashrafi tells the class.

To my surprise, the students are not laughing at me. Instead, they're following my lead.

"Well, that looks perfect, Azadeh," Khanoom Ashrafi says as I put the chalk down and turn. "There isn't a single thing that I need to change. You did a great job. You may take your seat."

With a slight limp, I walk back to my seat, my entire body blazing with pride as if I were sitting at the Caspian shore basking in the afternoon sun.

The Summer of Hell

Three years of middle school slowly pass without a single teacher taking a personal interest in me. I would have loved to discuss Tolstoy's and Dickens's works in class with Khanoom Ashrafi instead of teachers who seemed not to care much for their students or the tales they assigned for class readings. Through the stories, though, I learned that Najmieh is not alone in this world. Like her, many children in Russia or even England don't live with their own parents and have to work hard for little or no pay at all.

How Much Land Does a Man Need?—a tale by Tolstoy—stayed with me long after I read it, particularly the last scene where a serf is digging a grave to bury his lord. It is stated that, in the end, six feet from his head to his heels was all that the landlord needed.

The final words in the story ring true to anyone, from a serf in the slums to a king in the grandest palace of them all. Rich people like us may own a lot of land, but in the end, we're all the same, hanging on to just about six feet of dirt. The world may not see it my way, but in my heart and in my mind, Najmieh and I are equal now, not when we are dead, no matter how our class may separate us today.

Oliver Twist, an orphan in Dickens's novel, went through so much hardship until his life changed, for a few good people of wealth offered him shelter and care. There are so many children like Oliver Twist living in Iran. I have seen them with my own eyes, skinny and frail, begging for food in the streets of south Tehran, working in leech-infested rice paddies in Shomal, and making finely knit carpets with their tiny fingers in the factories of Esfahan and Kerman. It's the class these children are born into that binds them into a gloomy existence until their deaths. The will of many good people of wealth is what the world needs to wipe poverty off the face of the earth.

I wonder why no author has yet written about poverty in Iran. Maybe an Iranian aristocrat ought to write a novel about the lives of poor children in Iran, like Tolstoy and Dickens did when they were wealthy men themselves. But that can't possibly happen, since the shah seems to punish anyone who questions his ways of governing Iran. I bet if I ask Mamman, she'll give me her standard answer that I live a great life and should *never* speak against the shah.

What Mamman doesn't know is that I'm aware of all the horrible things she's protecting me from—the imprisonments, tortures, and murders at the hands of SAVAK, the shah's secret police.

Last spring, after I promised to keep my mouth shut, a neighbor told me about the shah's recent disastrous visit to America. The Iranian media, as usual, had declared the visit a huge success, a monumental step to bring the two nations to form closer diplomatic ties, but the truth was far from all that hype. Apparently, when the shah and his wife, Queen Farah, met President Carter and his wife, a large number of Iranian students were gathered outside the White House demanding the immediate release of all political prisoners in Iran. I could tell that the shah, standing behind President Carter, had tears in his eyes during the entire TV broadcast. But his tears, according to my neighbor, were caused by tear gas thrown at the demonstrators behind him, not overwhelming emotions of joy as newspapers and broadcasters claimed in Iran.

Unfortunately, the rally didn't help to free my neighbor's brother Hassan from Evin, Tehran's most notorious prison. Hassan is a member of the Tudeh Party, a communist opposition group, the same one that my uncle Mahmood, who now lives in Germany, belongs to, and that's why my parents say it's unsafe for him to set foot in Iran.

After *four long years*, I'll finally get a chance to see Uncle Mahmood and his new wife, Elizabeth. They have plans to visit us in England, where Mamman, Grandma, my siblings, and I will be by then.

Last summer, my parents bought a two-story Victorian house in Bedford, a small town near London, where Mamman knows a few Iranian families. Originally, my parents intended for us to spend summer vacations in England to learn English, but lately, they have been talking about moving to Bedford for good. I bet their decision has a lot to do with the shah and his awful ways of ruling Iran. If it were up to me, though, I'd rather finish high school in Iran and start college in America, since the weather in England often sucks, cold and gloomy with a great lack of sunshine. Also, I have a few cousins attending college in Maryland, and they can help us settle once we get there. However, Mamman says America is too far from Iran, making it difficult to travel back frequently to visit Grandma and Grandpa, so I'm sure we'll end up in England, since my mother always seems to get what she wants.

ᔕ ᔕ ᔕ

Apprehension fills my head the closer we get to leaving for England. This could very well be my last year of living in my homeland. To put my mind at ease, Mamman told me that if we were to stay in England, she would arrange for Najmieh and Peggy to join us there in the fall. Still, that means they both have to stay at Aunt Akram's house for almost three months while we're gone.

It's no secret that Aunt Akram is a difficult person to live with. She has only been married for a few years, and her husband has been to our house numerous times complaining about her. I once heard him tell Mamman, "Azar, I can no longer stand watching Akram discipline Payman. He's only a toddler. Please ask her to stop."

Payman is my vivacious, curly-haired cousin. I too cannot bear to watch my aunt slap and spank him or drag his little screaming body on the floor to lock him in the bathroom because he forgot to change his outside shoes to his inside shoes as he stepped into the house or because he wet his pants. Afshan still peed her pants until she was almost four, and Payman is not even three years old.

My aunt's cleaning rituals are also flat-out bizarre. She repeatedly washes her hands in scorching water and cleans her house, as if everything is always filthy, no matter how spotless it may appear to a pair of sane eyes. I'm worried about Najmieh cleaning daily under my aunt's watchful eyes, since she'll never be satisfied with what Najmieh can do to disinfect her home from germs, bacteria, or whatever else she's so desperately trying to get rid of.

If my aunt weren't so beautiful and so well put together, I don't believe any man would have ever asked for her hand. Sometimes I wish I had inherited her large, almond-shaped eyes, her long, curled eyelashes, and her soft, flowing hair, but only if that meant I wouldn't turn out to behave like her someday.

Grandma once told me, "You know, it's all my fault that your aunt acts crazy sometimes."

Curious, I asked, "Why would you say that, Grandma?"

"Well, it's a long story." She sighed, getting ready to spill her guts. "When your aunt was an infant, we took her on a train trip to Mashhad."

"Mashhad. Isn't that where the shrine of Imam Reza is?" I asked, already knowing the answer.

Imam Reza's shrine is the most sacred place of worship in Iran, since he is the only Shia Imam buried in our land. Mashhad is also known as "the Land of Miracles" because, true or not, Imam Reza has the reputation of healing the lame, the blind, the crippled, the mute, and many in need who come to him in prayer.

"That's right. Imam Reza, God bless his mighty soul, is buried in Mashhad."

"I don't think I have ever been to Mashhad."

"Oh, yes, you have," Grandma said, nodding. "Your parents took you and Jahan to Mashhad when you were just born, on the same train that Grandpa and I took your aunt sixteen years earlier when she was just born."

"On the same train?" *Wow, what a coincidence*, I thought.

"Yes, the same one. I'm sure of it." Grandma paused to catch her breath. "On the train, your aunt cried out loudly, like a lamb wounded, and nothing I tried—nursing, cradling, or singing to her—seemed to soothe her troubled soul. At last, I swaddled her tight and laid her on the floor that grumbled and rumbled under my feet, rocking her back and forth between my two soles. I begged Imam Reza, God bless his soul, to ward off the evil that was torturing her soul. Soon after, she fell into a deep sleep, resting peacefully until we arrived in Mashhad, safe and sound, or so that's what I thought."

Grandma let out a big, heavy sigh, shook her head, and went on.

"All that rattling overnight must have scared her spirit off, for the moment she opened her eyes, I could barely recognize her as my own flesh and blood. Since then, a renewed spirit, different from the one God had blessed upon her at birth, has taken hold of her soul. I should have known better."

While listening to Grandma, I wondered if my own spirit had fled my soul in the dark of the night when I was an infant on that train, rattling along. I hope I won't become a person like my aunt, constantly worrying and complaining about cleaning this or that. However, it's possible that my brother's spirit might have escaped him on that night, for he too, like Aunt Akram, can lose his temper if his clothes are not hung or folded exactly as he wants them each time. I would never ever get upset over such petty things. While Jahan's closet is always nice and neat, mine looks as if the Mongolian tyrant Genghis Khan has just rumbled through it all, so maybe I'm not like my aunt, after all.

৯ ৯ ৯

I wish Najmieh could come with us, but it's too late, for we'll be on our way to England shortly after the sunrise.

Before turning in for the night, I pull out a used stamped envelope from underneath my mattress and hand it to Najmieh. "Keep this somewhere safe and don't tell anyone about it. There are two hundred tomans inside."

"*Wow!*" she says with sparkle in her eyes. "That's a lot of money, Azadeh. Why are you giving it to me?"

"Well, who knows? You might need money to buy something for yourself or Peggy. We are going to be gone for a *very* long time." I pause and look her straight in the eye. "Najmieh, you have to promise me something."

"What?"

"You have to promise me that you'll agree with my aunt no matter how nutty her instructions may sound when it comes to cleaning the house or caring for my cousin Payman."

"I will, I will, I know. Don't worry. Let's go to bed before your mamman hears us."

Najmieh shuts the light, gets on the floor, and crawls into her bed, a rollup mattress next to my bed.

"Good night, Azadeh."

"Good night, Najmieh," I say, remembering the moment when I asked Najmieh to stop calling me Azadeh khanoom. Three years have passed since then, but I know something inside me changed on that day, something that made me realize Najmieh had been my most loyal confidante without me recognizing it for years.

God, please have my aunt behave herself. I sigh, staring at Najmieh lying curled up with her hands tucked under her cheek and the full moon shining on her face.

§   §   §

Since our plane took off, Grandma's eyes have remained closed, but she's neither asleep nor fully present in this world. Her slim body gently rocks back and forth as she chants the same words.

"Almighty God, giver of all that is good, the end is upon me, forgive me of my sins, forgive my son Mahmood for his unbelief. *Ya*

Imam Reza—God bless your soul a million times—I wish my last wish upon you, the greatest healer of all. Shine your light through my son; make him a believer in God before his spirit leaves him behind."

As I hear Grandma's pleas, anger stews inside of me. She's literally up in the air, frightened to death, just for a chance to see her son. It should be the other way around, Uncle Mahmood visiting her in Iran, but I know he can't. Four years earlier, an informer from SAVAK, the shah's secret police, had snapped a Polaroid of my uncle somewhere in Europe in the midst of a heated protest against the shah. Later, someone who knew Baba told him that Uncle's name was blacklisted in SAVAK's files.

The news devastated Grandma, and she began cursing at the shah, and that's how I learned of my uncle's bad luck. If I were the shah, I would be afraid, really afraid, for Grandma says the curse of a mother with her heart broken in half is a like a snake in pursuit of an attack, full of venom and deadly at last.

The shah must have broken many hearts before Grandma put the spell on him to pay for his crimes, but maybe more hearts need to be broken for the curse to grow in strength and strike at the shah.

After a few hours, Grandma opens her eyes and peers through the window. "Look out there, Azadeh. Goodness gracious, we are in clouds. It feels like heaven is just above us. Are we alive?"

"Of course, Grandma. We are alive. Trust me—nothing will happen to you. I have been on planes before, and nothing has ever happened to me. Planes are safe, even safer than cars, Baba says."

Slight turbulence rattles the plane, and Grandma begins chanting again. She truly believes the end of her life is only minutes or at most hours away. I'm starting to think that Uncle Mahmood may be right about Grandma being superstitious sometimes, though I hope she's right about the curse of the snake taking hold to topple the shah. Only then can Uncle Mahmood once again visit Iran, so Grandma won't have to bear the scare of sitting through another long plane ride.

§ § §

By the time we arrive at our town house in Bedford, Grandma seems well—a little tired but very much alive. As soon as Mamman unlatches the creaky, wooden door, Grandma jumps in and asks, "Azar jan, where is the bathroom?"

To her dismay, the only toilet in the house looks the same as the one she couldn't stand but had to use on the long plane ride. She walks out complaining to Mamman about the toilet as I go in. The pink *farangi* toilet even features a cushiony seat that I happen to like. I walk out as Grandma walks back in, sighs, and locks the door behind her.

"Do you think Grandma is squatting or sitting down?" I ask Mamman, hiding my smile behind my hand.

"Only God knows," she says, and we burst into laughter.

From what Grandma says, I can tell she dislikes two things about farangi toilets: touching the seat before using it and the lack of access to a hose nearby to ritually rinse off her private parts. An hour of listening to Grandma's rant is all it takes for Mamman to run to a nearby gardening store. She returns with a cardboard box full of disposable plastic gloves and a small metal pitcher that I assume the British would likely use for an entirely different purpose.

My personal preference is by far the farangi type. The squat ones smell gross, and you have to always aim right; otherwise, your shoes and socks will get sprayed and splashed with you know what. Afshan also prefers the farangi type, for she fears the hole in a squat toilet can swallow her whole if no one is standing nearby. That's why, I think, she always makes up excuses not to spend time at our grandparents' house, where she has no other option but to use a squat toilet with an unusually wide rim that I, too, believe could swallow her whole if she did slip and fall.

A week later, I miss everybody back home—Baba, Najmieh, Peggy, Grandpa, my cats, and my friends. Now I know why the British call Bedford a sleepy town, for there's nothing fun to do but to wait for the afternoon's arrival. Hearing that soothing melody makes my mouth water for an ice cream cone, a sandwich, a cup, or one of the zillion variations on display to choose from, but honestly, the ice cream truck is the one and only thing that I love about this town.

Come to think of it, though, Peggy would have loved this place, for more dogs than children live on our block. So far, I have seen a few that look just like Peggy, minus the colorful, tight-fitting outfits they have on. I don't get why most dogs in Bedford are dressed in clothes. The old lady across the street and her little white fluffy dog even dress alike. That dog just cracks me up, swaggering the neighborhood in flashy clothes with her head held high and her fluffy tail standing straight up.

I'll ask Mamman to take Afshan and me clothes shopping for Peggy before she arrives. In a few months, Najmieh might well be asking Peggy, "Now, Miss Peggy, tell me, what would you like to wear this morning—the royal purple-and-red satin outfit, the knit pink-and-gold sweater, or the ensemble that matches mine?"

ৎ ৎ ৎ

Uncle Mahmood's loud voice fills the air outside before the bell rings, and he stomps into the house.

Grandma jumps in front to greet Uncle first as his wife, Elizabeth, stands back, waiting her turn. He is a little wider in the waist, but his hair looks exactly the same, curly and full, blocking my view to see how Elizabeth looks. As always, his bushy mustache and large, black-framed glasses cover most of his face. When Uncle and Grandma's long embrace ends, he steps back, giving me a full view of Elizabeth's face.

She looks surprisingly young, maybe not much older than I am, dressed in a loose lavender summer dress, soft brown leather sandals, and thin-framed burgundy glasses. Her hair is lovely, silky light brown, straight with bangs. Her skin is fair, but it's hard to tell much about the size of her green, magnified eyes. I'll bet she can't see a thing with her glasses off.

We spend the rest of the day chatting, laughing a whole lot, and feasting on scrumptious food that Grandma has worked tirelessly preparing over the past few days.

In the following week, Uncle and Elizabeth take Jahan and me, and sometimes Afshan, to parks and museums in London. On their last day, as we walk around the Natural History Museum, Uncle stops in front of a display case and motions me over.

"That's Marie Curie, Azadeh. She was the chemist who discovered radioactivity in elements that I've been telling you so much about."

From listening to Uncle's long tutorials in the past week, I now understand what radioactivity means—the decay process of an atom's nucleus to make it become more stable.

"But that's a woman, Uncle," I say, looking up with my mouth open.

"So? What's wrong with that?" he says, twirling his mustache.

"Nothing." I shrug, staring at the display case. For some reason, I had assumed all famous scientists were men, like Galileo, Newton, and Einstein.

At the museum shop, I ask Uncle to buy me a small booklet that shows a black-and-white picture of Marie Curie and her husband experimenting in a laboratory on its cover. Inside, the history of radioactivity is discussed, along with diagrams explaining how it works to date objects from the past, like a dinosaur bone or an ancient artifact.

A few hours after we return from the museum, I find Jahan and Uncle in the family room watching live World Cup games on TV.

I show Jahan the booklet and say, "There, you can see for yourself. Men are not smarter than women."

"They are, Azadeh, but as usual, you aren't smart enough to realize that." He puffs out loud. "So, let me enlighten you again for the zillionth time. Who invented electricity? Edison. Who invented the phone? Bell. Who invented cars? Ford. And the list goes on and on. Tell me one thing that a woman has invented."

Electricity, phone, and cars are all big inventions. My mind goes blank. I can't even think of a small invention to name by a woman.

"Well, unfortunately, Mamman invented you," I vent out. "Edison was also invented by his mother." I sigh, feeling embarrassed in front of my uncle, who has been watching us over the rim of his glasses.

"Wait a second, young man," Uncle interrupts our discussion. "Do you know who is on the booklet cover you're holding?"

"No, I don't know either of them," Jahan says and shrugs.

"Well, that's Marie Curie and her husband, Pierre Curie."

"So?" Jahan says, rolling his eyes.

"They won a Nobel Prize for their discovery of radioactivity. Radioactivity has led to so many wonderful inventions like …"

Jahan and I listen to Uncle and interrupt him often to ask questions. He tells us how the discovery of radioactivity has impacted humanity both positively and negatively, naming cancer therapy and the construction of the atomic bomb as extreme examples. As I hear him talk, I ponder over the power of a common set of principles that, when applied, could save a person's life but in the same breath destroy the entire planet.

"Now, let's go back and reevaluate to see if men are indeed smarter than women. Marie Curie, for example, has won two Nobel Prizes, and her husband has won only one. So, isn't she *then* smarter than her husband?" Uncle looks at Jahan, pushing his glasses up his nose.

"I don't know, Uncle," Jahan blurts out. "She might be smarter than him, but she is not smarter than Einstein, for sure."

"Well, are you sure about that, Jahan?"

"No one on this earth is smarter than Einstein, Uncle."

"I don't know about that, Jahan. Einstein won only one Nobel Prize before he died, so I'm not sure if he's smarter than Marie Curie or not."

Jahan stays quiet, just like me a while back when I couldn't think of a woman inventor to name.

"Uncle, has anyone else won two Nobel Prizes besides Marie Curie?" I ask, hoping that she would be the only one so far.

"Yes, I think so. Two more scientists, I believe," Uncle says as Elizabeth walks in and sits next to him on the couch.

"Were they men or women?" Jahan asks, eager to hear the answer.

I know he's hoping for both to be men, so statistically he can still declare himself the winner of this argument.

"Well, I don't remember off the top of my head," Uncle says as he puts his arm around Elizabeth's shoulder. "But I know one thing.

This woman right here," he points to Elizabeth, "is without a doubt ten times smarter than her husband. Her Farsi is much better than my German, and she hasn't even been to Iran yet."

"He's 100 percent right," Elizabeth says, kissing his cheek. Then she gets up, grabs his hand, and pulls him off the couch. "Let's go, Mammoth. We have to pack and leave soon."

"*Mah-mood*, dear, not Mammoth. They became extinct five thousand years ago," Uncle says, once again teasing Elizabeth for mispronouncing his name.

As I watch them climb the stairs, I promise myself that I'll never again allow myself to get upset when Jahan claims he's smarter than I am, though I must admit that he is partly right; I can name so many smart men—Edison, Bell, Ford, Einstein, Galileo—but only *one* smart woman, Marie Curie.

ॐ   ॐ   ॐ

The next morning, no one is up early, for Uncle and Elizabeth are gone, not in the kitchen making delicious breakfast for everyone. Life is back to normal in this sleepy old town. Now there is nothing fun to do but to wait for the afternoon ice cream truck.

I hear Mamman's voice calling Jahan and me to come downstairs at once. Minutes later, we are sitting on the sofa, rubbing our eyes. Mamman is standing over us, scratching her head.

"This better be important, Mamman," Jahan says. "I'd rather go back to sleep, if you don't mind."

"There isn't an easy way to tell you this, but Aunt Akram just called with bad news." Mamman takes a deep breath and sighs. "I'm sorry, really, very sorry to tell you that Peggy is lost."

Jahan springs to his feet, shouting at Mamman, "Lost? Where? When? We have to go back right now to find her, this afternoon, tonight, the sooner the better!"

Tears choke up in my throat as I watch Jahan screaming for both of us. He is right. We must leave at once. Unlike Bedford, Tehran is not a place where most citizens show kindness when their paths cross that of a fluffy wandering dog.

"I'm sorry, kids," Mamman says, tucking her hair behind her ear. "We can't go back. Baba wants us to stay in England for now."

"Well, then, let's call Baba," Jahan says, flaring his nostrils and breathing heavily as Grandma walks into the living room.

"Now kids, what's all this loudmouthing about?"

"Peggy ran way, Grandma," Jahan says, staring at Mamman. "And Mamman doesn't care one bit."

"Who is Peggy?" Grandma asks, shooting up a brow.

"She's our little dog, Grandma," I sniffle. "You don't remember Peggy?"

"So that's what all this fuss is about," she says as a wry smile plays on her lips and her hands lift up in prayer. "Thank you, almighty God. At last, you heard my vows. Dogs are demons in disguise …"

This time, Grandma's soothing storytelling voice shoots flares of anger up my spine. I stomp out distraught, in tears, flaming inside. They're both making me mad—Mamman for not doing anything, although she can, and Grandma for once again taking pride in being so almighty right.

A few lonely weeks dwindle away, during which I hardly exchange any words with anyone inside or outside our Victorian town house. Our house in Tehran doesn't have a fancy name, but it's one hundred times better than this house, which looks exactly the same as any other house on our block. I miss our huge yard, swimming pool, indoor patios, and the bright roomy kitchen back home. My only wish is to be there now, gossiping with my girlfriends, going to Samad movies with Baba, sleeping on the rooftop with Najmieh at nights, and spending a few carefree weeks at our villa on the Caspian shore before school starts in September. I'd rather go back even if Iran is not as safe as it once was.

§ § §

Late one afternoon, near dusk, I hear Mamman talking to Baba on the phone. I get close to her and whisper, "Can I talk to him after you're done?"

"Just a minute," she says, covering the receiver with her hand. "Here is Baba."

She hands me the phone and walks away. Soon I realize this is just another dreadful call. Baba is telling me Iran is unsafe, and we are better off staying in England.

"What about Najmieh?" I ask him.

"Be patient, Azadeh. She doesn't even have a birth certificate. I have applied for one, but it will take months for it to arrive. I'll bring her with me as soon as I can."

I slam the phone down, feeling angry at my parents. If they had kept their promise, Najmieh and Peggy should be in Bedford by now. Najmieh cried so much into the phone last week that no matter what I said, she still blamed herself for Peggy's loss. But I could sense she was holding something back, something more sinister than feeling guilty about losing our dog. Hearing my aunt's screams in the background as we spoke sent chills down my spine, since I knew it wasn't in her character to be nice to Najmieh or anyone else. What if she is beating Najmieh like she beats her own son? We have to go home and save Najmieh from my aunt's unruly hands.

That night, Mamman tells us Cinema Rex, a popular movie theater in Abadan, a southern city in Iran, was burned to the ground last Thursday while over five hundred people were locked inside, screaming for their lives. According to her, riots broke out throughout Iran after the incident, blaming the SAVAK for staging the accident. Mamman says she doesn't believe the shah's secret police were involved, but why are people rioting and risking their lives to say that the SAVAK had done this horrible thing?

I had once been to that theater when Baba's construction company had contracts to build roads and highways near Abadan. What if I were there with my family when it went up in flames? I can vividly imagine the horror of that night, helpless people piled up behind locked emergency exits, screaming to get out, but I can't see them burning alive. Who would or could do such a horrible thing? Mamman thinks a radical Islamist group had likely set the fire to make the shah look bad, but how could a person of faith—of *any* faith—be responsible for such a heinous act? Now I understand why Baba said Iran is unsafe, but I'd rather go home and start school in September than stay in England. Besides, we need to go back and make arrangements to take Najmieh with us if we are to move to Bedford for good. But I hope that's not my parents' plan, since I feel completely out of place in this town and can't imagine myself settling here for the rest of my life.

§ § §

On yet another gloomy, overcast day, I walk into the house, back from my afternoon visit to the ice cream truck. Mamman is on the phone with Aunt Akram.

"Oh my God. When did this happen?"

The pale look on Mamman's face tells me this is far worse than Peggy's loss. I quietly sit down and listen with my ears perked up, my mouth open, and my head down.

"I can't believe she ran away, poor girl. This is all my fault," Mamman continues in a shaky voice.

Tears stream down my face as I watch the ice cream cone slip through my numb fingers and hit the ground. Realization washes over me like waves crashing down. That's it. I may never see Najmieh again. Mamman is right. This is all her fault. She is the one who left her behind in a madhouse. Aunt Akram's frantic cleaning spurts and temper tantrums probably drove Najmieh insane, and she ran away, just like Oliver Twist. There's only so much a person can take before the fear of dying out there, alone, outweighs the prospect of living a miserable life.

God, lately I have been thinking that Uncle Mahmood may be right and that You may not exist, but I know now that I was wrong. Please forgive me for my doubts. Please bring Najmieh home unharmed.

"Mamman, we need to go home and find Najmieh *now*. No more excuses, *please*." My voice is loud, like Jahan's when he's arguing with Mamman.

A tender expression spreads across Mamman's face. "I know you are upset, Azadeh. Believe me, I'm so worried for Najmieh too, but we can't go back, and you know why."

Mamman tries to stroke my hair, but I recoil and shout, "No, I don't! What if I were missing instead? Would you go back then? You know the answer to that, don't you? Live with it!" I choke up and collapse into tears.

"Azadeh, people are looking for her. She'll turn up. I'll promise you."

"I don't want to hear your voice, your empty promises. I'm not getting up from this couch until we're ready to pack and go home."

"Well, then, sit there for as long as you wish," she says, turning to leave.

I remain seated with my eyes closed, my heart broken into pieces, bawling. Grandma walks in to talk with me, but I ignore her. She sighs and starts to pray as agate prayer beads pass between her fingers.

That night in my sleep, I see Najmieh lying unconscious, curled up on the ground with Peggy standing over her, licking her face, trying to wake her. When she doesn't wake up, I scream, and the next thing I know, Grandma is shaking me awake.

"Stop screaming, child. Close your eyes and dream of God. His light will chase the demons back into the depths of darkness where they belong."

It was not the demons but my conscience that was catching up with me, for I had failed my friend in every possible way. It's my fault that Najmieh is gone. Where is she now? Is she alive? I should have insisted on bringing her along with us to England. I will likely never see her again. I sink my face into the pillow and cry myself to sleep.

During the next few weeks, I plug my ears whenever I see Mamman approaching to have a conversation with me. Often, I phone Baba at his office, asking about Najmieh, begging him to come to England and take me home.

My persistence finally pays off. We're going home tomorrow, three long weeks after my aunt's dreadful phone call. Thank God the summer of hell is about to end.

ဩ ဩ ဩ

While walking down the long international hallway at Tehran's Mehrabad Airport, I see Baba waving at us from outside the security area. He's smiling from ear to ear, and I can't wait to hug him and ask about Najmieh.

When we meet, Baba picks Afshan off the ground and says, "I have good news."

"Najmieh is back?" I ask, holding my breath.

"Not quite, but she has mailed you a letter."

"A letter? Where is it?"

"At home."

"What does it say, Baba?" I ask, angry at him for not bringing the letter along.

"She is in Rasht."

"Rasht?" Mamman asks. "How did she get to Rasht?"

"Well, Azadeh knows all about that."

"I don't," I say, pondering over what Baba said.

"You gave her a lot of money, Azadeh, without asking us. She used it to buy a bus ticket to Rasht."

"Good for her," I say, fuming. "I would have fled too if I were stuck living with Aunt Akram for that long. Is she coming back soon?"

"I don't think so," Baba says, putting his arm around my shoulder.

"Why not?" I look up at Baba.

"She is getting married in a few weeks."

"She is only sixteen. That's way too young to get married."

"Not for a village girl, Azadeh." Mamman sighs. "Thank God she's alive."

As Baba pulls into the driveway, I don't feel like I'm home. Najmieh is not out on the driveway, smiling, eager to help us unload our belongings. Peggy is not out there, either, jumping three feet high in the air, letting everyone know how excited she is to see her family again.

Once inside, Baba gives me Najmieh's letter. It bears no return address, so I know I can't write back if she doesn't mail another letter. I rush to my room and close the door, turn my back against it, and slide down to the floor. I never imagined our friendship would come to such an abrupt end. For some reason, I always thought Najmieh would be in my life forever, moving in with me after I got married to help me raise my own family.

Najmieh's handwriting puts a smile on my face. She still writes like a child—bubbly letters, misspelled words, no punctuation—in spite of all the hours we spent together to work on her writing. To my surprise, she's not living in her village near Rasht. Instead, she and her mother are working as dishwashers at a motel in Rasht where her husband-to-be is the cook. In her words, I sense a newfound happiness; the love for this tall, broad-shouldered man, as she describes him, somewhat assures me she's better off living with him than with us in Tehran as a servant. Tears roll down my cheeks as I read her final words:

> *Dear Azadeh don't be sad for me becuse my fater died I am not sad for that I feel sad only becuse of Peggy only becuse I didn't say goodby to you and your famaily plese forgive me have a good life I am happy very happy my mother is happy too.*
>
> *By the time this leter reachees you I have taken a last name never had one before with a handsom husband wish me good luck and healtee babies.*
>
> *Your friend always,*
> *Najmieh*   *August 25, 1978*

The realization that she left out her last name and the return address on purpose makes me feel like the scum of the earth. She doesn't want to be rediscovered by people like us, people who have a lot of money but no conscience about her way of life. Once again, Najmieh shows me she is a better person than I am by asking me to forgive her, since I am the one who needs to be forgiven, not her. I knew damn well how much she wanted to go to school, learn new things, and grow up living a life of a spoiled city girl like me, but I did absolutely nothing to make that happen for her. I hope God can forgive my parents and me for not treating Najmieh as an equal member of our family.

As I place Najmieh's letter underneath a pile of old photographs in the top drawer of my nightstand, I think about her dreams and my dreams. She wants to be like me, and I want to be like Marie Curie. Chances are she'll never be like me, and I'll never be like Marie Curie—not because we are not good enough or smart enough but because we were born in a place where women just don't get what they want from life.

Black Friday: The Aftermath

I arrive home from a slumber party, hoping against hope that Mamman will have good news to share, a phone call or a letter from Najmieh to let us know where she lives in Rasht. But today is no different from yesterday, or ten days earlier when we came home from England. Oddly, in spite of Najmieh's disappearance, our household is back to normal. Mamman is busy getting things ready for us to start school in two weeks, while Baba chats nonstop about the uprising that he believes may topple the shah. Frankly, I couldn't care less for my newly sewn high school freshman uniform, but the prospect of a revolution looming intrigues me. Maybe that's what needs to happen for someone like Najmieh to realize her dream of becoming a city girl like me.

My overnight bag slides over my shoulder and drops onto the floor in the hallway as I head for the family room, where Mamman is watching TV with my siblings. The shah is on live, addressing the nation.

"I hear your voices and sympathize with you. I understand the reason for this uprising. I promise you, we will all live in a free society from this point on. The nation's military force will never be used against the people of Iran again … Today, I fired General Oveisi for ordering the military shootout yesterday without my knowledge. Please accept my sincere apology ..."

His words make me realize what I heard at my friend's house this morning was true. Yesterday, military tanks and helicopter gunships opened fire on a large group of protestors at Zhaleh Square. I can't believe many people were killed only because they stayed out past curfew imposed by martial law. That's not right. The shah must have ordered the shootout himself, for he is the commander in chief. I don't understand why he is blaming General Oveisi, his chief commander, for this atrocity. *How could the shah order the killing of so many people on a Friday, the weekend in Iran?*

After the shah's public apology aired, I phone Homa, a close neighbor, and we agree to go out for a walk around the block.

Street corners, bus stops, delis, and coffee shops are filled with clumps of people, whispering, some are even talking out loud as if they intend for others to hear them out. Apparently, the shah himself was in one of the helicopters, hovering above the crowd and directing the operations as he witnessed the carnage unfold in Zhaleh Square. Soon we find ourselves telling others about what we've heard.

In my head, the rumors create a brutal image of the shah—a lunatic in a helicopter shooting at innocent people as if they were nuisance ants on a kitchen counter, deserving to be sprayed to their deaths. More than ever, I find myself searching for the truth, the whole truth about the shah, his regime, and the massacre. Getting information, though, is not easy with a state-controlled media and with parents and relatives who are fearful to share more than just a few words: *Always remember, the walls have mice, and the mice have ears. You are never to speak against the shah. If you do, horrible things will happen to you and your family.*

But this time, my gut tells me something is terribly wrong, and I need to rely on myself to figure things out.

ᕗ ᕗ ᕗ

A week after the massacre, my friends and I are standing at the curbside near the entrance to Shemiran Mall, where we often meet to go clothes shopping on weekends. I feel lucky to have not one but four best friends, and except for Jessica, we come in matching pairs. Neda and I are olive skinned, tall, and skinny; Bita and Lily are dark skinned, short, and already full-figured; and Jessica is the only blonde, of average height and somewhere between skinny and full figured.

Today, the Shemiran Mall is closed, so we're not here to spend money. Instead, we're on our way to catch a taxi to Zhaleh Square. Bita has secretly organized this outing, and we are not to tell anyone about it. I just hope no one sees me wandering about, for my parents will ground me if they ever find out.

"Zhaleh Square! Zhaleh Square!" we yell out to hail a taxi.

Jessica and I quickly jump in the front to share the passenger seat, while Lily, Neda, and Bita crawl in the back, huddling next to an elderly woman.

In the car, I balance myself by sitting half on the passenger seat and half on the gearbox as the driver weaves his way through heavy traffic, zigzagging and honking to barrel ahead. At one point, our taxi almost hits a policeman, standing and whistling in the middle of an intersection to guide traffic. Peering through the window, rows of tanks and truckloads of soldiers with machine guns pass before my eyes, making me wonder if the imperial army is now for or against the people of Iran.

"Can these soldiers shoot at people on the streets and get away with it because of martial law, like they did last week?" I whisper in Jessica's ear, and she shrugs.

The taxi driver turns to face me. "Technically, they can, but they won't."

"Why not?" Jessica asks, leaning closer to hear his answer.

"Because they all despise the shah just as much as I do." He sighs. "My son was almost killed last Friday at Zhaleh Square. That bastard."

A mile up from the square, I ask, "Can you stop here, please?"

Should I also ask him if it's safe for us to wander about this place? Probably not, since Bita will persuade everyone to ignore his warning if he offers one. Unlike me, a coward, Bita is a true Spartan, just like her brother, Behnam, a political prisoner at Evin, Tehran's most notorious prison. She once told me that her mother goes to Evin almost every morning and begs to see Behnam, but the guards always send her away, telling her not to come back again.

Each of us pays an equal share for the ride and steps out, but the elderly woman remains in the backseat, adjusting and tightening the knot on her flowery silk headscarf while haggling away, "Dear son, you can charge me only one-fifth of what you charged those girls. I'm not paying a toman more."

Like Grandma, this old lady is full of surprises, bargaining to get the best deal in town even in the midst of an uprising and martial law. She looks eerily familiar, but I can't remember where I have seen her before. What is she doing here alone in this dangerous part of Tehran?

We make our way down a road lined on both sides with beautiful, mature maple trees. I love the way maple looks in spring, gold leaves with bright red-orange veins and curly dark tips. The air is filled with a pleasant, refreshing aroma seeping out of gurgling gutters that separate the sidewalks from the main street. A glorious glow shines through and above the trees, making me wonder if its creation has something to do with sunlight meeting the reflection that's coming off the streams.

This beauty is suddenly marred as traces of blood appear on the walls behind the trees. The scene immediately clues me in, like an abstract painting that's left blank except for a few patches of red to make a bold statement. Closer to the square, blood is smeared on the walls as if the artist has now gone completely mad, covering the canvas with stroke after stroke of red.

With each step forward, the image of an armed soldier popping out of thin air to shoot us all dead grows more vivid in my head, making my heart race faster, as if I were climbing up a steep mountain gasping for air.

"Shouldn't we go back?" I ask, hoping that everyone would agree.

"No. I want to see the square with my own eyes," Bita says, determined as ever.

"Me too. I want to go on," Neda agrees.

A few blocks from the square, we stop and look at one another in a daze, unable to speak, unable to grasp the reality of what we see before us: bloody handprints, bloody signatures are everywhere.

"Can you believe these courageous people actually took the time to write their names before they died?" Bita asks as she squeezes her eyes shut and rubs her forehead. "They're all God's angels—my heroes."

She bursts into tears, as we all do. Lily wipes tears away from her face as I embrace Neda, sobbing hard on her bony shoulder. Visions of injured people, dipping their fingers in their own blood to sign their names, flash before my eyes again and again. I don't believe any woman was gunned down, for all I can read on the bloody walls are men's names: Reza, Ali, Massoud, Akbar ... Even with my eyes closed, I can see their names, shining bright like neon signs in my head. Staring at a large handprint, glowing red but unclaimed, makes me wonder what happened to the person who left it behind. Did he run from the bullets or die, crouched up against that wall, struggling to sign his name for the very last time? Tears roll down my cheeks as I think of this nameless, faceless man—a man who meant everything to his parents, maybe even a wife and children—who is now likely dead. But why did he have to die? Why did his life mean nothing to the shah? Why didn't they arrest him and throw him in jail instead of shooting him dead?

When we reach the square, army tanks have barricaded all entrances, but dried blood is everywhere—on the concrete, pavement, walls, shop windows, and doors. As I take a deep breath, my nostrils fill with a moist, rusty scent. I'm probably imagining the smell rather than inhaling it, because I know the smell of fresh blood comes from the oxidation of iron II (ferrous) to iron III (ferric) once it's exposed to air. As always, chemistry can take my mind off almost anything, even a gruesome scene like this. If Najmieh were here, she would have loved to hear all about iron II and iron III, but I know that's not the case with Bita. In fact, she'd be furious if she found out what just ran through my head.

"This looks like a war zone." Bita says and sighs as she clasps her hands behind the back of her neck with her head down, shedding more tears. "A scene from a big-budget Hollywood movie. Words can't even describe how much I hate the shah."

Bita is right. This once bustling neighborhood is almost burned to the ground. I look around for the small ice cream shop where Baba often took my siblings and me for a treat in the weekends, but all that's left of it now is a hole in the wall. A few stores and eateries are spared, hidden behind sliding aluminum doors that are locked near the ground by heavy metal chains. But the ones that are not sealed off suffered the fate of the ice cream shop—doors bashed, windows shattered, livelihoods smashed, and just about everything covered in black dust.

Fluttering flyers, banners, and paper waste litter the ground, twisting and twirling in eddies. My eyes wander and focus on a row of unattended books nearby, their pages flipped open, turning fast in the wind.

"Look. These are all censored literature," Bita says, bending over to pick one up.

The cover of the book in her hand is graced with a black-and-white photograph of an attractive young man. The title is the biography of this *shaheed*, a martyr, published by the Mujahedin Party, the largest anti-shah organization in Iran. Curious, each of us picks up the biography of this handsome shaheed, as well as other literature published by the Mujahedin Party and other opposition groups, stuffing our bags with material that will no doubt shed light on our government's darkest secrets.

Across the street, the old lady who rode with us in the taxi is nervously looking around as she rolls down an aluminum door that seals off a stationery/gift shop, the same one Mamman often took my siblings and me to buy goodies and decorations for our birthday parties. Now I remember her face and her soft, engaging voice helping me pick stamps for my stamp collection last year. I hope she gets home safely and won't venture out again to check on her store.

Dusk is beginning to gather as we board a taxi back to the Shemiran Mall. On the way, while thumbing through a biography of a shaheed, I begin to worry about the books and brochures in our bags. What if our taxi driver is a SAVAK agent? No one will likely hear from any of us again if he decides to drive us to a SAVAK interrogation house instead of the mall.

As our taxi slows down and stops at a familiar curbside, I breathe a sigh of relief. We pay for the fare and clump together on the sidewalk for good-bye kisses and hugs.

Lily looks up and asks, "Can I share a poem before you all go? It's called 'Birds of Storm' by the famous poet Shafi'i Kadkani."

I've never heard his name, but Lily seems to know every poet who ever lived or is still alive. During the taxi ride, while each of us skimmed through mostly shaheed biographies, Lily had her eyes glued on a small booklet of revolutionary poems.

"Go ahead, Lily jan. Please, enlighten us," Jessica says, and as always, Lily gears up to passionately recite.

O birds of storm! May you fly high.
How did you so lovingly accept
In your own blood
The impact of lead bullets so kindly?
I want to question the breeze.
How will the sea move today
Without the tide of your heartbeat?
O birds of storm! May you fly high.

"Do you do know what this poem means?" Lily asks as the rest of us exchange baffled looks. "The people who died kindly accepted the bullets for us so we can become free, like birds of storm, and fly high."

"That's so beautiful, Lily," I say, my voice trembling. "Every soul in Iran has to stand up for the innocent lives lost in Zhaleh Square."

Lily squeezes my hand and says, "Let's take an oath. Repeat after me the words of the great poet Kadkani."

She begins to recite the poem again. As our voices harmonize, powerful emotions wash over me like the warm waves of the Caspian Sea. I feel an immense connection to my friends—strong love, loyalty, something profound that I have never experienced before in my life. I know they can read my mind, and I can read theirs, for we are all thinking the same thoughts. Now that we have seen the truth with our own eyes, there is no other way but to participate in this uprising somehow.

ဢ ဢ ဢ

After the massacre, Tehran becomes a ghost town. Shops, movies, amusement parks, restaurants, almost everything is shut down. Instead, the street protest against the regime is slowly but surely moving indoors. Like Baba and his colleagues, many people are on strike, and at night, it seems, all citizens are out on their rooftops shouting slogans into the dark.

A few days earlier, I heard Baba tell his friend in a cheerful voice, "That's it, Faraydoon. That's the end of the shah. He can never regain power after his lifeline, oil, is cut off. He took a lot of heat when the national newspapers, railroads, and airlines went on strike, but the oil strike is something he can't recover from."

To show solidarity with the movement, my brother and I, along with our cousins and high school friends, become frequent moonlight chanters on rooftops. The slogans we shout out every night convey a religious message, but none of us is truly a devout Muslim. We're just a bunch of teenagers having fun on rooftops, hoping that our rebellious activities can somehow topple the powerful shah.

My handsome cousin Mammad, a good dancer, often brings with him a portable cassette player. Unlike most Iranian boys, Mammad's complexion is fair. His soft hair is almost blond, and his large, honey-colored eyes are set inside a pair of arched brows that look as if they have been plucked. Sometimes Jahan teases Mammad by telling him that if he were a woman, he would have had hundreds of suitors by now. I agree with Jahan, because Mammad looks a lot like his eldest sister, Homa. She had so many suitors in high school that she finally agreed to wed a high-ranking military officer in the summer of her junior year.

Almost every night, a group of us dance to American music, particularly the *Saturday Night Fever* sound track, while chanting, "*Allahu Akbar*"—God is great.

One night on our rooftop, Mammad shouts, "Death to the shah! Death to the dictator!"

The entire neighborhood quickly joins in, chanting Mammad's slogan.

Mamman quickly appears on the roof in her red robe and brown slippers. "Do you want SAVAK to storm in and shoot us all? All of you come down this minute. This night marks the last day of your bravery on this rooftop."

We march down the staircase, one by one, while Mamman stands at the very top, frowning and ranting with her hair standing up in disarray, making it hard for us not to chuckle as we pass her by.

"Guys, listen! You can come over to my rooftop from now on and shout whatever pops into your creative minds. You have my word; my parents won't wake up," Mammad declares.

"How come?" I ask, thinking of my own mother, who's awake around the clock.

"Because every morning, the alarm clock in their bedroom literally blasts for hours before Haj khanoom finally turns it off to recite her morning prayers."

Three years earlier, Haj khanoom became Aunt Banoo-Azam's official nickname after she completed the Haj ceremony, the annual pilgrimage to Mecca, Saudi Arabia. Grandma says every able-bodied Muslim must participate in the Haj ceremony at least once in a lifetime, or dire consequences may result. In spite of Grandma's warnings, though, none of her children has yet agreed to accompany her to Mecca during her many sacred journeys to confess her love and devotion to God and Islam.

After enjoying a few nights of freedom on Mammad's rooftop, he writes a slogan: *Arm me, then shoot me, you imperial man; only a coward shoots at an unarmed man.*

The euphoric voices, chanting Mammad's words, fill up the night sky with so much hope and optimism that I can imagine myself on the streets shouting in bright daylight without fearing the shah and his armed entourage.

$$\mathfrak{H} \quad \mathfrak{H} \quad \mathfrak{H}$$

"Meet me at the small square near my house," Bita says over the phone on a cloudy morning in November. "I have also called Lily, Neda, and Jessica, and they have all agreed to come."

I put the phone down and sneak out, feeling excited and nervous at the same time. Apparently, posters are nailed onto walls in and around Bita's neighborhood, inviting citizens to join a march.

At the square, we exchange hugs and kisses before setting out to participate in our first rally, something that we've been talking about for a while. We are all dressed in comfortable clothes—jeans, skirts, sweatshirts, and sneakers with our hair up in ponytails, except for Lily, who has short hair. Overhead, dark, puffy clouds cover most of the sky, nearly blocking the faint sun from reaching the ground.

On the way, we pass a line of almost barren trees, fashioning only a few crinkly, token leaves. Their nakedness makes me think of my own mortality. Unlike their dead leaves that cover every inch of the ground, my body can't rejuvenate next year if I die during a bloody shootout.

Four blocks over, we spot a large group of protestors marching on, shouting slogans against the shah. Dried leaves crumble and crush under our feet as we quickly walk toward the screaming crowd, passing by locked-up shops and restaurants, a strong indication that most Tehranian merchants are still on strike against the shah.

The crowd swells and shouts, "Allahu Akbar—God is great! *Marg bar shah*—death to the shah! Ayatollah Khomeini is our Imam, our divine leader."

My heart bursts with pride as we take our place at the end of the march. Soon my elation deflates as I notice a few chadory women frowning at us with their eyes moving up and down.

"Why is everyone dressed in a black chador?" I whisper in Jessica's ear.

She shrugs. "The stares are freaking me out. Let's get out of here, *now*."

"I agree. Tell Bita we must leave right away."

As Jessica reaches to tap on Bita's shoulder, I hear a woman shout, "Whores! Go home! How dare you disrespect Islam, the ayatollah!"

The next thing I know, another woman slaps Lily and shoves her back. She loses her balance and tumbles into a puddle of water. Desperate to find a way out, I survey our surroundings, but all I can see are closely packed faces, men and women, filled with rage, shouting, "May God bless your hand for slapping that bitch! That whore deserves not just slapping but lashing for flashing her bare legs!"

Jessica helps Lily stand up, and the four of us instinctively huddle around her to protect her from further assault. With my knees shaking and my heart pounding, I repeatedly apologize, and so do my friends, as we get shoved and pinched to make our way through the crowd. When we finally break loose, a bearded man hollers from across the street.

"This is your lucky day, you foolish, stupid imperial girls! The next time you dare showing up like this, I will personally throw acid onto your worthless faces! The days of whoring the streets are over!"

Indignation flares up inside me like a cobra coiled up, ready to attack at the slightest sound. Just one more insult is all it will take to set me off. They are all liars. We are not whores. We are not even allowed to date boys. I'm not going to wear a chador to show them support. That's not who I am, and I'll never dress like that, never in a million years, never.

The wrathful crowd is now a few blocks behind us. We stop for a few minutes to catch our breath. Each of us is sobbing hard into our hands or on a friend's shoulder, defeated, confused, and heartbroken.

"How could this be?" Bita says, sniffling and rubbing her large, red nose with the back of her hand. "The flyers we collected at Zhaleh Square stated clearly that this movement belongs to every Iranian citizen, not just those who believe in extreme Islam."

"You're right, Bita," I say, looking down at a black-and-blue pinch mark on my arm.

We walk and talk among ourselves, coming to the grim conclusion that, either way, Iran is doomed. The shah is brutal, but so are these fanatic revolutionaries. Sadly, it looks like a no-win situation, the end of the road. I'm afraid my life as I have lived it up to this point is about to change in ways that may even be worse than before.

Bita's house is now minutes away. We pass through a maze of alleys and enter a small, winding street toward her house. Her apartment is on the third floor of a six-story concrete building at the end of a narrow cul-de-sac.

It's near dusk when I phone Baba at his office. My shaky voice gives my feelings away, and he leaves promptly.

An hour later, I'm sitting with Baba in the car, telling him about the rally—the women and men who hated us, how frightened and sad we all were.

"I'm very disappointed in you," Baba says in his usual calm voice, shaking his head. "Why didn't you ask me if it's safe for you to attend that rally?"

Guilt snakes up my legs and twirls in my stomach. "I'm sorry, Baba. I would have asked, but you never answer my questions. I want to know the truth about the shah. I really do, Baba. I am not a kid anymore."

"I'm sorry for keeping you in the dark, Azadeh. Naturally, I worry about your safety, but I can see now that we need to be more open with you. Tell me what you want to know, and I'll truthfully answer all your questions," Baba says as he starts the car.

On the way, we continue our discussion, exchanging information as if we were two adults rather than a teenager arguing with a reluctant parent. I trust Baba enough to tell him about the censored books and brochures hidden in Mashti's unit at our house.

Mashti is an elderly man who lives with us. He has a small room with a private bathroom in a separate unit on our property. In exchange for rent, he tends the garden and the yard, always dressed in the same tattered, dark-brown clothing, raking up leaves in the backyard or scooping them off the pool into trash cans for disposal. Underneath the water heater, against the back wall of Mashti's windowless unit, my books and pamphlets are hidden inside a large plastic garbage bag.

When we arrive home, heavy rain is splashing hard against the windshield. Baba removes his keys from the ignition, pauses for a moment, and turns to face me.

"Look, Azadeh, I go to rallies too."

"You do?" I say, shocked by his admission.

"The rally that you foolishly went to was organized by a radical Islamic group. Something terrible could have happened to you and your friends. I only go to rallies that are planned and advertised by Tehran University students."

I knew Baba was a graduate of Tehran University, but I had no idea that he was still involved with the school and student activities.

As we walk briskly toward the house, a hard, freezing rain lashes us with its sharp needles. Baba pauses at the doorstep and looks at me.

"The next time I attend a rally, I may take you along, but I need to check with your mother first."

Once inside, Mamman, as usual, has imagined the worst, looking frantic in her thick burgundy glasses, red robe, and white socks, screaming.

"Azadeh, where have you been? Your eyes are puffy and red!

What has happened to you? Tell me the truth! Were you arrested? Raped?"

As I move my lips, Baba tells me to go to my room. I quickly oblige and disappear without answering Mamman's questions.

An hour later, Mamman comes in and sits on my bed; her face looks uncharacteristically calm. She grabs my hand and says, "I know how you feel, and I'm here to offer support. I want you to know that I'm not an advocate for this revolution. I disapprove of many of the shah's policies regarding human rights and censorship, but I still believe Iran is better off under his rule than a bunch of *mullahs*."

"Why do you say that?" I ask, surprised by the irony in her words.

"Well, mullahs only care about money. Even Baba agrees with me on that."

"Isn't the shah the same way?"

"He is, but he gives more to people. Listen, I know your father is very enthusiastic about this revolution, and that is his business. I don't expect you to take sides, but please be careful from now on. Baba and I have agreed that you may participate in rallies if you wish, but *only* with Baba."

I promise Mamman that I will respect her wishes. She thanks me and kisses me on the cheek. When she gets up to leave, I feel closer to her than I have in a while, for I still harbor a lot of anger toward her for leaving Najmieh in the care of my crazy aunt. I wonder how Najmieh and her husband feel about the revolution. Would their lives be better with the shah gone? I don't know what to think anymore; even Mamman and Baba don't seem to think alike.

Bewildered, I get up and walk to the hallway, grab a towel, and head for the shower. As the warm water washes over my body, my bruises begin to sting. Staring down at black-and-blue pinch marks on my arms takes me back to the rally, to a reality that could become my future if the angry people who assaulted us earlier take charge of Iran. *God, please, please don't let these people win over the shah.*

On a cold, cloudy morning in late November, Baba delivers on his promise. In a few minutes, Jahan and I will leave with him to attend a peaceful protest at Tehran University.

As I step into Baba's car, I ask, "Should I bring a scarf?"

"Why?" Baba asks, raising a brow.

"To hide my hair," I say, thinking of the Islamic rally last week.

"Don't be silly, Azadeh. Just come as you are. Let's go."

En route, Baba tells us about all the different political groups that have helped to organize the rally we are about to attend. I listen to him and keep quiet, although I know the names of almost all the organizations he's talking about from the literature I picked up with my friends at Zhaleh Square a few months earlier. I still haven't told Baba about that day, and I am not about to tell him now, for he might change his mind and not take me along.

Twenty minutes later, Baba pulls into a parking lot of an office building six blocks away from Tehran University. By now, the clouds have partly disappeared, enabling a pale sun to shine through. On the ground, brittle leaves are scattered everywhere, drifting in the afternoon breeze.

On the way, Jahan kicks pebbles into a gutter that runs parallel to the sidewalk. Closer to the rally, the sound of wind whistling and water rippling in gutters intermingles with voices, shouting, "*Azadi, azadi* is what we seek!" I love hearing the sound of my name—Azadeh—a person who seeks freedom, azadi. A warm feeling of euphoria washes over me as we join the crowd and shout, "Azadi, azadi is what we seek!" with our fists up, punching the air. I am so happy to be present, to be here in this moment, witnessing all this. The people of Iran are finally free to say what's on their minds.

The atmosphere feels completely different from the Islamic protest I attended the week before. Many women are dressed in street clothes, and a few in black chadors don't seem bothered by the *Western* look—short skirts, jeans, fancy hairdos, and makeup.

Standing alongside Baba, I feel safe and included but still perplexed, for it appears to me that the crowd at this rally is unaware of how people dress at Islamic rallies, so I ask Baba, and he replies, "Don't worry, Azadeh; the details aren't important. The educated people will run the new government. Most people in the rally you attended with your friends were illiterate and uneducated."

"But what about the ayatollah? Isn't he the leader of this revolution?"

"Well, technically he is, but the intellectuals believe his supporters are mostly uneducated people. Those people don't really know what's best for them. They'll come along when the new establishment forms. Just enjoy the moment and stop analyzing everything. You're just like your mother, an endless worrier. Trust me—we're making history."

A cloud passes behind another as I look up, pondering over what Baba said. If the main supporters of the ayatollah are illiterate, then Najmieh and Mashti must be among them, but Najmieh wasn't religious at all. She never prayed and loved to show off her flowing hair and feminine curves. There isn't an ounce of doubt in my mind that Najmieh's aspirations are more aligned with the crowd at this rally than the Islamic one last week. I can only hope that Baba is right and that when the intellectuals resume power, they can help people like Najmieh and Mashti to become equal citizens of Iran.

Revolution Madness

"Ladies and gentleman, at this historic moment, on January 16, 1979, the shah and shahbanu are about to board a plane for Egypt ..."

I take my eyes off the booming old radio in the corner of the kitchen and glance up at the large white-faced clock on the wall. It's a little past noon. My family and I have been sitting around the breakfast table since ten this morning, awaiting this much-anticipated news.

"*Yes! Yes!*" Baba shouts, jumping up and down, the same way he does when his favorite soccer team scores a goal.

Mamman shakes her head and sighs. My siblings and I stay quiet, watching our parents' strikingly opposing reactions.

The newscaster ends the program by stating that the shah's departure is due to extreme exhaustion, personal reasons, and so on, but I don't believe a word of it. He left because he was afraid for his life.

Minutes after the broadcast, the staccato blast of car horns fills the air. The familiar sound brings back fond memories of my aunt's wedding the summer before, where a train of honking cars trailed behind the bride and groom's car, cheering them on. Today, the whole nation is in a festive mood to celebrate the end of the shah and the beginning of the ayatollah. Just like a wedding, one chapter closes as another one opens, but no one really knows if it's for better or for worse.

I wonder what's running through the shah's mind as he flies over Tehran. Does he have any regrets for exiling Ayatollah Khomeini, the Islamic leader of this revolution, for speaking out against him? He might still be in power if he hadn't ordered the ayatollah to leave Iran fifteen years earlier, right before I came into this world. Strangely, I had never heard the name of this ayatollah until just a few months earlier. Why is he so popular, and what is it about him that so many people are willing to risk their lives to bring him home?

To show solidarity with the rest of the honkers in our neighborhood, Baba puts on his robe and slippers, grabs his car keys, and runs outside. Soon after, loud beeping noises emerge out of our backyard, in harmony with other horns that are going off in distinct intervals of three beats. *Beep-beep-beeeep, beep-beep-beeeep …*

Mamman springs to her feet and walks to the window. As the pale-blue velvet curtains move to each side, a full view of Baba sounding his horn like a cheerful toddler in his toy truck appears before us.

Mamman shakes her head and sighs. "Look at him, a grown man acting like a child. He has completely lost his mind."

A good ten minutes pass before Baba runs inside. "Kids, let's go and show our support for the revolution. Go on, change quickly. Hurry up," he tells my siblings and me in a firm, joyful voice.

After a brief argument, Mamman allows Jahan and me to go along with Baba, but not my eight-year-old sister, Afshan. She insists that Afshan must stay home where it's safe and sane. Meanwhile, Baba is too antsy to see firsthand what's unraveling on the streets to fight for Afshan's liberation, so in spite of her pleas, we leave home without her.

On the way, I think of my parents' constant arguments over this uprising, fearing that our country's unrest may break them apart permanently. As we drive farther away from our relatively quiet, posh neighborhood, roads and sidewalks begin to jam with cars and crowds. The sound of horns blaring, coupled with the sight of thousands of windshield wipers standing upright, moving from side to side, is an image that will forever live in my mind. It looks and feels as if the cars have come alive, shouting and waving with the people to celebrate the shah's demise.

After searching for hours, Baba finds a parking spot and flattens the windshield wipers against the glass, and we emerge into a sea of noise and chaos. Swarms of people cheer and holler about, carrying signs, banners or newspaper headlines that declare in large print: THE SHAH IS GONE. Compared to the rest of the crowd, we came unprepared with no signs, no banners, and no newspapers to show off.

Unflattering caricatures of the shah and Jimmy Carter, glued onto sticks, heave up and down in massive crowds as people shout, "*Marg bar shah!* Death to Shah! The Western puppet, Carter's puppet! *Marg bar* Carter! Khomeini is our Imam, the divine leader!"

But not every person is marching and shouting slogans. Some are working in groups to drag down, destroy, and burn picture frames and statues of the shah and his family, while others are climbing tall monuments and buildings to hang posters—some as large as or even larger than billboards—of the ayatollah. Unlike us, many people must have anticipated and planned for this event. Otherwise, I don't understand how they could have prepared thousands and thousands of larger-than-life posters of the ayatollah in the blink of an eye, just a few hours after the shah fled Iran.

I glance up at a large poster of the ayatollah, and instantly, his stern black eyes pierce right through me, sending chills up and down my spine. That's not a flattering picture of him with his lips curled into a mocking smile, forehead furrowed and eyebrows frowned. The same image of him appears everywhere, inside the display window of shops, posted onto walls, and draped over the sides of many buildings, making it impossible to escape his penetrating gaze. *A picture is worth a thousand words*, a popular saying, pops into my head. For my sake, I hope it's not true in this case.

It is past midnight by the time we arrive home. The house is pitch black except for the side lamp burning in the family room. Next to it, Mamman is sitting impatiently on the sofa, knitting a red-and-white sweater for Afshan. As my parents begin to argue, my brother and

I flee the scene, for we do not wish to get caught in the middle of a heated discussion.

Once in my room, I take my shoes off, pull the covers back, climb in, and fall asleep in a flash.

ৡ ৡ ৡ

Two weeks later, the ayatollah's plane is in the sky above, due to land any minute at Mehrabad International Airport in Tehran. I can't take my eyes off the TV set in our family room, where thousands and thousands of people fill the screen, awaiting his arrival. Whatever the cameras allow me to see is draped in snow: the streets, sidewalks, cars, poles, and trees. I turn and glance at the crackling flame in the fireplace and sigh. *It's good to be home watching the events unfold on TV.*

At nine fifteen, the chartered 747 Air France jumbo jet begins taxiing to the gate. Soon after, the plane stops, and the TV camera zooms in on its exit door as a portable staircase quickly appears beside it. Minutes later, the frail Ayatollah Khomeini, clutching a flight attendant's arm, emerges through the door wearing a large black turban, two ankle-length robes, black wool socks, and dark slippers. The jubilant crowd roars in excitement, shouting his name, as he smiles and waves, triumphantly marching down the stairs.

While staring at the ayatollah, Baba sheds tears of joy, Mamman sheds tears of sorrow, and I feel neither happy nor sad to shed tears of any kind, since I don't know if he's any better than the shah if he ends up claiming his spot.

I glare at the TV, thinking that if it weren't for the landmarks on the streets, I wouldn't have recognized this place as Tehran, the city I grew up in. Mostly women in chadors fill the screen, and only a few are dressed in warm pants, coats, and jackets, something that I would be wearing if I were out there screaming. That's not the Tehran I remember, where mainly elderly women wore chadors. I wonder if the younger and more modern women, like Mamman and me, are at home watching the events on TV.

The ayatollah, now on the steps of the jumbo jet's staircase, appears to smirk rather than smile at me. Like Mamman, I don't trust him. Maybe it's because I'm a woman, or will be one soon, and his supporters look nothing like me or anyone associated with me—except for Grandma, of course.

At the bottom of the staircase, a reporter asks, "Ayatollah, how do you feel now that you are finally home after fifteen years in exile?"

"I don't feel a thing. Not a thing, really. Nothing," he blankly replies.

His callous response bothers me, as he must know many people watching him now have risked their lives to make his journey back home come true.

Mamman's face puckers and turns red. "Did you hear what this stupid mullah just said? 'I feel not a thing for Iran.' I guess according to his idiotic philosophy, the *Hezbollah*, the party of God, must rule upon all nations of the world. God save us all." Then she turns and snarls at Baba, "Modjtaba, it's people like you who brought this monster home."

Baba remains quiet as Mamman storms off, letting off some steam by calling a grand ayatollah a simple mullah, which is equivalent to demoting the pope back to early priesthood. Watching them fight makes me feel helpless, for there isn't a thing I can do to make them stop.

I take my eyes off the TV and look out into the garden. Large icicles hang from tree branches and windowpanes, water dripping slowly from their ends. While staring at the drops falling one by one, my mind wanders off. What if Mamman is right and Baba is wrong? How will my life change if the Islamic fundamentalists instead of the intellectuals—as Baba hopes will eventually happen—take control of Iran? I don't think I have what it takes to survive if Iran becomes like Saudi Arabia, a place where women's bodies are completely masked in dark clothing from the top of their heads to the tips of their toes.

§ § §

A few days after the ayatollah's return, I walk into the kitchen, minding my own business. Mamman is sitting at the breakfast table fuming, cursing at the ayatollah. The radio is on, announcing news that she obviously can't stand to hear.

"This mullah hasn't even been back for long, and he's already electing our prime minister," she says and looks straight into Baba's eyes. "The Koran is the only book this man has ever read in his life. How could he possibly know a thing about the ins and outs of running a country—a civilized one, if I may say?"

Mamman is referring to the ayatollah's latest decision of appointing Mehdi Bazargan to the post of prime minister. I wonder what will happen to Shapour Bakhtiar, the prime minister appointed by the shah a few months before he fled to Egypt. I know he's still in Iran and has not yet resigned.

Curious, I ask my parents, "Which prime minister is in charge?"

Once again, they begin to argue over my head. Baba says the one appointed by the ayatollah, while Mamman insists that only the one appointed by the shah is legitimate. What I gather from my parents' arguments is that both prime ministers are to the far left of their respective parties, which I assume means neither Mehdi Bazargan nor Shapour Bakhtiar is extreme in imposing his own personal beliefs. Bakhtiar supports the shah but strongly advocates for a government much like that of the United Kingdom, where the prime minister is democratically elected. In fact, Bakhtiar recently called for an election so the people of Iran, instead of the shah, can vote to appoint a new prime minister, which he said might turn out to be neither him nor Mr. Bazargan, the ayatollah's appointed prime minister.

According to Baba, Bazargan is a well-respected, liberal Islamic thinker. I'm not quite sure what liberal means politically, but it has to be better than being closed-minded like the shah or perhaps even the ayatollah. Nevertheless, no matter how liberal these prime ministers are supposed to be, just like my parents, they don't seem to compromise, and as a result, people take sides and die every day on the streets of Tehran.

The horrific scene at Zhaleh Square that I witnessed five months earlier with my friends has now become the face of Tehran. It's impossible to walk on the streets without witnessing blood on the walls, pavement, trees, and just about anywhere and everywhere. I'm sick of seeing blood, smelling blood, and imagining what happened to the people who left it behind. I desperately want my life to go back to the way it was before the revolution, for my parents to stop fighting, and for people of Iran to stop killing one another over leaders that seem not to care for them at all.

৯ ৯ ৯

Ignoring Mamman's warnings, Baba often leaves home alone to participate in organized activities against the shah. One day, when Mamman is out visiting Grandma with Afshan, Baba asks Jahan and me to go out with him on the streets. Feeling overwhelmed with guilt, I hesitantly say yes, knowing that if Mamman were home, she would not have allowed me to go.

Right before getting into the car, Baba says, "Azadeh, run back inside and put on your headscarf."

As I rush back to my room, I vividly remember Baba's voice a few months back. *Don't be silly, Azadeh. Just come as you are. Let's go.*

Confusion fills my head as if the scarf covering my hair is sending vibes to dumb down my brain. As I step into the car, Jahan turns his head.

"Azadeh, in your case, I think *hijab* is a real good thing."

"Why?" I ask, feeling a stab of indignation.

"Because there will be less of you to see," he says and cracks up.

"Just shut up, Jahan! You aren't funny!" I shout, hitting the back of his head with my hand.

Jahan turns around to retaliate, but Baba insists that we stop. As always, we calm down in front of him, but I know Jahan will hit me hard once we are out of the car and Baba is preoccupied. I wish he would just talk to me intelligently about the revolution instead of insulting me all the time. Maybe there is something wrong with me that always brings out the worst in him, but I don't think I'm ruinous by nature. Left to my own devices, I believe I would have chosen to be his ally, not his adversary.

Everywhere we go, piles of sandbags line the streets. Bloody walls, pavements, and trees stand witness to deadly scenes of recent assaults. Torched cars, tires, books, and imperial flags and memorabilia litter most avenues and sidewalks, some still burning, releasing smoke that stings my eyes. The sheer number of imperial army tanks left abandoned in front of roadblocks tells me that the shah is gone for good and the ayatollah is here to stay.

Large numbers of imperial soldiers with machine guns crisscrossed around their shoulders wander the streets, either alone or in small packs. I glance around and cannot spot a single soldier without a red carnation plugging the barrel of his machine gun.

Jahan rubs his chin and asks Baba, "Those soldiers are simply stupid. Aren't they afraid that someone might shoot them in the head or stab them in the back? What's up with the flower?"

"No, they are not. They are on our side," Baba says, smiling.

"How do you know?" I ask Baba.

"The red carnation sticking out of the barrel signals a change in faith."

"Well, I say it's about time, brother, to wake up and smell the roses—I meant the carnations." Jahan chuckles.

The soldiers don't scare me, but armed pedestrians and passengers inside crowded cars, on motorbikes, and in the back of pickup trucks do. I wish they would stop waving their firearms with so much zest. One may accidentally go off and kill someone, like it does sometimes in the movies.

After a few hours of wandering the streets, a crazed-looking man standing not too far from us points his machine gun up and fires a magazine of bullets into the sky, shouting, "Allahu Akbar!"

A horrific, deafening sound fills the air as Baba pulls Jahan and me next to his chest, covering our heads with the palms of his hands.

Tears run down my face as I beg Baba to take us home, and he quickly agrees. A sigh of relief escapes my body as we turn and head for the car. *I am never going out on the streets with Baba again. I have seen enough of this madness.*

§ § §

Three weeks after the ayatollah's arrival, Prime Minister Bakhtiar resigns. The ayatollah, now confident of his divine power, appears behind a pulpit on several TV broadcasts preaching *Shariat*, the Islamic law.

"Shariat is now the law of our land with no exception. Those who disobey will be punished ... The family protection law is inconsistent with Shariat ... A devout Muslim woman must dress according to Shariat. Conservative. Unappealing ... Based on Shariat, a woman can't be a judge. The witness testimony of a man in court is equivalent to that of two women."

Mehdi Bazargan, the so-called liberal prime minister appointed by the ayatollah, publicly objects to many of his demands, but to no avail. In our home, Mamman fumes whenever she hears the ayatollah mouthing off on TV or radio. I agree with Mamman wholeheartedly, for I too believe the ayatollah's views are unfavorable to women. Why shouldn't a woman's testimony in court have the same credibility as that of a man? With that statement the ayatollah is implying that men are smarter than women.

One night, as we all watch TV in the family room, Mamman shakes her head and tells us, "Look at what this mullah is saying. He makes me sick. This revolution has taken us backward in time. Our daughters aren't going to be veiled." She pauses and glares at Baba as if *he* was the person who toppled the shah. "Now it's my turn to speak up, and I'll show you, Modjtaba. I'll show you how it's done. We should have stayed in England."

She sighs and turns to look me straight in the eye. She has every right to blame me for leaving England last September. In hindsight, we should have stayed there instead of returning home, since I never got a chance to see Najmieh, anyway. I wonder how Najmieh is holding up with all this revolution chaos. I bet she's probably out on the streets of Rasht with her fists up in the air shouting for equality and justice for all.

"That woman, Margaret Thatcher," Mamman continues, "will probably become the next prime minister of England, as day by day we amount to less and less in this damn country of ours. I'm not going to let this man get away with veiling us."

During the next week, Mamman and her chic friends, dressed in high fashion European clothes and dark sunglasses, become regular participants at street rallies, protesting against mandatory veiling. According to her, they have to wear ridiculously large dark sunglasses to disguise their faces from the enemy—the regime insiders—individuals who are dressed in civilian clothes to secretly photograph people. It seems as if a turban has replaced a crown, but nothing fundamental has changed in Iran. Before, people were scared of SAVAK, the shah's secret police. Now, just a month after the revolution, the same people are again afraid of yet an unnamed secret police of some kind.

One day, Mamman is late coming home from one of her frequent outings with her girlfriends. Worried thoughts grow in my head as I watch Afshan play with her Barbies. She has setup her two-story pink Barbie house at the corner of the kitchen and is pushing Ken's camper truck to approach and park in front of the house. Today, he's a lucky man, for I can see five well-dressed Barbies around the dining table waiting to have dinner with him. Last September, right after we returned from England, I gladly donated my Barbie collection to Afshan, basking in her love for weeks afterward. For Afshan's sake, I hope the ayatollah doesn't declare war on Barbie and Ken.

For the zillionth time, Afshan looks up and asks, "Where is Mamman, Azadeh? Don't you think it's getting too dark out there? Are you sure she's okay?"

Before I have a chance to respond, we hear Mamman's car

grinding and growling outside. Afshan runs out as I sigh and stare up at the clock and then at the large, empty bag of potato chips in front of me next to a bottle of consumed Coca-Cola.

Minutes later, Mamman walks into the kitchen and puts her notepad down. "I'm sorry to be late, Azadeh. I went to a craft store after the rally to pick up some materials."

"To pick up what?" I ask, staring at her. "We were so worried about you."

Mamman tries to stroke my hair, but I recoil and look down, only to see the words on her notepad, written neatly in oversized letters in her handwriting: *We Have Two Choices—Freedom or Death—Nothing More, Nothing Less.*

The realization that I may soon lose my mother at a rally cuts through me like a knife. My eyes well up with tears, thinking I'd rather have my mother alive and veiled rather than defiant and dead.

"Azadeh, would you like to help me make a banner with these words?" Mamman asks as she tucks my hair behind my ear.

I wipe my nose on my sleeve and nod. Mamman unrolls a white piece of fabric on the kitchen floor and asks me to arrange large red letters on its surface, each printed individually on waxed paper.

"*Wow*, Mamman, you are so brave," I say as she irons the seventh word, *Death*, onto the banner while I stretch the fabric around it. "Are you really willing to die if they force us to veil?" I ask, wondering why she chose the word *death* instead of defiance or something like it, for *death* sounds too final, too scary to think about.

She sighs. "No, not really, but only because I have you, Jahan, and Afshan to worry about. I want to be around to see you all grow up. Hopefully, the ayatollah will back down."

"But I don't want to wear the veil, either. Can I go with you to a rally next time, just once, please?"

"No. It's too dangerous. In the last rally, the police shot bullets up into the air to scare us," she says, shaking her head. "I even saw a few unshaven, Islamic-looking men walking around with knives and batons."

"Are they waiting for the ayatollah's orders to attack?" I ask, shivering inside at the thought of Mamman standing near men who bear weapons of death.

"I think so. If he gives the orders, I won't go anymore. You have my word."

"Well, then, it's safe for now. You said it yourself. That means I can go? Right?" I ask in a pleading voice.

"Okay, I'll think about it. It's time to go to bed," she says, folding the banner.

We clean up the mess in the kitchen and go to bed.

The next morning, I peek through the window and watch Mamman step into a friend's car, a black cherry Mercedes-Benz. The gold hood emblem sparkles in the sunlight as the car backs out of our driveway. Six women in disguise are on their way to have their voices heard. I'll do just about anything to be a passenger in that car.

ŞŞŞ

A week later, I'm getting ready for bed when I hear Mamman's voice calling my name. In the kitchen, I find her sitting alone next to a large glass of steaming hot tea.

"Come here and sit down, Azadeh." She pats the chair next to hers. "You know, tomorrow is a very special day, and I'm thinking of taking you with me to a big rally."

"Is it special 'cause I'm going with you?" I ask, playing with my ponytail.

"No, silly. Don't flatter yourself. Tomorrow is March 8: International Women's Day."

I didn't even know such a day existed, but that *is* indeed a very special day. I'm a woman, or will be one soon, and based on what Mamman has been telling me, my personal freedom is at stake.

That night in my dream, I see myself standing in a large crowd of unveiled women, our fists up punching the air, shouting, "We have two choices—freedom or death—nothing more, nothing less!"

The next day, Mamman and I arrive at the rally early in the morning, our faces masked by large, dark sunglasses. Mamman meets a group of friends and begins to chatter as I unroll our banner, the same one that we made together a week earlier.

After a few minutes of examining the crowd, I ask, "Mamman, why are some women wearing chadors? Aren't we here to protest against veiling?"

"No, we are here to protest against *mandatory* veiling. Most women in chadors here are like Grandma—they like to cover up but don't want it enforced upon others like you and me. Look at that banner." She points to two women wearing headscarves and holding up a banner a few rows behind us. It says: *We are in hijab, our daughters are not. Let us be who God made us to be.*

"That's exactly right," I say. "Let God, not the ayatollah, judge if we are sinners or not."

"Well said, Azadeh."

Mamman and a couple of her friends applaud, making me feel proud inside.

"Azadeh, pay attention when I'm talking to you," Mamman says firmly.

"What? Did I do something wrong?" I ask, looking around.

"I just told you not to tuck your hair behind your ears. Let it loose."

"Why?" I ask, feeling disoriented, like a small child lost in a crowd.

"Don't ask why. Just listen, and do what I tell you."

I release my hair to fall over part of my face.

"That woman, over there," Mamman points to someone in a navy-blue cloak and matching headscarf, "is taking our picture. Be aware of your surroundings."

"Sorry, Mamman; I didn't see her. I'll be more careful," I say, worrying about the picture in her camera.

A large crowd has now gathered in and around Sepah-Salar Square—a large square housing several government buildings—awaiting the speaker to take the podium in front of the parliament. From where we are, I can see a group of men and women struggling on the stage to assemble the communication apparatus for the program.

After fifteen minutes, a gentleman holding a loudspeaker comes down from the podium and says, "Many wires to our speaker system have been cut, and we are unable to continue with our scheduled program."

The nearby crowd roars, "Death to censorship! Death to censorship!"

Moments later, groups of people begin to chant among themselves, delivering the gentleman's message from the podium to the ends of the crowd. Within a few minutes, everyone is shouting, "Death to censorship! Death to censorship!"

Banners rise, and marching begins. "Women's freedom is neither Eastern nor Western, but universal!"

The people in the crowd move out of the square and into Shahabad Street, shouting slogans with their fists raised and banners waving in the air. After passing several streets, we turn onto Hassanabad Street, where many nurses in white uniforms and caps appear on patios of Sina Hospital.

In solidarity, the nurses raise their fists and yell out slogans.

In return, the crowd shouts, "Salute to the nurse! Salute to the nurse!"

The nurses bow as tears stream from my eyes, Mamman's eyes, and the eyes of most women and men striding along.

"I hope the government won't arrest them," one of Mamman's friends says as we pass Sina Hospital.

I turn back to look at the nurses one last time through large, dark sunglasses, wishing that I could smash the sunglasses under my feet and tuck every strand of loose hair behind my ears to claim my identity. I'm just a coward, that's who I am, always afraid of what may happen to me next if I do this or that. They're so brave to take a strong stand by exposing their identities like that. *God, please keep them safe.*

In the middle of that night, I wake up to the glare of chandelier lights. Baba is sitting on my bed, tapping on my shoulder.

"Wake up, Azadeh. Stop screaming."

"I had a nightmare," I say, rubbing my eyes.

"About what?"

"I don't remember."

"Drink some water and go back to sleep."

"I'll try, Baba."

Baba kisses my forehead and turns off the light.

I bury my face under the sheet and recall my dream—tall, unshaven men beating petite nurses with batons and stabbing them with knives. I didn't tell Baba anything, since I'm not sure if he still believes in this revolution.

Six days after the large International Women's Day protest, the ayatollah backs off and appears on TV.

"Veiling is not obligatory but highly recommended ..."

As I listen to him, I feel like a bird set free from a cage. He has no right to enforce his religious beliefs on half the population. I'm grateful to Mamman and women like her for standing up to him. Otherwise, veiling would have become the law of our land.

ৡ   ৡ   ৡ

A few weeks pass without the ayatollah making any more demands on mandatory veiling. Instead, he focuses his attention on men, especially the ones with a long history of service in the previous administration.

A newly established revolutionary court begins to prosecute the shah's top officials. Amir-Abbas Hoveyda, a long-serving prime minister of Iran, is among the first group of individuals to be tried. He, alongside a number of ranked military officials, is quickly convicted and placed in front of a firing squad.

Tears pool in my eyes as I glare at pictures of Hoveyda in *Kayhan*, the primary newspaper in Iran—his eyes closed, his mouth half-opened, his naked body ungracefully wrapped in a small piece of white cloth just long enough to cover his private parts.

My stomach tightens as I read the charges brought against him. The first two are spreading corruption on earth and fighting God. None of the seventeen charges listed as reasons for his execution makes any sense to me, a fourteen-year-old teenager. I don't understand how our government can allow a national newspaper to publish such humiliating pictures of a dead man, even if he were guilty of all charges. Unlike the shah, he wasn't even a criminal to deserve such an awful punishment. I used to always watch him on TV, respectfully dressed in a suit and tie with a large pipe sticking out of the corner of his mouth. *Zan-e Rooz (Today's Woman)* magazine often featured his progressive views regarding women's rights, which made me feel hopeful about my future in Iran. I'm afraid what Mamman said last night is true. They killed him only because he was a Bahá'í.

Many religious people in Iran consider a Bahá'í to be a *kafar*, a disbeliever, since Bahaullah, who founded the religion in the nineteenth century, is an illegitimate prophet in their eyes. According to the Koran, Muhammad is the last prophet sent by God and—to a zealous worshiper of Islam like the ayatollah—no one other than Muhammad can possibly claim that holy spot. Even Grandma says a Bahá'í will burn in hell if he doesn't see the light of Islam before his death.

Sweat covers my body as images of my Bahá'í classmates race before my eyes; their safety is now in jeopardy with the prime minister gone. I lay the paper with the headlines facedown and run outside, weeping. I don't understand how the ayatollah, a man of the cloth, can remain so nonchalant watching all this cruelty going on.

Under the Ayatollah's Spell

Nowadays, everyone on the streets of Tehran or at bakeries, restaurants, food markets, and private gatherings is asking the same question. *Did you see it last night?*

Like Grandma and Baba, I may have seen it too: the profile of the ayatollah's face shining in the full moon.

A few days after the moon sighting, as we eat breakfast around the kitchen table, Grandma tells Jahan and me, "My dearest grandchildren, let it be known that God has commanded the ayatollah to prepare the earth for Imam Mehdi's resurrection."

Shia Muslims believe Imam Mehdi, born over ten centuries ago, is in occultation, awaiting God's order to return and save the world.

"I can feel the rift," Grandma continues with sparkle in her eyes as agate prayer beads pass between her fingers.

As usual, I stay put to hear the rest while Jahan rolls his eyes and flees the kitchen.

"Imam Mehdi is almost here. The resurrection signs are slowly but surely unfolding, like pearls sliding down a broken thread. The emergence of the shah, the beast—the *Yazid* of our time—widespread adultery, bloodshed …"

Yazid, a hated personality in Shia Islam, is known to have beheaded Imam Hussein, Prophet Muhammad's grandson, during a bloody battle in Karbala.

"And now, my dear, the splitting of the moon." She nods, rocking her slim body back and forth on the chair. "Soon, the sun will rise from where it sets, closing the door of repentance on its way. Then the fire will drive us all to that final place on earth. *Boom! Bang!*"

She shouts the last two words, scaring me half to death that I almost fall off my chair.

"Three blazing blasts—resurrection, judgment, and at last—*at last*, my dear child—the end of this world as we know it today. *God will forgive you!*" she exclaims with a glow of expectation in her eyes. "*But* you have to make up all the prayers that you have missed since you turned nine."

Nine rings in my ear as I stand up to leave. Nine is that magical age when a Muslim girl is expected to begin the ritual of praying three times a day. I'm now fourteen, so that means I have to make up $5 \times 3 \times 365$ prayers. A cold sweat sweeps over me as I grab a notepad and pencil to do the math behind my desk.

The sight of 5,475 prayers in black ink takes my breath away. That's way too many prayers to make up. Technically, I have to make up fewer prayers than 5,475 since I have spent almost every weekend with Grandma in the past five years. While at their house, we prayed together, so that would make up for $5 \times 3 \times 52$ missed prayers. On paper I subtract 780 from 5,475.

"But 4,695 is still a huge number of prayers," I whisper under my breath, letting my head fall back against the chair. In units of time, that's roughly $4,700 \times 5$, since each prayer takes about five minutes, which translates to approximately 292 hours or about 16 consecutive days of nonstop praying.

Gosh, what shall I do? I sigh, stabbing the desk with my pen. I love God, but praying that much is not in my bones, in my makeup. I don't even understand what I tell God when I pray in Arabic. Why can't I pray in Farsi instead? That'll make it so much easier and faster for me to fulfill my religious duties and make Grandma proud.

Grandma, I think, may be right about the ayatollah's profile splitting the moon, but the sun rising from where it sets can't really happen as she explained. For her to be right, Galileo has to be wrong.

Galileo's theory, in my book of planets, explains why the sun rises in the east and sets in the west. In fact, the sun is a star, so it neither rises nor sets. It's planet Earth that's moving, rising, and setting over the sun. I had never thought about how time is measured until I saw it explained in that book. Suddenly, everything about time made perfect sense. For instance, there are 365 days in a year because it takes Earth exactly that many days to circle the sun. And there are twenty-four hours in a day, because, as Earth orbits the sun, it also rotates like a spinning top, and the period of each spin is exactly twenty-four hours.

A rush of excitement ran through me the moment I realized it's the spinning that creates sunrise and sunset. The sun appears to rise from the east simply because Earth spins toward the east as it circles the sun. How could the sun possibly appear to rise from the west as Grandma claims? What has to occur physically between the sun and Earth for the sun to rise in the west?

I beat my brains out for hours, playing with the globe on my desk, trying hard to imagine what needs to happen in space for sunrise to appear in the west as Grandma says. Suddenly, a lightbulb clicks in my head. I shut my eyes and can visualize that likely scenario. Nothing will happen to the sun, I think, but Earth has to abruptly change course and spin in the opposite direction, toward the west instead of the east. In that world, Iran will be dropped all the way down into the Southern Hemisphere. Can God flip Earth upside down like that without killing all the living things on the top of it?

If that ever happens, then everyone will die in that instant and won't be able to walk over to the final gathering place to witness the fire, the resurrection, and the end. It makes no sense. Maybe Grandma just mixed up the order of the events preceding Judgment Day. The sun rising from the west has to be the very last thing that can happen on Earth, which means resurrection has to come before our planet is flipped on its head.

Why can't science and religion agree on this simple point—the passage of day into night and vice versa? Either the sun or Earth has to physically move in time for the sunrise and sunset to occur. I believe what I read in my book of planets is correct since nothing in the Koran can explain to me why there are 365 days in a year and 24 hours in a day. Galileo was such an amazing man to unravel all this complicated stuff over three hundred years ago, and no one has yet been able to prove him wrong. I wonder if he was a religious man or even believed in God. I know Uncle Mahmood is an atheist, but what about other scientists? Are they mostly atheists too?

After nightfall, I slip outside to look at the moon, determined to examine it from a scientific point of view. It's not split into halves. Maybe I just imagined it to be because of what Grandma has been feeding me. The shadowy profile is still there, but I can't tell if it's the ayatollah's face or not. In fact, it looks more like a lion with a fluffy mane or a bird with a large, round crown. If the moon is not split, then the sun can't rise from the west anytime soon, since Grandma said the events of Judgment Day proceed in order, like pearls sliding down a broken thread.

I crawl into bed thinking about what Uncle Mahmood told me once: "If you believe in science, then there is no God. Hopefully, as you grow older, you'll wise up and understand."

In my dream that night, I see the ayatollah hopping on the moon, dressed in a full-length white spacesuit. Behind the glass that encloses his face, he flashes a smirk down at Earth. Earth looks like the globe, the same one that sits on my desk. As the sun peeks over Earth, the moon and the ayatollah's face slowly fade away. Now, I can see the cat-shaped outline of Iran all the way down in the Southern Hemisphere instead of its usual place in the Northern Hemisphere, so the sun must have risen from where it normally sets. My uncle's face is projected onto the whole Earth, becoming larger and brighter as the sun soars higher and higher into the sky. Blinding light reflects off his large glasses as he mouths the words, "Wise up, Azadeh. Don't believe in Grandma's fairy tales," over and over again. *Boom. Bang.* Earth explodes, landing me right in the middle of my favorite Disney fairy tale, where Lady and the Tramp are eating the opposite ends of a single strand of spaghetti.

The next morning, I wake up in a twilight zone: half-asleep, half-awake. Vivid images of the ayatollah hopping on the moon, my uncle's lips moving, and Lady and the Tramp smiling flash in my head.

All through middle school, I struggled to understand what's behind the order of elements in the periodic table. None of my science teachers could ever explain to me why until I had that dream. It was a hot summer afternoon, and I had fallen asleep with a thick college chemistry book opened in my lap. When I woke up, somehow I knew the order had a lot to do with how lonely the last few electrons were away from the nucleus—one, two, or three made metals and four or more made nonmetals—with a few exceptions, of course.

I ponder over my dream, searching for a profound meaning of something that's unclear to me. Maybe the chance of the moon splitting into halves is as likely as Lady and the Tramp sharing a single strand of spaghetti. Maybe Uncle Mahmood is right. Maybe all the stories in the Koran are nothing but a bunch of fairy tales. Why don't I put off praying until the day the moon splits into halves? According to Grandma, the splitting occurs before the door of repentance is closed, which comes right after the sun rises from the west. Since I don't believe the latter can physically happen, maybe the former will never materialize to prompt me to pray.

My head throbs each time I argue with myself to find a good reason as to why I don't pray. There is no logical explanation, and God can see right through my lies. I don't pray because I can't stand it. When I read, finish a science project, or watch a good movie, I learn something. When I pray, I learn nothing. The incomprehensible Arabic words that pour out of my mouth can't touch my heart, hook me in, and make me think.

God, I hope you can forgive me on Judgment Day if I worship you in Farsi, the language of my birth, instead of Arabic, the language of my faith.

It won't be long before I find out if learning Arabic in school is a requirement now that the ayatollah is in charge of Iran. The schools are scheduled to open tomorrow after being closed for almost five months since October of last year when the shah was still in power. Thank God for Mamman and women like her in organizing protests to stand up against the ayatollah's call for mandatory veiling earlier in the year. Otherwise, I would be wrapped in a chador tomorrow, stumbling over myself a zillion times before the day's end.

§ § §

"You're going to be fine, Azadeh," Mamman says as I step out of her BMW in front of the large, brick-faced Maryam High School. "If a school official gives you a headscarf to wear, just say no and come home."

"Should I go to the principal's office first before coming home?" I ask, throwing my schoolbag over my shoulder.

"No. Just take a taxi and come home," she says, reaching inside her purse pocket for cash.

"Okay, Mamman. Good-bye," I say, shoving the bills inside my bag.

I shut the door and walk toward the school entrance, anxious to see what's awaiting me inside.

Students, all dressed in uniforms—white dress shirts, navy-blue pleated skirts, white socks, and black shoes—enter in large numbers through a wide-open space framed by a pair of heavy ornate iron gates. To my surprise, almost all faculty and staff in the school yard are in regular clothes—suits, shirts, skirts, and dresses. A few students and staff are wearing headscarves, but thank God no one is in a full-length chador. I breathe a sigh of relief—one less thing to worry about for now.

I glance around the school yard for a sign of the ayatollah, a picture, a poster, but none catches my eye. Everything looks the same as before, except for the imperial flag; it's no longer hanging from its post.

I liked our flag just the way it was before—horizontal stripes of green, white, and red with a golden lion right in the middle. Many Iranians consider the lion to be our national symbol since ancient times when Iran was called Persia, the largest and most powerful empire on the earth. I hope that picture of the ayatollah, the one with his eyebrows frowned, won't replace the symbol of our country's glorious past. I would like to see the golden beast returned to resume its rightful place at the center of our flag, holding a sword above its head with the sun shining on its back.

"Did you see it last night?" Bita asks, tapping me on the shoulder.

I take my eyes off the post and turn my head. "Yes, I saw it. Did you?"

I lied, because I know Bita wants me to see the face of the ayatollah in the moon. She is a big fan of the revolution, because her brother, Behnam, a political prisoner at Evin, was released on the same day that the shah fled Iran for Egypt.

"Isn't that something? What a magical scene to close your eyes to night after night," she says as she tightens the knot on her flowery headscarf.

"Why are you wearing a headscarf, Bita?" I ask. "You look much prettier without one, you know."

"And why aren't you wearing one?" she asks in a mocking voice. "Looks aren't everything, you know, Khanoom Professor Wannabe."

"To tell you the truth, Bita, I haven't seen the ayatollah in the moon. I just said that because that's what you want to hear—a bunch of lies."

"You're only saying this now because you're mad at me." She smirks.

"Believe what you want to believe, Bita. I don't care what you believe," I say, feeling relieved to have been honest with her. I'm done pretending to see the world through her eyes.

Jessica walks over, interrupting our heated discussion. "What's up? What are you two arguing about?" she asks as she tucks her thick, curly blonde hair behind her ears.

"Do you see it or not?" Bita asks Jessica, glaring at me.

"See what?"

"The ayatollah in the moon, brainy."

I shake my head, tired of hearing Bita's sarcastic comebacks.

"No, not really," Jessica says. "I don't see him, but my grandma says he's there, so I guess something must be up there in the moon."

"I'm done talking to you both," Bita says and storms off.

"What's with her?" Jessica asks and shrugs.

"Forget about her, Jessica. You know how she is, always trying to get her way on everything. What does your grandma say, exactly?"

The two of us exchange knowledge throughout the day. Her grandma also believes Judgment Day is fast approaching. I explain to her why our grandmothers are probably wrong, and she agrees with the reasons I present. We are both into science and enjoy our time alone, away from Bita's loud mouth and obnoxious comments.

At first, Jessica claims that she doesn't pray because her mother is Christian and her father is Muslim, making it difficult for her to decide how or which way to pray. At the end of the day, we both admit that we don't pray because it takes too much time, and it's boring as hell. We also agree that it is more fun to be a Christian than a Muslim, because you don't have to cover up your body, and God will accept your prayers in any language that you wish to recite them.

During the following weeks, Bita's headscarf moves farther and farther down her head, covering more of her shoulders and less of her jet-black hair. As she unveils, our friendship begins to mend. I'm mostly at fault for what happened between us on that day. I would have acted as though the ayatollah is a supreme being too, if Behnam were my brother instead, since the revolution is the reason her brother is alive today.

On the last day of school, Bita's headscarf does not even hang loosely around her neck. It's tucked inside her purse, peeking out from the inside of a small side pocket. In my mind, Bita would have been the very last woman on this earth to submit to the wills of men and veil. Her self-assured and confident ways make it impossible to imagine her happy, content, and veiled. Pretending to be someone you are not takes so much away from the person you are or hope to become. I'm glad to see the old witty Bita back again with her black hair up in a ponytail and colorful beaded jewelry hanging around her wrist and neck. She doesn't need to veil to show the depth of her gratitude for the ayatollah. We all know that about her, with or without a headscarf poking out of her purse.

Just like Bita's scarf, the myth of the ayatollah's face in the moon slowly fades away, for whatever others and I once saw on its fluorescent surface is no longer there.

 # The Hostage Crisis

Tehran, April 1980

" The power of Allah against which no plot can win ..." The ayatollah's frail voice warns the nation the day after the United States' secret mission—Operation Eagle Claw—fails to rescue the American hostages in Tehran.

Soon the nonstop media coverage informs every soul about that doomed Operation Eagle Claw: a secret military mission, ordered by President Jimmy Carter, to free the fifty-two US citizens who were held captive inside the American embassy in Tehran since November of last year. The plan called for the arrival of eight helicopters and six Hercules aircraft at a desert site near Tehran where an elite group of rangers were to be deployed to carry out the rescue mission. Battling dust storms and heavy winds, one helicopter crash-landed, and a second one collided with a refueling aircraft during takeoff. The ensuing explosion and fire killed eight US servicemen and destroyed two aircraft on-site. The remaining US crew fled the scene, leaving behind five helicopters that were captured by the Iranian armed forces the next day.

The saga had begun six months earlier when a group of university students ambushed the American embassy in Tehran. A *nest of spies* was what the captors called the embassy during TV interviews while

132

standing in front of the hostages who were handcuffed and blindfolded. Even with their eyes covered, I could tell they were afraid, standing still, shoulder to shoulder, not turning their heads as reporters' voices and nonstop chitchat in Farsi filled the air on the screen.

I looked hard at the hostages and could not spot a single tall, broad-shouldered man resembling Sean Connery or Roger Moore, the actors who play James Bond in the spy movies. Likewise, the captors, mostly bearded men in oversized white shirts, didn't appear like a group of students to me. A serious student would be neatly dressed for college, carrying books in a handheld or over-the-shoulder leather bag like all those pictures in our album of Baba and his colleagues when they were students at Tehran University. Maybe the captors told the reporters that they were students to scare us, to fool us, to have us believe that even the intellectuals were now on the ayatollah's side.

Outside the embassy, a large American flag burned as a group of men shouted, "*Marg bar Amrica!* Death to America!"

"Mamman, are they really spies?" I asked.

"Probably not. Like a spoiled child, the ayatollah is playing a game."

"What do you mean?"

"He has asked President Carter to return the shah back to Iran, but so far, the United States has refused. However, with the hostages in his custody, the tables are now turned. He has the upper hand, something to bargain with, something to show the world that his word would always be the last."

"What will happen if the United States returns the shah?"

"The charges against the hostages will be dropped without a trial, and they will be released at once."

"What about the shah?"

"Have you not seen the gold cage the government has built for him? It's all over the papers, Azadeh."

"No, I haven't, Mamman. I don't look inside papers anymore. I can't bear to see photographs of dead people."

"I know, Azadeh jan," Mamman said, stroking my hair. "That's a terrible thing for a young person to see, for anyone to see. I'll promise you, we'll find a way to get out of this hellhole soon—the sooner the better." She shook her head, watching the hostages on TV.

"What about the gold cage, Mamman? What are they going to do with it?"

"Well, I think the plan is to exchange the shah for the hostages. Once he is back, the ayatollah's disciples would likely throw him in the cage and parade him all over Tehran before hanging him in a public square. Barbaric. That's what this regime is, barbaric."

"That's an awful way for him to die." I swallowed, fearing that the shah's children might soon see a dead photograph of their father flashed in all the newspapers. I'd rather die than see a picture of my father hung from a post in a public square. I would never be the same after seeing something as horrific as that.

As I looked up and glared at the burning American flag on the TV screen, I wished that I were one of the hostages, handcuffed and blindfolded inside the embassy. Unlike me, they had a good chance to leave this madness behind and go on living the rest of their lives in a peaceful country.

ဢ ဢ ဢ

The failed American rescue mission soars the ayatollah back to his supernatural status of the year before when his face was first spotted on the moon. Religious scholars and the mullahs, interviewed in newspapers or on TV and radio programs, claim that it was the ayatollah's spell that had brought down the American choppers. One mullah after another compares the events of Operation Eagle Claw to *El-Fi sur*, the elephant verse, in the Koran:

> *Have you not seen how your Allah dealt with the People*
> *of the Elephant?*
> *Did He not bring their plan to naught?*

And sent upon them birds in flocks,
Striking them with stones of baked clay,
Turning them into an empty field of stalks and straw.

The verse describes the failed attempt of an army of forty thousand men and elephants that were sent out to destroy Kaaba, the house of Allah in Mecca, Saudi Arabia—the most sacred place of worship in Islam. According to the tale, Sultan Abraha, the king of Yemen, builds a grand church in honor of his ally the Negus, a Christian Ethiopian emperor. For months, he tries to convince the Arab tribes in the region to worship at his new church instead of Kaaba, but his words fall on deaf ears. At last, he sits tall and proud on the back of a large white elephant, leading a massive army of men and elephants toward Kaaba. Along the way, many Arab tribes put up a fierce fight against him, but none can withstand the power of his grandiose army. Close to Kaaba, Allah sends birds, equipped with stones of baked clay, to attack the sultan's army and the elephants he brought with him to stomp over his house.

"You see, the choppers are the elephants of our time," one scholar of Islam says in discussing his interpretation of the failed American rescue attempt on live radio. "The ayatollah, may Allah bless his soul, has put a curse on the People of the Elephant ..."

"All mullahs are stupid," Jahan says, sipping tea. "This fool is basically claiming, as they all do, that the Americans are like the People of the Elephant and have plans to destroy Kaaba if not stopped. I bet Grandma is loving all this, savoring over each and every word. For God's sake, it was bad weather, not divine intervention that brought down the choppers. Why the hell was I born in this backward place?" He sighs and gets up to leave the kitchen.

For once, I wholeheartedly agree with my brother. To me, it's amazing that the Americans were able to land helicopters and planes at a site near Tehran without the Iranian air force shooting them down. I can't believe the ayatollah is taking credit for this blunder instead of blaming himself for it. His regime has placed so many trained imperial pilots in front of a firing squads that none are left to protect Iran. What happened in that desert could not have taken place two years earlier when the shah ruled Iran. He was a tyrant, I know, but we had the best and the most feared military force in the entire region. No country, including the United States, would have dared to cross our borders in the dark of the night to set up a secret camp near our nation's capital without being noticed. There is no doubt in my mind that the choppers came down because of *grains* of clay, not *stones* of clay thrown by angry birds as the mullahs claim. Unlike Sultan Abraha's mission, President Carter's target was the American embassy in Tehran, not Kaaba in Saudi Arabia. But does it really matter what I think? All this media propaganda has now convinced many steadfast believers that the Americans are the People of the Elephant in our times. With all this nonsense going on, how could I ever make it to America? Like my brother, I wish I were born somewhere else, anywhere but Iran.

§ § §

"Azadeh, my dearest granddaughter," Grandma says one night as we prepare dinner together. "You should start praying soon, for there isn't a shadow of doubt in my mind who the ayatollah really is."

"Who?" I ask, turning to face her.

"He is the Messiah, my child." Grandma sighs while dicing a cucumber on the cutting board. "The ayatollah is Imam Mehdi. The end is upon us soon, very soon."

The year before, Grandma told me the ayatollah was Imam Mehdi's agent, who was ordered by God to prepare Earth for his resurrection. Now, she's claiming the ayatollah is Imam Mehdi himself. It's hard to believe what Grandma says anymore, since she also told me the end of the world was only weeks away after the ayatollah's face appeared on the moon. Here we are, fourteen months later, and the world is still intact. I wonder if all elderly think the same way as Grandma does, believing—or even wishing, it seems—for the end to materialize in their lifetimes. To me, it feels a little selfish to think that way since they have lived almost their entire lives, where mine is just beginning, and I don't want to see it end soon, although my dream of attending college in America seems unreachable now with all this chaos surrounding us.

The month before, my cousin Ibrahim wrote about how his life, too, has taken a turn for the worse in America. He has lost many of his friends in Maryland, where he attends college, and on several occasions, ripened tomatoes were thrown at him on his campus. In a recent letter, he wrote, "In a few months, I may be walking the grounds of a new college as a flamboyant Turkish scholar instead of a marked Iranian target."

Now that's a thought. Maybe I can change my nationality first and then move to America. If and when I get to America, all I want is to study science and forget about politics. It's odd that in English the study of politics is called political science; the two subjects at the opposite ends of my range of interests. There is nothing scientific about politics to call it political science. In Farsi, we call it *seeyasat*. A student who studies seeyasat becomes a *seeyasatmadar*, a good negotiator, not a scientist per se. Unlike a seeyasatmadar, a scientist cannot alter the truth and lie to promote his agenda.

§ § §

A few months after the American disaster, the ayatollah appears on TV. His frail, monotone voice once again fills the screen while Mamman, my sister, and I are having tea and sweets around the breakfast table.

"A Muslim woman must wear the veil. If you resist, Allah will defeat you in the same way He defeated the Americans in the desert. Remember, the power of Allah is one against which no one can win."

Mamman shakes her head and says, "Can you believe what this crazy mullah is saying? He truly believes that it was his divine intervention that brought down the American choppers. It's all over for us, the poor, weak, helpless women of Iran. How dare we stand up to him now that he has single-handedly defeated the powerful Americans? This time, we can't protest on the streets as we did last year to take a stand against him. I'm sure his disciples are already out and about, ready to throw acid, stab, or shoot any woman who dares to disobey him."

The thought of acid blinding my eyes and eating through my flesh makes my stomach twist and turn. I'd rather mask myself in dark clothing and become invisible than run the risk of turning into a living monster. I wonder if all religions are like Islam, where your obedience is sought through fear and revenge rather than love and forgiveness.

Not long after the announcement airs, all women on the streets of Tehran are veiled. Now only the triangle of my face sets me apart from others dressed in dark cloaks, baggy pants, and long headscarves. I'm wearing exactly the same clothes, but in my mind, I can only picture my old self in a loose-fitting summer dress with the sun on my skin and the wind in my hair. That's exactly how I should look and feel on a scorching hot August day. I'm afraid the only way out of this madness is for America to step in and declare war against us, like they did against Germany in World War II. In the process of freeing the hostages, they can potentially set the women of Iran free, much as they rescued the Jews from the hands of the Nazis. I can even imagine myself surviving the blasts and standing and waving a flag as the American troops roll into town, just like it happens in the movies. But most importantly, I can imagine myself in my favorite summer dress with my hair up in a ponytail, buckling up on a plane headed for the United States.

$$ \text{ও} \quad \text{ও} \quad \text{ও} $$

"Azadeh! Let's go! Hurry!" Baba shouts from downstairs.

"I'll be there in a minute!" I shout back, feeling excited for my cousin Roya. She's probably all dolled up by now, wearing a glamorous heavy wedding dress with tons of makeup.

I admire my reflection in the mirror, dressed in a charcoal-brown, form-fitting silk dress and Mamman's antique emerald jewelry set with my long hair flowing over my bare shoulders. It took me at least two hours to tame my unruly curls, but it was all worth it. I love my glossy straight hairdo and the glow of emerald in my eyes. Grandma says my hazel eyes—which, according to her, I have inherited from Grandpa's eldest sister—change color depending on the light or the color of the outfit or jewelry I have on.

When I hear a couple of honks, I grab my black cloak and headscarf, adding the layers on my way out.

As I step outside, the summer heat hits me like a brick wall.

"Damn this headscarf," I curse under my breath. My hair will be a complete mess by the time we arrive at my aunt's house.

I crawl in the backseat and glance up, catching a glimpse of myself in the rearview mirror. The glow of emerald in my eyes has turned dark, a reflection that matches my feelings buried deep down inside.

# The Iraq War

Tehran, September 1980

"Wake up, Azadeh. It's almost noon. The whole nation is awake," Mamman says as she walks into my room and pulls back the drapes.

On a hot summer day like today, I'd rather stay home than go out dressed in a cloak and a long headscarf. Even if I'm fully covered up, bearded men, standing at every corner of every street in Tehran, stare at me like a hawk as if I have done something wrong. This new breed of men—dressed in army fatigues and holding machine guns— call themselves the Revolutionary Guards. I have seen with my own eyes how they cuff and shove women into cars if they aren't dressed according to the status quo.

"You won't believe what happened yesterday," Mamman says as she sits on the edge of my bed.

I roll over to avoid the blinding sun streaming through the window.

"Saddam Hussein's army invaded Iran last night," Mamman says, shaking her head. "This morning, that coward has declared war against us. Can you believe it! This would never have happened if the shah were in power. He wasn't just the king of Iran. He was the king of the Middle East. He kept peace in the region."

I rub the sleep from my eyes and mumble, "Good. I'm glad he attacked us."

Why can't Mamman just leave me alone? Can't she tell that I've been wearing the same pajamas for five straight days without taking a shower and brushing my hair?

"That's a terrible thing to say, Azadeh," Mamman says and yanks the sheet off my body.

"Why, Mamman? The ayatollah doesn't give a damn about me. Why should I care what happens to him? I hope the Iraqis drop an atomic bomb on Tehran and kill us all. I don't know about you, but this is not how I plan to live the rest of my life." I sit up, grab the sheet, and pull it back over myself.

"Get up this minute, Azadeh!" Mamman sighs, standing by the door and looking flustered. "You have slept enough. Baba just brought home kebab sandwiches for lunch. You'd better hurry before it's all gone."

What Mamman just said is sadly true. When the shah ruled Iran, we were the America of the Middle East. Iranian women, like pop star Googoosh, were the fashion icons of the region, and all the countries in the Persian Gulf feared us. Saddam Hussein, practically a nobody in anyone's book, has now attacked us because he knows the ayatollah has executed all the elite imperial officers and pilots that could have easily defeated him in this war if they were still alive. I must have been about ten years old when Saddam first attempted to invade Iran, but the shah's imperial air force crushed his troops before they even got a chance to reach our borders in the south. I'm afraid nothing good can come out of a war with Saddam, for he and the ayatollah are cut from the same cloth.

Jahan is just about ready to take a bite out of my kebab sandwich as I walk into the kitchen. I let him have half of it and sit down to eat the other half.

"Do you know what happened yesterday, sleepyhead?" Jahan asks as he opens a bag of potato chips.

"Yes. Mamman just told me," I say, pouring myself a glass of Coca-Cola.

"Who do you think is going to win this war, sis?" he asks between bites.

"I don't know, probably Iraq. We don't have a strong military to fight back as we did when the shah ruled Iran."

"Well, I don't really care who wins this war. Baba told me not to worry too much, as he has made plans to ship me out before my eighteenth birthday rolls around."

"Ship you to where, Jahan?" I ask, angry at Baba for favoring Jahan over me.

"Whoops! I shouldn't have told you all this. Keep your big mouth shut for now. I'll tell you later when I know when and where."

Jahan gets up and leaves the kitchen as I ponder over his words. I want to be shipped out too before school starts. Maybe, if luck is on my side, the schools will remain closed because of the war with Iraq. I'd rather stay home and vegetate instead of attending school dressed in a cloak, baggy pants, and a long headscarf. I can't imagine learning a thing in a place that can't accept me for who I am or desire to become.

§ § §

To my dismay, in spite of the war with Iraq, schools are scheduled to open for the 1980/1981 academic year. This is the first year that veiling is mandatory for schoolgirls ages nine years and up. Just the thought of waddling around in the school yard with my friends like a flock of crows dressed in dark clothing and fully covered up sends chills down my spine. A herd of sheep is what we have become, mindlessly following the shepherd, too afraid of the wolf to stray behind. The wolf, it seems, is capable of winning all kinds of wars. In just two years, the ayatollah has defeated the shah, has made veiling mandatory, and has somehow managed to keep the American hostages locked up in Iran. I won't be surprised if he captures Saddam Hussein and makes him beg for his life. But I'm not going to let this man win over me for the rest of my life. There has to be a way for me to get out of Iran.

§ § §

A quiet tension hangs over my head as I step into the school yard, covered in dark clothing from the top of my head to the tips of my toes. To my surprise, unlike previous years, clusters of girls are not huddled together gossiping or chitchatting about how summer vacations were spent.

After a few minutes of looking around, I feel like a small child lost in a crowd, trying to recognize a familiar face in a sea of dark scarves and cloaks. *What should I say when I find that someone?*

Hair, ears, and entire bodies are covered up, making it hard to make small talk. It's unbelievable but true that I can no longer say, "I love your new hairstyle," or ask, "Where did you get those amazing earrings?" Veiling, it seems, has taken more from us than just the excitement to look hip and shine in a crowd. We have become more docile and quiet, unsure of where we stand in a society ruled by mullahs.

Lines begin to form as our new principal, dressed in dark clothing and a long headscarf, takes the podium.

"Welcome back to school, young daughters of the revolution. May Allah bless you and your families. In addition to our regular curriculum, each student is now required to take lessons in the Arabic language ..."

My head starts to spin as I consider the deeper meaning of her statement. English is what I need to learn to be prepared for college next year, not Arabic.

"Also, each student is required to attend the prayer at noontime in the school yard. If it's that time of the month for you, you may be excused. Just report to the disciplinarian of your grade. Each grade is assigned a disciplinarian, and in a minute, I will introduce each of them to you ..."

Disciplinarian? As I hear the description of this new staff position, I realize that this person is hired to make my life hell while at school, especially outside the classroom.

"And one last thing before you are excused. During PE periods, you will each knit scarves or sweaters that will be shipped to your fellow brothers to keep them warm in the upcoming winter months as they fight the Iraqis on the front lines. You may begin marching to your classrooms now."

Knitting scarves and sweaters during PE is replacing exercise? I can't wait to get home and hear what my brother has to say about what the regime has cooked up for the boys to do during PE periods. They probably have them do jumping jacks and go through hoops in preparation for the battleground. If that's the case, then they at least get a chance to exercise more parts of their bodies than just a few fingers bending and stretching to make knots.

On the way home from school, to my astonishment, I am not thinking about veiling and the war with Iraq. Instead, my mind is filled with chitchat that I heard during recess and lunch—a parent, a relative, or a family friend of this or that student killed by the regime, gone missing, or imprisoned somewhere in Iran. The horrors others have endured make me feel grateful that God has chosen my family to escape unharmed.

That evening, as we sit down for dinner, Jahan hands me a large white plastic key and says, "I bet you didn't get one of these at your school today."

"What is this?" I ask, turning over the key. "Made in Taiwan" is printed on the back.

"That, right there," he points to the key in my hand, "is my ticket to paradise." He smirks and rolls his eyes.

"Can I see the key too?" Afshan asks, and I hand it to her.

Mamman shakes her head as she puts down the food on the table. "I can't believe the garbage they're feeding you at school these days."

"What are you talking about, Mamman? This is not garbage.

You'd better sign me up for this war. I can't possibly wait till I'm eighteen to use my key to paradise." Jahan chuckles.

"Why? Are you out of your mind?" Mamman asks, furrowing her forehead.

"No, not really. I want to become a martyr of this war."

"Stop your nonsense, Jahan," I say. "What's the rest of the story?"

"Well, if I die, I'll use this key," he picks up the plastic key off the table, "to unlock the gates of heaven, but that's not the best part."

"What do you mean?" I ask, thinking that the government could have at least spray-painted the plastic key in sparkling gold or silver to make it look more like an authentic key to paradise.

"Well, once I unlock those heavenly gates, beautiful women will be chasing after me, competing for my love."

"How many women?" Afshan asks, staring into Jahan's eyes as though she believes his every word.

"Seventy-two women, and all virgins, if you know what that means."

"What's a virgin?" Afshan asks, but no one answers her question.

"Stop it, Jahan," Mamman says, laughing. "I guess you don't believe any of this garbage, do you?"

"Well, that all depends," he says, rubbing his chin.

"Depends on what?" Mamman asks, a frown wrinkling her forehead.

"Depends on what you and Baba can offer me instead. More women, I suppose?"

Except for Afshan, the rest of us burst into laughter. Her pleas to understand what this conversation is about fall on deaf ears, since no one seems to have the energy or the patience to explain all the nonsensical changes to a ten-year-old child. She still has a hard time understanding why she couldn't wear her uniform to school this morning like she did last year or why she had to wear a headscarf that made her scalp itch all day long.

§ § §

A few weeks later, each girl in the eleventh grade has noticed that Khanoom Khorshide, the disciplinarian of our grade, isn't quite all there.

A jokester among us often teases her. "Hey, Khanoom Khorshide, your face is glowing like the rising *khorshid* masked in a sea of clouds."

"Thank you. I have heard that so many times," she says as her lips twitch with a half grin, half smile, making us wonder if she's happy or not.

Another simple matter that Khanoom Khorshide cannot figure out is why each girl in the eleventh grade always seems to be on her period. Being on your period provides a perfect excuse to be excused from noontime mandatory prayer in the school yard. In Islam, a woman on her period is exempt from praying, because—in God's eyes—she's ritually unclean to recite prayers. That's about the only thing that I can think of in which a woman is favored over a man in Islam because, unlike us, they have to pray every single day of every month.

The girls in the twelfth grade, however, aren't as lucky as we are, since their disciplinarian is smart enough to know that the period excuse can't be used for an entire month. She keeps records on each girl and sometimes even asks to see evidence if someone requests to be excused too many days out of a month. I hope she resigns before I graduate eleventh grade. It makes me sick to think of her standing over my shoulder as I pray in the school yard every single day, minus the days that I'm actually on my period.

There is one thing though that Khanoom Khorshide is dead serious about. Each morning, she barks at us to line up in a row facing her. Then she walks up and down the aisle while hitting the palm of her hand with a soft ruler like a madwoman, shouting, "No makeup is allowed! No makeup is allowed!" If she sees a face she dislikes, the pacing abruptly stops. "You are despicable, despicable. Step forward, despicable, despicable …"

Her mannerism reminds me so much of that crazy cartoon character Daffy Duck from the Looney Tunes. Like Daffy, she appears completely black and loves to shout *despicable* with her eyes bulging out for no apparent reason at all.

Poor Jessica gets pulled out of the line almost every single day, accused of wearing too much makeup. Her only fault is that, unlike the rest of us with olive skin, her skin is fair like her Russian mother, Olga. I don't understand how many times Khanoom Khorshide has to rub her delicate skin with a white piece of cloth to realize that Jessica's rosy cheeks are a gift from God, the same God that we are expected to worship at noontime in the school yard. I'm surprised that the school officials have not yet replaced her, but maybe she is exactly the type of woman that the Islamic Republic wants us to become—fully covered up with no brains and no desire to look nice.

Months later, early in the morning, Khanoom Khorshide is pacing up and down the aisle, slapping the palm of her hand with a soft ruler while shouting, "No makeup is allowed! No makeup is allowed!"

Suddenly, she stops right in front of me. The next thing I know, her white cloth is in my face, aiming for my eyes. I laugh at her in my head as her sweaty hand rubs against my cheeks and the white cloth moves up and down around my eyes. Once again, she can't stop herself from spitting out *despicable* not just once or twice, but way too many times.

I do have baggy eyes because I was reading the novel *For Whom the Bell Tolls* late the night before, which I couldn't put down. It's a pity that what matters to Khanoom Khorshide the most is my physical appearance, not what's playing in my head—Robert and Maria, the unmarried characters in the novel, making sweet love. This government of ours has got it all wrong. To make us believe in Islam and pray like we should, they need to change the way we think, not the way we look.

For Whom the Bell Tolls by Hemingway is one of my favorite novels. The Spanish Civil War portrayed in the book reminds me so much of how things were a few years earlier in the midst of the revolution. But it's not the political situation that draws me to this book; I can't get enough of the love scenes between Robert and Maria. When I read and reread the scenes, I can feel what Maria feels when Robert holds her, touches her, and makes love to her. Maybe if I were in love, like Maria is in this book, I could somehow forget about my miserable life in Iran.

§ § §

Fall turns into winter, snow covers every inch of the ground, and far away in America, President Carter loses his seat to Ronald Reagan, a B-grade movie actor turned politician in Hollywood, California. He may not be a superstar by Hollywood standards, but minutes after his inauguration, the hostages are released and are on their way back to America. It's hard to believe that nearly fifteen months have passed since they were ambushed inside the American embassy in Tehran.

Just about anything and everything American movies have to offer is magical, be it on or off the screen. A retired B-grade movie actor has just performed a miracle in real life, while his predecessor failed even with a full-blown secret military operation backing him up. Baba says this new president is good news for Iran. I don't understand why most Iranian men believe a Republican president is always better for us than his Democratic counterpart. Maybe Baba and his friends are right this time. Maybe this movie actor can perform another miracle and rid Iran of this ruthless ayatollah. Only then could we once again watch movies on the silver screen as we used to when the shah ruled Iran.

Nowadays, we still watch movies, but only on the small screen and in secret at someone's house. Movies like *Saturday Night Fever*, *Going Steady*, *Over the Edge*, *Thank God It's Friday*, and *Grease* are just a few favorites that my friends and I have watched many times. I don't know how our parents get hold of black market movies, but every upscale household seems to have a collection of hip American films in stock.

If Iran were like America, I think I would go steady with Hamid, one of my brother's friends. He has a pretty large nose, but overall, he's tall, dark, and handsome. We are like Sandy and Danny in *Grease*. While many girls like the bad-boy greaser Danny, he's only into nerdy-looking Sandy. I'm kind of like Sandy, looking nerdy most of the time, but when I let my hair down, take my glasses off, and wear something nice, most guys notice me in a crowd. I wish I could dress up and go out on a date with Hamid; at least once would be nice. What's wrong with Hamid and his friends and me and my friends dancing wildly on the streets like Sandy, Danny, and their friends in *Grease*?

But we can't have fun like that on the streets of Tehran, because they're owned by the ayatollah, and he considers dancing a crime. Thirty-five lashes is the minimum punishment I'll get if I'm caught dancing with a man who's not yet my husband. I have no intention of breaking this law, but it makes me sick to think that we have a law that prevents us from moving our body parts when we hear pleasant, rhythmic sounds. Even an infant dances to music well before she's ready to walk or talk. Dancing is a natural instinct, a gift from God. The ayatollah has once again got it all wrong. God has no problem seeing us dance and have a good time. It's only he and his disciples who think otherwise, depriving us from exercising our God-gifted rights.

On most nights, to escape from it all, a group of us gets together at someone's house to watch movies and go crazy wild. We often practice the dance scenes played in films to perfection as we giggle and make fun of the ayatollah, Khanoom Khorshide, or any other idiot we can think of. I tend to always be cast as John Travolta, because I'm the tallest one in our bunch and can toss the others over my shoulders and in between my legs without falling flat on my face too many times.

Some nights, as we watch movies late into the night, sirens sound, electricity shuts off, and bombs begin to fall on Tehran. All the commotion brings us back from the dreamy land of movies to our homeland, where being happy is considered a crime.

"Wipe that smile off your face!" my principal shouted at me once.

"How could you smile like that when your brothers are dying in the war?"

What my principal doesn't know is that I weep almost every day when I see young men on the streets of Tehran with missing parts: limbs torn off, eyes gouged, faces burned and disfigured. The truth is that I do care for my brothers a whole lot, but I don't give a damn if my principal and the ayatollah think otherwise.

One night, in our dark, damp basement, hours pass as I huddle together with a bunch of friends and family, listening to music out of a boom box, waiting for the lights to come back on. When the chitchat quiets down, I keep staring at the candle burning out, thinking that I know why it's blue at the core and yellow all around. It's all chemistry. It's all about how matter interacts with light.

Sometimes I think I'm weird to think for hours and hours about why nature looks the way it does. I bet no one in this basement knows that the sky is blue because of how air molecules interact with sunlight. Nitrogen and oxygen molecules in the air are capable of scattering more of the blue and less of the remaining colors that are coming at us from the sun. In a way, an air molecule can act almost like a tiny prism, bending and separating the blue from the rest of the colors in sunlight. I wonder what else is in the air that makes a rainbow stand out in the sky. It has to be something that acts just like a prism, something that can equally bend and separate all the colors that, when combined, make up the white, bright sunlight.

Once again, my mind gets stuck on esoteric topics to avoid thinking of real life: my bleak future in Iran. Would it be so bad if a deadly bomb finds its way to where I'm hiding now? Isn't dying in an instant a better option than living in fear of dying night after night with no end in sight? I bet someone else in this basement is thinking the same crazy thoughts, not the ones about the color of the flame or the color of the sky—those I know are exclusively mine—but the more serious thoughts.

Grandma's Last Wish

Mamman's quiet cries creep all the way into my room. My heart feels heavy as I follow the sound of her weeping into my parents' bedroom and peek in. Baba is there too, cuddled next to her at the edge of the bed, his lips pressed against her ear, speaking words of comfort that I can't hear.

"Did someone die?" I ask, stepping into the room.

Baba sits up on the bed and looks me straight in the eyes. His dreary eyes tell me I'd rather not hear what he's about to say.

He rubs his forehead and sighs. "Uncle Reza was arrested last night. He's in Evin."

My knees feel weak as the voice inside my head screams *no* before I'm able to speak. "Is he still alive?" I ask, tears rolling down my face.

Mamman bawls.

"Why do you ask that?" Baba frowns at me. "Of course he's alive. We'll get him out soon. I'll promise you."

I don't understand why Baba always promises things he can't deliver. He told us the revolution was a good thing for us, and look at where we are now. He doesn't know if Uncle is still alive to make an empty promise like that.

As Baba continues to comfort Mamman, my mind races back in time. Horrific tales of what goes on behind those feared walls echo in my head from the mouths of friends and close neighbors, stories

151

of loved ones snatched in the middle of the night to be tortured at Evin for many long months. Some even faced a firing squad before they had a chance to say their good-byes. I never thought this could one day happen to me.

It's not hard to imagine how the ayatollah's disciples ambushed my uncle the night before. It has happened to too many families before us. I know their kids; some go to my school; some live on my street.

Uncle probably woke up to the sound of loud voices approaching. "Go! Go! Go!"

Seconds later, the door to his bedroom slammed against the wall as men in disguise stormed in and switched on the light. He focused his eyes and saw guns—two, three, or more pointed directly at him.

"Get up! Get dressed!" a gunman shouted as another pulled the covers off his bed, whacking him with a gun at the back of his head.

"Why? What did I do?" Uncle pleaded, not knowing what he had done wrong.

"Traitor, you know what you have done."

"Who are you?" Uncle asked, dazed and confused.

"Shut up. Get up, or I'll shoot you."

Uncle got up in haste and put on his robe and slippers. The gunmen handcuffed and blindfolded him as he stood next to his bed. They hustled him out the bedroom door, down the hallway, and into the frigid, snow-covered terrace. In the middle of the yard, his slippers sank into deep February snow as he struggled to follow orders to quicken his pace. Outside, the gunmen shoved him into a car and headed for Evin. If he is still alive, he is sitting in a cell awaiting a mock trial.

Images of Mandana and Nadia, my young cousins, flash in my head. It's not right to take their father away from them. They're only ten and four. That's not how things happen in real life. Fathers are supposed to be around to watch their daughters grow up, get married, and have children of their own. Only a monster like the ayatollah would dare to interfere with God's wish for every person to live a prosperous life.

Jahan steps in, hears the news, and bursts into tears. Baba tries to console him, but I can tell he knows, as I do, we may never see Uncle again.

"What is he charged with?" he asks Baba, wiping tears with the back of his hand.

"He is charged with a serious crime: assisting an infidel to escape prosecution."

"Who is the infidel?" I ask, stroking Mamman's hair.

"Uncle Muhammad."

The news strikes me like a lightning bolt. This is far worse than I thought; my other uncle is in grave danger too.

Baba goes on. "The revolutionary court has convicted Uncle Muhammad of organizing an underground army of militants to fight against the new regime."

I had no idea Uncle Muhammad was an antirevolutionary. If I were an adult, I too would have turned into a zealous antirevolutionary by now.

"What if they find Uncle Muhammad?" Jahan asks Baba, holding back tears.

"His sentence is execution by a firing squad," Baba says, looking down.

Jahan breaks out crying a second time.

"Where is he now?" I ask, staring at Baba.

"We don't know." Baba sighs. "He is most likely out of Iran."

"How did Uncle Reza help Uncle Muhammad escape?" I ask.

"I don't think he helped him at all," Mamman says, sniffling. "That's just a scare tactic to coerce Uncle Muhammad to turn himself in."

"He might have helped him out, Azar," Baba says. "But that doesn't matter now. What matters is Reza. We have to find a way to get him out of jail."

Baba leaves the room, telling us that he's off to work to make some important phone calls.

I stay with Mamman in their bedroom. She weeps as I stroke

her hair and think of Baba. This must be very hard on him. Baba and Uncle Reza have been best friends since grade school. Rumor has it that Uncle Reza planted the seed for my parents to tie the knot. My insides clench as I imagine the ending of our saga. Which uncle will die? Should Uncle Muhammad turn himself in to save Uncle Reza and then face the firing squad? I don't know what to think anymore. I love them both. It's like choosing between losing my left or right eye.

§   §   §

Ten days pass, and Uncle is still in jail. I'm sitting alone in the family room, recalling the day I turned fourteen. It was exactly two weeks after the ayatollah had returned home from exile. Today, I turn sixteen. Two years of my life has been wasted living under the ayatollah's thumb, and there isn't a damn thing I can do to stop time from moving forward.

I look over at the rolled-up newspaper on the coffee table and weep. The voice inside my head shouts at me. *Come on! Don't be a coward, Azadeh! Unroll the paper!*

My hand shakes as I reach for the paper, frantically flip through the pages, and pause for a quick glance at the list of names under the execution column. A sigh of relief escapes my body as I throw the paper onto the ground and thank God for sparing my uncle. Since his arrest, I can't stop my mind from picturing him dead in the paper—his eyes closed, his mouth half-opened, his body ungracefully wrapped with a small piece of white cloth—just like the images of Prime Minister Hoveyda published in *Kayhan* shortly after the ayatollah resumed control of Iran.

§   §   §

My siblings and I collapse into sobs as Mamman tells us about Grandma's grim diagnosis. She has terminal breast cancer. All this worrying for Uncle must have taken its toll on her. I feared that something terrible might happen to her, but I wasn't expecting it to be this soon, just a month after Uncle's arrest. According to Mamman, Grandma quickly opted to have a mastectomy to extend her life, hoping that it would buy her enough time to see Uncle before she takes her last breath.

After the operation and weeks of cancer treatments, Grandma looks nothing like herself. Her scalp is almost bare, and she feels even lighter than my skinny eleven-year-old sister, Afshan. I can easily lift her off the bed to set her in a wheelchair for a quick stroll around the neighborhood. She now lives with us, since Mamman has to drive her to the hospital twice a week for radiation therapy.

As Grandma and I stroll the streets in our neighborhood, she doesn't talk to me much, no matter how hard I try to cheer her up. I wonder if she knows or cares about who I am anymore. I understand that it's natural for her to love her son more than she loves me; she was a mother first before she became my grandmother, but I wish she would talk to me like she used to before all this happened to us. I want her to know that I care a whole lot for her, but I don't think she wants or needs my help.

When Grandma is awake, she sits on her bed and prays nonstop, as agate prayer beads passing between her fingers until Mamman shows up. The second she sees Mamman, her mumbling stops, and words begin to spill out.

"Azar, I have to see Reza before I die. You are my only hope; my future is in your hands."

The highlight of my day arrives each morning when Grandma asks me to bring her the paper. That's the only time I think she may recognize who I am, sitting by her bed holding her hand.

I give her the paper and stand quietly by her side.

"Thank you, sweetie," she says while spreading the paper in her lap.

I watch as a magnifying glass moves up and down in her shaky hand until she finds that perfect spot for a close look at a lifeless, blown-up face underneath the glass. Then she moves on to a new picture, either below or on the next page, without looking at me once. When none of the photographs matches Uncle, she smiles, sighs, and puts the paper down. Once again, rosaries pass between her fingers as she anxiously waits for Mamman to come home.

I can't help but wonder why Grandma smiles when she looks inside the paper. Maybe all this trauma and radiation has changed the person she once was. The Grandma I knew would have wept staring at pictures of dead men, as if they were her own flesh and blood. I pray that her sweet, loving spirit is still alive and has not yet left us.

Staring into Grandma's sad, droopy eyes always takes me back to that safe place, my grandparents' home in Shahran, when her eyes would sparkle with joy every time she saw my brother and me. Jahan and I often spent the weekends with our grandparents, who lived in a small town twenty miles northeast of Tehran.

Their house had a spectacular view of the Alborz mountain range, with its highest peak, Mount Damavand, clearly visible on most days. At sunset, the Damavand peak appeared as a giant purple pillar partly submerged in a hazy orange glow, a glow that Grandma had me believe was nothing other than an act of almighty God.

When I was a kid, I believed everything my grandma told me. As I grew older, I realized she wasn't always right. Grandma believes everything in the sky—the sun, the moon, the clouds, the stars, the rainbows, the sunset glows—are all the work of God. According to her, the golden gates of heaven are way up in the sky. When they open to receive a worthy soul, the blue of the sky blends into a blinding light, lifting one's spirit into a magical world unlike any seen by a pair of mortal eyes.

Two years earlier in my physics class, I learned that clouds are not just magical objects in the sky as Grandma had me believe. They're tiny droplets of water or grains of ice that float in the sky, reflecting sunlight, which makes them appear fluffy and white against a blue background. I wonder what else is in the air besides nitrogen molecules, oxygen molecules, water drops, and ice crystals? The first two make the sky blue, and the last two create clouds, but there has to be something else in the air that makes rainbows and sunset glows stand out in the sky. I plan to find out all there is to know about how nature works, and the ayatollah is not going to stop me from learning things that are most important in my life.

At my grandparents' house, my brother and I often went for a hike with Grandpa while Grandma made her delicious cuisines. We always took the same path up a few sloping trails that opened into a valley of small rivers. In the summertime, we would spread a soft blanket on the bank of a river and sit down next to Grandpa as he told us stories from *Shāhnāmeh: The Epic of the Persian Kings*. Simurgh, one of *Shāhnāmeh*'s best-known characters, a benevolent, mythical flying creature strong enough to lift an elephant off the ground, lived at Mount Damavand, the summit of the Alborz mountain range. Often in my dreams, I would see the three of us riding Simurgh from these same riverbanks all the way up to the summit.

On the way back from the hike, we always stopped at the bakery to pick up fresh bread handed to us right out of a burning *tanoor*, a clay oven carved into the wall. We ate almost half the bread on the way home, which often angered Grandma.

"How many times have I told you not to allow the children to eat?" she would ask Grandpa. "Now they are not hungry, and I have to throw away all this food."

Usually, Grandpa ignored her, but sometimes he would complain, "Woman, just quiet down. Lower your voice. In forty years, I have yet to see you throw food away."

On one occasion, while ranting, she followed him outside as he was preparing to water the garden. He turned the hose on her instead, and we all had a good laugh, including Grandma.

I never understood why Grandma always gave Grandpa such a hard time. My brother and I did eat a lot of bread on the way with Grandpa, but the minute we walked into the house, the smell of sautéed onions and fresh-cooked rice made our stomachs rumble anew.

After dinner, we often watched comedy shows on their ancient TV set and sometimes played *passor*, a popular card game, or backgammon with Grandpa as Grandma smoked her smelly hookah, puffing out tiny rings of black smoke.

Every day at their home, Grandma and I prayed side by side behind Grandpa before sunrise, at noon, and after sunset while Jahan slept or played. I often told him, "Get your lazy bones up and pray!" but he never did.

One time when I kicked Jahan to get up and pray, he warned me, "If you pray too much, you'll get a big scar on your forehead like Grandpa, and no one will ever marry you."

"That's much better than going to hell," I replied.

Grandpa had a brownish, oval-shaped scar in the middle of his forehead from pressing it forcefully against the *mohr*—a matchbox-sized piece of clay imported from the holy city of Karbala in Iraq—when he prayed.

In the bathroom mirror, away from my brother's prying eyes, I checked my forehead up close and personal several times, but so far, there was no scar. After that, I never pressed my forehead against the mohr while I prayed.

Grandma and I also fasted together during the month of Ramadan. We spent the whole day cooking what we anticipated to eat right after the sunset. Ramadan is a holy month during which Muslims believe God revealed the Koran to Prophet Muhammad. Every day during this month, we rose before sunrise to eat a meal and perform our first prayer of the day. Then we fasted, no food or drink, for the entire day until sunset. We ate our second feast right after sunset, followed by the last prayer of the day.

I once asked Grandma why we had to fast, and she told me, "Fasting brings you closer to God. It makes you feel the pain of hunger suffered by many who aren't as fortunate as you are. And as a result, you'll become more generous, more giving to your fellow human beings."

"How can it make me more generous?"

"Well, you are expected to hand over the food that you don't eat during the day to those who are needy."

"Oh, now I understand. Do you and Grandpa do that, as well?"

"Yes, of course we do. All Muslims comply."

"Where do you take all the food?"

"Usually to a mosque. Grandpa takes either food or money to the mosque every day during Ramadan. That's why he isn't here at noon to pray with us. He prays at the mosque with the rest of the men in the neighborhood."

"Can we go with him next time?"

"No, dear. Women are not allowed."

There we go, I thought then and again now. My biggest complaint against Islam is that women can't do this or that, but men are free to do whatever they want. No wonder the ayatollah thinks he is God and can do no wrong.

ৡ   ৡ   ৡ

The intense sadness in Grandma's eyes drives Mamman insane, crazy enough to spend every second of every day on Uncle's case. His freedom from Evin has become her only passion in life. That's all she talks about when we arrive home from school in the afternoon or when Baba comes home from work at night.

Six weeks after Uncle's arrest, Mamman's determination pays off; she has an appointment with Mr. Asadollah Lajevardi, nicknamed "the Butcher of Evin," the chief prosecutor of Tehran and the warden of Evin Prison.

Hairs on the back of my neck stood up the second I heard Lajevardi's name. One of my close friends told me recently that Lajevardi had personally tortured someone her father knew well. Our next-door neighbor had an even more horrific tale to tell. Lajevardi had murdered a young woman with his bare hands while my neighbor's uncle watched with his hands tied behind his back. I don't understand why my mother thinks this monster can help us bring Uncle home.

The next day, Mamman comes home from her meeting with Lajevardi, sobbing into her hands, sickened with worry that her brief conversation with Lajevardi might have brought unwanted, possibly deadly attention to Uncle's case. It doesn't take a future hopeful rocket scientist to know that things didn't go quite as well as she had hoped.

"I saw my poor brother just before I left Evin," she tells Baba as she yanks a navy-blue scarf off her head and throws it onto the ground.

"How did he look?" Baba asks, trying to calm her down.

"Awful, just awful. I saw him through the plexiglass. He had just endured thirty or so lashes. I barely recognized him, Modjtaba. His face was severely bruised. What am I going to do now? My mother is dying, my brother is in jail, and there isn't a damn thing I can do to help either of them. I wish I were dead," she says, collapsing in tears.

Baba hugs her and kisses her forehead. "Don't say that, Azar. I'll promise you, we'll find a way to bring Reza home."

Mamman shakes her head. "What am I going to tell Gisela now? She wants to come back from Germany to help her husband somehow; only God knows how!"

"Don't worry about Gisela, Azar jan. I'll call her tonight and explain why she should not come back at this time."

"Please do, Modjtaba. I have told her several times that there isn't a damn thing a blonde-haired, blue-eyed German woman who speaks Farsi with an incomprehensible accent can do in Iran other than get herself and her family into more trouble."

Mamman gets up, lets out a heavy sigh, and heads to Grandma's room. I follow behind and stand under the door frame.

She sits by Grandma's bed and holds her hand. "Mamman jan, Reza will be home soon. We're making a lot of progress. It can be any day now."

"When?" Grandma asks in a faint voice. "When can I see my son?"

I walk away wondering how much longer I can keep myself together and act as if I can handle things like an adult. Why can't Mamman ask me how I feel about all that's going on—Grandma dying, Uncle in jail, and Mamman always gone?

Minutes later, I fling myself onto my bed. No one seems to notice if I'm missing for long periods of time, no one knocks on my door or calls my name to show up for meals, not even Mamman. After crying my eyes out, I drag my body to the kitchen and sit down for dinner with my family.

I glance across the table at my sister and brother. They appear just as miserable as I do: untidy hair, mismatched clothes, and puffy eyelids as if stung by a bee. My brother no longer cracks jokes, and my sister no longer begs for more Barbie clothes. Meanwhile, my parents are busy, as usual, discussing what matters to them the most.

Mamman is telling Baba about her meeting with Lajevardi earlier that morning. "First, he scorned me for not wearing proper hejab in his presence, although I was showing only my hands and a small triangle of my damn face. Then he went on to tell me that in the eyes of Islam, royalty and peasants have equal rights."

Baba sighs and shakes his head. "Equal rights. That sounds strange coming out of his bloody mouth. He doesn't even believe in human rights."

Mamman continues, "Just before I left, he told me, 'You are an ignorant, selfish woman. Every day, we bury thousands of martyrs who have volunteered to fight in this bloody war with Iraq so rich people like you can have a roof over their heads. Most martyrs of this war aren't even eighteen years old, and you have the gall to come here and talk to me about your mother's aches and pains. I don't give a damn about you, your mother, your brother, and your entire family. Frankly, if it were up to me, your brother would be under six feet of dirt.'"

"This man has no soul, no humanity," Baba says as he rubs Mamman's shoulder. "You did your best, Azar jan. We'll find another way to get Reza out."

I leave the table unnoticed and head for Grandma's room. I don't know if she's unconscious or asleep, but her eyes are closed, and she appears peaceful.

Gazing at her still body takes me back to the carefree years when Najmieh and I stayed up late watching movies, exactly where she is resting now. People, it seems, are able to forget their pasts and move on, even after tragic events they can neither understand nor overcome. I will never know why Najmieh and I met and became friends, but I have moved on with my life without getting over her loss. With God's help, I hope I can carry on after my sweet grandma is gone; at least in her case, I know she will be in a better place.

I plop myself on the edge of Grandma's bed, hold her hand, and begin to pray.

God, please bring my uncle home before Grandma dies. If you do, I'll believe in you with all my heart. I'll even believe what Grandma has been telling me for years about rainbows and sunset glows in the sky. They are all your creations, after all.

§ § §

After Mamman's failed meeting with Lajevardi, the phone becomes her best friend until Baba is home from work, anxious to hear what she has to say. She constantly speaks into the receiver to people with last names unrecognizable to my ear. I don't dare talk to her anymore, for she yells at me the minute she sees me approaching while she's on the phone jabbering away.

In the search to find Uncle's savior, Mamman leaves the house at the crack of dawn and returns well into the night.

One day when I come home from school, I'm surprised to see Mamman home early, sitting on a chair next to Grandma's bed, stroking her hair. I stand by the door and listen.

"Mamman jan, Reza will be home soon, very soon. Do you remember Akbar Kateri, Ahmad ahga's nephew? He is a now Mullah Kateri. He has promised to help us."

Ahmad ahga is married to my aunt Banoo-Azam, Baba's second sister. The last time I saw Akbar at my aunt's house, he wasn't dressed in an ankle-length robe, turban, and black slippers. But maybe now that he's a mullah, a man of the cloth, he can help us get out of this mess. A newfound energy surges within me, filling my heart with optimism and hope.

A few days later, Ahmad ahga arranges a meeting at his house for Mamman to present her case to Mullah Kateri.

The morning of the meeting, Mamman dresses in a full hejab and walks over to Grandma's room. She kisses her on the forehead and says, "Mamman jan, don't worry anymore. Reza will be home soon."

When she steps out of Grandma's room, I hug her tightly and follow her outside. She steps into a taxi and waves good-bye as I cross my fingers and pray for everything to turn out just right.

Later that evening, we are all ears as Mamman tells us of her experience.

"I met the plump mullah in Ahmad ahga's dining room. He was sitting on a fine carpet, resting against a *motaka*, an oversized carpet-faced pillow. He didn't get up to greet me but continued to slurp freshly brewed Persian tea from a saucer as a large chunk of sugar moved around in his mouth. During our conversation, Mullah Kateri often poured hot tea from a delicate, hourglass-shaped, gold-rimmed teacup to a saucer and whistled the steam away. He told me, 'Your brother has committed unforgivable sins against Islam,' and he went on and on.

"'Dear Mullah Kateri,' I told him, 'I am on the same page as you are, but my mother is dying of cancer, and she is begging for Imam Khomeini's forgiveness. Her last wish is to see her son.'

"You know, I have never met a mullah who doesn't see food as a rare commodity," Mamman tells us. "Kateri's mouth was stuffed with sweets as he kept rambling on, spitting bits of pastry here and there. Can you believe that a few bits of pastry even landed on the tiny triangle of my exposed face?"

Baba laughs hard and says, "Azar, come on. Stop exaggerating."

I can even see a faint smile on Grandma's bony face as Mamman continues to make fun of the mullah's improper table etiquette.

At the end of Mamman's meeting with the mullah, he agreed to talk to the ayatollah in person about Uncle's case, but only if he received one million tomans in cash, about sixty thousand American dollars in 1981.

"You know what the mullah told me about the money?" Mamman asks. "He said, 'You understand, Azar khanoom, the money I'm seeking, of course, is not for my own personal use. I will donate it all to an Islamic charity.' Who does he think I am, a fool? The money is either going straight down his pocket or the ayatollah's."

"It doesn't matter, Azar. It's money well spent," Baba says.

Mamman shakes her head. "Modjtaba, you don't know how many times I had to bite my tongue to ask him if I may offer the money in his name to a charity of his choice to save him the unnecessary burden of transferring the funds."

"I'm glad you controlled your urges, Azar," Baba says and laughs. "Beggars can't be choosers, you know."

Tension in my shoulders loosens as I watch my parents joke around and feel excited about life like they used to when I was a child.

§ § §

A week later when I come home from school, Mamman is in the kitchen, crying.

"What's wrong?" I ask, feeling a knot tightening around my stomach. "Did something happen to Uncle or Grandma?"

"No. It's not Uncle. It's not Grandma. It's Baba. He is in the hospital."

"Why?" I gasp and burst into tears.

"He'll be okay. Don't worry." She sighs. "While he was on his way to hand deliver the cash to Mullah Kateri, a motorcycle ran him over in the middle of a busy intersection and fled the scene. Thank God a Good Samaritan picked him up off the ground and rushed him to a nearby hospital in his car. His right leg is crushed, and he needs to stay in the hospital for surgeries and follow-ups."

The day after the accident, my siblings and I accompany Mamman to the hospital to visit Baba. He looks pale and dreary and doesn't want to talk about what happened to him the day before. Instead, he asks about Uncle and tells Mamman to stay on the mullah's tail and call him at least three times a day.

Looking into Baba's tired eyes, I realize it's not just his children he has forgotten about; what was he thinking running in front of a speeding motorcycle? It makes me sad to think that he can no longer be the messenger of good news—the person who shows up behind the plexiglass to tell Uncle over the phone, "Pack your bags, buddy. It's time to go home."

A few days later, Mullah Kateri calls Baba in the hospital to inform him that the ayatollah believes my uncle is guilty as charged, and according to Islam, he must pay for his sins. He doesn't return the money he owes my parents, and they believe he never even presented Uncle's case to the ayatollah in person. I don't understand how a man of the cloth could allow himself to get rich from a family in the midst of so much chaos. I worry that my grief-stricken parents cannot bear what is coming our way next—a lifeless picture of my sweet uncle in the newspaper with Grandma still alive staring at it in horror. If that ever happens to my family, I too, like Uncle Muhammad, will turn into a zealous antirevolutionary.

ى ى ى

After a month of absolute despair, Mullah Mohsenni-Ejei, the minister of information in Iran, calls our home to talk with Mamman. She leaves quickly and returns with stars in her eyes.

"Azadeh jan, Mullah Mohsenni-Ejei has agreed to release Reza on bail!" she exclaims, walking briskly to Grandma's room. Her whole face brightens with hope as she sits next to her bed and fills her in.

As I hear Mamman speak, I feel numb and can't believe my ears. I never thought anyone would read the letters my mother was mailing out in piles. Maybe she wrote of Uncle's years of education, and this mullah thought he should be out on the streets building roads, bridges, and factories for Iran. Maybe I was wrong in assuming that all mullahs are crooks and criminals.

"How much does it cost to bail Uncle out?" Jahan asks.

"Nothing, but Grandpa has agreed to put his house up for bail."

My heart feels heavy as I think of my grandparents' home in

Shahran, where I spent most of my weekends growing up. I can't imagine Grandpa living much longer if he loses Grandma and his beloved garden at the same time.

The next day, Jahan and I are sitting quietly in Mamman's car, parked in the rear parking lot of Evin Prison. My heart pounds in anticipation of seeing my uncle after he had spent five months behind those feared walls—the same walls that the ayatollah once criticized the shah for building to keep people who opposed him locked up. It's tragic but true that Iran will likely never change; Evin has been and will always be filled to the brim with innocent souls no matter who is in charge of the law.

Mamman and Grandpa left hours earlier to sign the bail papers for Uncle's release. I'm thinking of Grandma when Mamman, Grandpa, and Uncle show up. I only know the emaciated man is my uncle because he's standing next to Mamman and Grandpa. He looks old, skinny, and frail; his hair is completely grayed, and a four-month-old white beard covers most of his face.

Jahan and I look at each other in shock before turning our heads to say salaam to Uncle as he sits in the passenger seat.

"Salaam, kids," he says without turning his head.

En route to the hospital, Mamman tells Uncle about Grandma's health. "I hope she'll get to see you and know that's you before she's gone."

"I hope so too. I want to tell her not to worry anymore," Uncle whispers.

Grandma is near death but still conscious when Uncle appears at her bedside. Standing next to him, I can see a glimpse of happiness shining in her dying eyes. Watching Grandma and Uncle together washes away all the resentment I'd let pile up inside me toward Mamman. It's because of her that Grandma will take her last breath knowing that her son is still alive. Someday, I'll be there for Mamman like she has been there for Grandma if she ever needs me to make the impossible possible in her life.

The next time I go to the hospital, Grandma's eyes are closed.

I wait until the two of us are alone before sitting by her bedside. A million memories, sights, smells, and sounds race through my head as I reach out to grab her arm. Her hand feels warm wrapped inside my sweaty palms, but in my heart, I know her spirit is now in that magical place she often talked about, the place where the blue of the sky blends into a blinding light.

 **The Escape**

"**D**id you see Omar this morning?" Mamman asks Baba in a hushed voice as I walk by their bedroom.

Omar, what a strange name! I don't know of a soul named Omar in Iran. That's a popular Sunni name. Unlike Sunnis, Iranians are Shias and believe Omar is an illegitimate successor of Prophet Muhammad. Instead, they believe Imam Ali, Prophet Muhammad's son-in-law, is his legitimate successor.

Curious, I pause for a second to hear Baba's answer.

"Yes." Baba sighs. "He came to my office this morning. All the arrangements are in order to smuggle the boys across the border by the end of this month. Twenty-two thousand American dollars per head—half upfront and half after the job is done."

What boys? I get closer to the door and lean over to peek inside.

"For God's sake, Modjtaba," Mamman weeps as Baba sits next to her on the bed. "What are we doing with our lives? Omar is a Pakistani drug lord turned human trafficker because it's more profitable these days. I'm having second thoughts about all this."

So Omar is from Pakistan. That explains why he has a Sunni name.

"I don't know what to say, Azar. We have talked about this many times. The other option is to send Jahan to war, and we can't do that."

Jahan! A surge of anger rushes through my veins.

"I know we are doomed if we do and doomed if we don't. Thank God Jahan and Mammad will be together on this journey," Mamman says.

My cousin Mammad too! What about me? With my heart pounding, I march inside.

"Azadeh, you startled me. Is there something wrong?" Mamman asks, her face turning white. "Were you eavesdropping?"

"Yes, I heard everything!" I shout, growing hot with anger. "You are sending Jahan away with Mammad. What about me? There's nothing I can do here after I graduate from high school in two weeks. I'll run away like Najmieh did if you don't send me with Jahan."

"Calm down, Azadeh," Mamman says as I take a few deep breaths.

"Come and sit down on the bed," Baba says, but I refuse. "You know why we are sending Jahan and not you at this time, don't you? It's dangerous for him to stay in Iran. His draft papers arrived just a few months ago. He has to turn himself in soon to fight in this bloody war with Iraq. We can't allow that to happen to our family."

"Baba, I'm not an idiot," I say through gritted teeth. "I understand all that, but why can't you send me too? I can't just sit around and vegetate until this war is over."

"I'll promise you, Azadeh. We'll send you off to college abroad, but you have to be patient. We're taking a big risk trusting Omar to take the boys across the border. It's unwise to send a young woman off with a bunch of smugglers. We decided that it's best for Jahan to take this risk now, but not you. You are better off staying here with us for now," Baba replies firmly.

"I want to take the risk now. It's my life. It's my choice. I know what's best for me, not you. I'm not living the rest of my life like a prisoner, hidden inside dark clothing, too afraid to open my mouth."

"Maybe you can talk to Omar about taking Azadeh, as well," Mamman says to Baba with hesitation in her voice.

Baba snaps. "Absolutely not, Azar. We can't do that. She's too young, and it's too dangerous. This discussion is over," he says and turns in my direction. "Listen, Azadeh, you need to focus on your studies now. Your high school finals are in two weeks."

"Tell me, Baba, what's the point of finishing high school in two weeks?" I cry out, blood racing to my face. "What's next for me? I'm not going to school anymore. I'm not taking my finals."

I pause and let out a heavy sigh, feeling winded as if the words have taken my breath away. A few moments of awkward silence pass before I rush out, weeping.

The next morning when I look up and see Baba standing over my bed, I stuff my pillow into my face and ignore him. He gets flustered and leaves, but a clamor of his voice keeps ringing in my ears. *You can't go. Not this time. Grow up and act your age.*

My mind and body are too worn out to argue with Baba, but he couldn't be more wrong. There is a place I can go where he can't control me anymore. Sinking deep into my bed, I plunge into a bottomless sea of darkness and despair.

§ § §

With every passing day that I boycott school, my hope that Baba may change his mind withers away. On the fourth day, I reach for the top drawer of my nightstand, where three vials of medicine are hidden underneath a pile of my favorite photographs. I stole the vials from the medicine cabinet in the bathroom after Grandpa took his pills this afternoon.

At the very top is a Polaroid of our family in front of an old mosque in Shiraz, but that's not why the picture is there. Najmieh is in it too, standing next to Mamman and Afshan, smiling. I can hardly bear to look at her face.

Another photograph shows Grandma and me in the swimming pool. I'm holding her like a baby in my arms. I remember that was the day she had me touch a small lump in her right breast, a lump that grew fast into a large tumor and claimed her life. I wonder what happens to people after they die. Is Grandma in heaven now, waiting to reunite with her loved ones? I never asked Grandma what would happen to a teenager if she died. Once she told me that all children twelve years and younger would go to heaven if they died, but why should I, a seventeen-year-old, go to heaven after causing so much pain and suffering for my loved ones?

Underneath all the pictures, I see the letter Najmieh wrote me after she ran away from my aunt's house. As I read it, I sob at her words, her bubbly letters, how much I miss her, how I wish she were here sitting by my side, holding my hand, asking, "Tell me Azadeh. What's wrong? Maybe I can help." At the end of the letter, she wishes me a good life, and look at where I am now. I'm so miserable, so unhappy with my life. If I die, at least I can be with Grandma.

I look down at the three open vials of medicine. Pills of different colors are spread on my bed, but I have no recollection of opening the vials and emptying their contents. I scoop up the pills and let them drop, one by one, into a glass teacup placed on the nightstand next to my bed. Holding the cup in my hand, I think and hesitate before placing my hand on the opening and shake it hard until all the colors are evenly mixed up. I stare at the cup for a very long time, dazed, not thinking of anything at all, until I hear footsteps coming down the hallway. I quietly hide the cup in the bottom drawer of my nightstand, switch off the light, and lie down for the night.

I stay awake through the night, mostly thinking of people who love me a lot, while listening to the sound of the clock's ticktock. I can't bear the thought of Mamman discovering my body, blaming herself for the rest of her life. This is not her fault, but maybe she'll be better off without me around. I'm so confused about life, death, and whether I can wait for the day when God is ready to take me in His arms.

By morning, I'm no longer thinking of anyone else but myself. I reach for the teacup, pop the pills in my mouth, and wash them down with two bottles of sweet Coca-Cola.

Quietly, I sit on my bed for God knows how long, dazed, scared, confused, unsure of what I have done before running into the kitchen. Mamman is at the breakfast table, holding a large glass teacup.

"Mamman, I just took three vials of pills. I'm so sorry. Please help me. I don't want to die."

Her teacup smashes onto the floor and shatters into pieces. "You did what? How could you?" She jumps to her feet.

The next thing I know, I'm being shoved into Mamman's car. Sweat covers every inch of my body as I put my hand on my heart, listening to the beats, hoping that they won't stop. Strangely, I start to feel calm, ready to fall asleep after not sleeping for such a long time. It's okay if my heart stops. I don't want to wake up. It's too exhausting to stay alive. But it's hard to sleep with Mamman constantly turning her head and shouting, "Don't fall asleep, Azadeh! Don't leave me! Please, keep your eyes open! We are almost there!"

Once in the hospital, a crew immediately spreads me on a gurney and wheels me into a private room. My hands and feet are tied before a nurse inserts a large tube up my nose, down my throat, and into my stomach. My insides hurt, but I'm too worn out to complain, too distraught to care. A yellow, charcoal-smelling liquid circulates through the tube for a few hours as I watch pills, some still intact in their capsules, float in a large white bucket next to my bed. There are so many of them: red, yellow, blue, surfacing one after another. I am just a coward, too afraid to live, too afraid to die.

Mamman holds my hand the whole time and tells me over and over, "We love you, Azadeh. Why? Why did you do this?"

Baba is now standing next to my bed, crying quietly into his white handkerchief while stroking my head.

I come home the following day right before dinner is served. The medicine cabinet in the bathroom and the lock on my bedroom door are removed, but everything else appears normal, as if nothing has happened at all.

I look down at my plate and ask, "Mamman, would you like me to go to school tomorrow?"

"Yes. That's an excellent idea, Azadeh. I knew you would come to your senses," Baba says, blocking his face with a newspaper so I can't see his teary eyes.

Mamman doesn't say a word, but she looks pale and dreary. I understand why my parents don't trust me, for I have betrayed them so badly. But I don't understand why they don't talk to me about what I have done so I can tell them how sorry I am for putting them through it all.

I try to eat, but nothing goes down and nothing appeals to me, not even my favorite dessert that Mamman just placed on the table.

In the next week, as always, life goes on whether I like it or not. I drag my lifeless body to school and back, happy to be alive, not necessarily for myself but for my parents. No one except for Mamman and Baba knows about what I have done. At school, I pretend to be the same person I once was, but I know that person is long gone. I feel alone, disconnected from this world, unable to talk to anyone about my emptiness inside. *I wish I were dead and gone* is what I tell myself most of the time.

§　§　§

One day, I'm in a somber mood when Mamman walks in and sits next to me on the bed. She's holding a book in her hand, a collection of *ghazals* by Hafiz, a cherished poet of Persia. Soon, she'll ask me to make a wish or ask a question. Then she'll randomly open the book to foresee what the future may have in store for me.

I force a smile on my face as Mamman holds my hand in hers. "I have some good news to share. You can leave with the boys next Friday if you want."

My heart expands as I look into Mamman's eyes. "Baba agreed to send me along?"

"Reluctantly so," Mamman says as she tucks my hair behind my ear. "Azadeh, you understand that you can't mention this plan to anyone."

I feel a rush of blood to my face, excited but also scared. "I can't say good-bye to my friends, not even Grandpa?"

"No. You can't. The government will arrest Baba if they find out."

The realization of leaving my home, family, and friends in eight days is too much for me to bear. Tears pool in my eyes and roll down my face. I'm too embarrassed to tell Mamman that I know why Baba had a change of heart. He fears that I may end my own life, the same way Jahan's may end in the midst of a bloody battleground.

"Is this the right thing for me to do?" I ask Mamman with my head down.

"I don't know, Azadeh," she says and shrugs. "I just don't know anymore. That's why I brought Hafiz with me. Let's ask him for advice."

For centuries, it has been a Persian tradition to consult Hafiz when faced with difficult situations in life. When used in divination, it is widely believed that Hafiz's poetry will reveal the answer to your destiny.

Mamman closes her eyes and opens the book as I cross my fingers, hoping for a good reading.

> *In the spring, open your heart to joyous infusions,*
> *Like a flower bloom, or stay in muddy collusions,*
> *I cannot tell you to befriend this or drink that,*
> *For wit and wisdom will display their own solutions.*

"Bravo, Hafiz, bravo. Well said," Mamman says and smiles.

> *Harp strings chime in the same advice,*
> *When worthy, you will reach your own conclusions ...*
> *Worry not, or else you will lose your precious now,*
> *If encumbered in day and night's revolutions.*
> *Though the path of love is thorned with fears,*
> *Pass will come easy if free from destination's confusions ...*

"Mamman, just like the ghazal said, I feel stuck in Iran. I'm going to miss you, Baba, Afshan, Grandpa, and everyone, but I can't see a future for myself here."

"Then don't second-guess yourself. This is a very good ghazal,

Azadeh. *Death* is not mentioned anywhere, and *free* is stated directly. It couldn't have been any better. Hafiz has your back. He's advising you to go and not worry about your destination's confusions."

She weeps and holds me tightly.

"You're right. I should go," I say, sniffling. "I'm so sorry for what I did, Mamman, so sorry. Thank you for saving my life. I won't disappoint you. I promise."

"I know. I know you won't; enough crying now. Hafiz has never been wrong before, so you have nothing to worry about, right?"

"Right, right, you're right," I blurt out, feeling somewhat relieved that it wasn't a dire ghazal.

"Let's go out for a treat at the Paradise Café," Mamman offers.

Poor Mamman is trying her best to make it all seem normal, but what's happening to our family is anything but normal. Who knows where my brother and I will be ten days from now? I hope the auspicious foreshadowing by Hafiz will help Mamman not to worry as much about us.

"I would love that," I say, laughing and crying at the same time as we get ready to celebrate my newfound freedom.

Mamman, my eleven-year-old sister, Afshan, and I dress in mandatory baggy dark uniforms, long pants, and dark scarves and leave the house for the café. One thing I won't miss for sure is dressing up in such ridiculous clothes on a hot day like today.

On the way, Afshan asks why Mamman and I have cried.

"Afshan jan, we haven't cried," Mamman assures her. "Azadeh was helping me in the kitchen to chop onions for dinner tonight."

"Stop lying to me, Mamman. Just stop it," Afshan says and exhales loudly. "Jahan told me yesterday that I should be nice to him this week because I may never see him again after next Friday. Where is he going? Is he going to war? I want to know."

"No. He's not going to war, Afshan jan. He's going on a European vacation with Mammad, your cousin. He'll be back in a few months. How many cream puffs do you want? This time, you can have as many as you want," Mamman says, trying to change the subject.

"I'm not hungry. I want to go home," Afshan says, a frown wrinkling her brows and forehead.

In spite of all the turmoil in Tehran, the Paradise Café is still a place where you can leave your troubles behind. We enter the café, and Mamman puts her snakeskin handbag on a round marble-top table as we sink deep into lush, maroon velvet cushions. It's sad but true that a handbag has now become the only accessory by which a woman can express her individuality and sense of style.

After a few minutes, the waiter approaches to take our order.

"Two hot teas, a cup of milk, half a dozen creampuffs, and two éclairs, please," Mamman says.

Food and beverages arrive in gleaming, gold-rimmed white china. While Mamman and I drink tea and indulge in mouth-watering pastries, Afshan sits with her chin in her hands and her elbows on the table, refusing to drink or eat.

I feel a sudden urge to tell my sister the truth. She deserves to know. She is right. I may never see her again after next Friday, and the thought scares me to death. However, on the bright side, I am so grateful to my parents for giving me the strength that I desperately needed to keep on living and hoping for a better life.

ဪ ဪ ဪ

The clock strikes midnight, turning Thursday into Friday, the day that I have both dreaded and desired at the same time. I stay up the whole night thinking, tossing, and turning. At six in the morning, the doorbell rings, buzzing louder in my ears than it normally sounds.

I know who is waiting behind the gate: my aunt Banoo-Azam, her husband, Ahmad agha, and my cousin Mammad. My heart feels heavy as I pause for a moment to look back at my room, the desk where I set up my first science experiment, the carpet where Najmieh slept on her rollup mattress, the bed where I almost took my last breath. I shut the door and sigh. *I will likely never see my room again.*

Mamman buzzes our relatives in. Aunt Banoo-Azam shambles into the living room, sobbing and pounding her chest over and over with the palms of her hands.

Afshan walks in wearing a red, full-length nightgown. She is not supposed to be up, but I'm glad she's here. "What's going on? Why is everybody crying?" Afshan asks, rubbing her puffy eyes.

"Go to bed, Afshan. It's only six o'clock," Baba says.

"Is Azadeh going to Europe with Jahan and Mammad too?"

"Yes. I'm going with them," I say. "Can I have a big hug before you go back to sleep?"

We hug while I cry on her bony shoulder.

"Please don't go, Azadeh. I don't want you to go," she begs, pushing me back and staring into my eyes as if searching for the truth.

"Are you going with them too?" She turns and looks at Mamman, her face crimped into a frown of betrayal.

"I'm just going for a few days," Mamman assures her.

"No! You're not going anywhere!" Afshan screams. "You have to take me with you! You just have to!"

"Afshan, I'm not going with them. I'm only driving them to an airport that is far from our house. That's all. You have my word. I'll be back in a few days. Meanwhile, Baba will stay with you around the clock until I'm back."

"You're all lying to me!" she shouts and runs back toward her room.

Baba embraces me as he whispers in my ear, "You'll be okay, my lovely, brave daughter. You'll be okay."

Suddenly, I feel small in his arms like I did when I was a child, pleading with him not to leave for a long business trip. As Baba hugs Jahan, the realization that I may never see my sweet father again makes my heart sink to the core of the earth.

"God will be with you, my dear children. Take good care of one another," Baba says, standing next to Ahmad agha's car, his face crumpled in pain.

Car doors shut, and Ahmad agha steps on the gas. As we round the corner, I see Afshan running outside and Baba turning to pick her up.

On the way to Mehrabad International Airport, the car is silent except for inaudible Arabic prayers from the Koran that are whispered through Aunt Banoo-Azam's lips as she trembles on her knees.

At the curbside, Aunt Banoo-Azam sobs hard into her chador, whispering nonstop and appearing as if she is about to pass out.

"Ahmad agha, is she okay?" Mamman asks.

"Yes. As usual, she is overreacting. She has probably swallowed a few too many Xanax pills this morning. Azar khanoom, thank you again for saving our son. We owe you one," Ahmad agha says, stepping out of the car.

On the pavement, Ahmad agha lifts the Koran above and in front of his head. I walk under the holy book and turn to kiss its cover as Aunt Banoo-Azam throws water onto the ground after my passing. Mammad and Jahan follow the same ritual, which is performed to ask God to grant us a safe journey.

Mammad's parents embrace him for a few minutes each and give Jahan and me a quick hug. I watch Mammad stare at his parents' car until it disappears into a cloud of thick smog. Tears stream from my eyes, for I know that will happen to me in a few hours when Mamman has to leave us behind.

We walk inside the terminal and scatter into three groups, trying to avoid contact with armed soldiers who are walking around and randomly inspecting people. Mamman and I stay close together while Jahan and Mammad stand alone, waiting for our plane to arrive. Omar, the head of the human trafficking operation, phoned Baba this morning to instruct us how to conduct ourselves at the airport.

At ten thirty, we all board the same plane for Zahedan, a city in southeastern Iran located near the borders with Pakistan and Afghanistan. I sit next to Mamman in the middle of the plane, holding her hand. Jahan sits near the front, and Mammad is all the way in the back row. My gut tells me there are families in this plane sitting apart but closely connected in ways that make us all human: our conscious minds.

"Please don't cry, Azadeh," Mamman whispers, squeezing my hand. "It draws attention to us."

I close my eyes and try my best not to think about what lies ahead. As the plane takes off, I watch Tehran move farther and farther away—the runways, the Shahyad Plaza, houses with courtyards, parks, and highways trapped by smog, and at last the Alborz mountain range where many scenes from *Shāhnāmeh: The Epic of the Persian Kings*, are staged.

I remember sitting on Grandpa's warm lap many years earlier when he told me the story of Zal, a mythical hero in *Shāhnāmeh*. Zal was born albino and abandoned shortly after birth by his superstitious father, Sam. Simurgh, a benevolent bird with the head of a dog and the claws of a lion, raised Zal in her larger-than-life nest at Mount Damavand, the summit of the Alborz mountain range. I keep thinking of Simurgh—a visionary bird with godly strength that no earthly being can overcome—a creature that, if real, could save her beloved Iran from the bloody hands of the ayatollah.

About an hour later, the plane descends upon the arid, golden landscape of Zahedan. I stare out the window and look in the direction of Pakistan, a neighboring country I know almost nothing about, with ways more foreign to me than Europe and America. I also know nothing about how we will cross the border to Pakistan. Baba said that part of the escape plan is a top secret that Omar refuses to share with his desperate clients in Iran, mostly affluent families with sons drafted for war.

I wait with Mamman in the arrival terminal, looking around for a man holding a birdcage. This nameless man, according to Omar, will take charge of what comes next.

Suddenly, Mamman gestures toward a thin man carrying a birdcage and wearing a shawl around his head.

"That's him, Azadeh. Let's go."

To deflect attention, we walk slowly and stop just a few steps behind him.

Mamman whispers with her hand over her mouth. "Are you the taxi driver who's looking for his missing bird?"

He nods, and we stand where we are. A minute later, Mammad is nearby but as instructed he doesn't acknowledge the taxi driver or us. Mamman is now biting the insides of her lips, looking around for Jahan. Ten agonizing minutes pass before Jahan appears, playing with his curly hair, chewing gum, and smiling. If I could, I would slap him hard at the back of his head.

We all board the taxi with the birdcage man and take off. Fifteen minutes later, he pulls over to the curbside and stops. In less than a minute, a white pickup truck parks behind us.

The birdcage man turns his head and says, "Hurry up, kids. You have less than a minute to get your luggage out, change vehicles, and say good-bye. Go. Go. Hurry up."

Mamman pushes me out of the car. "Go. Go, Azadeh."

"I have less than a minute. That's not enough time," I say as Jahan and Mammad quickly grab our two small black suitcases and Mamman pushes me again to follow the boys.

"God be with you, Azadeh. Go. Go. Keep your eyes on *voojood* at all times," Mamman says, squeezing my hand one last time.

I am in charge of what the boys have nicknamed voojood, lifeline: a small black briefcase strapped around my shoulder, holding toothbrushes, toothpaste, our passports, my reading glasses, a few of my favorite Polaroid pictures tucked inside a small Farsi-English dictionary, and five thousand American dollars in cash. The night before, Mamman sewed forty one-hundred-dollar bills inside the fabric cover of the briefcase, and the rest is inside a small zipper pocket. She told my brother and me, "Don't tell anyone about the money hidden inside voojood. Use this money only—and I mean *only*—if you absolutely have to."

The next thing I know, I am sitting in the back of the white pickup truck, weeping as the engine roars, the gears click, and the truck slowly rolls away. Mamman is standing in the middle of the road, sobbing and waving good-bye. The sight of her figure merging with the dusty background makes my body go numb. I can't blink or breathe, but my mind is racing back in time to the moment when we drove off with Najmieh while her mother stood in the dark, holding a lantern, waving good-bye. It's true—what goes around comes around in this world. I wonder if Mamman is thinking the same thought. I can only hope and pray that our future will be different from that of Najmieh and her mamman.

A few minutes later, Jahan opens his mouth. "Boy, this feels like a real James Bond movie. Mammad, since you're not as handsome as I am, I'll play the role of James Bond. Unfortunately, Azadeh can't pass for a Bond girl. We'll just have to do without one for this episode."

"Just shut up, Jahan! Shut your big mouth!" I shout. "This is not the right time to kid around. This episode of James Bond may end very soon if the bad guys in the front decide to stop the truck and shoot us all. They have guns, right there." I point to the space between the seats in the passenger cabin. "Can you differentiate once in your life between what's real and what's not?"

I turn and stare out into the barren desert ahead as we leave the outskirts of Ahvaz, feeling the dry air sucking the moisture out of my mouth.

"Sorry. Geez, I was just trying to lighten up the mood."

"Please, Jahan, don't try to be funny. This is not the right time or place for it," Mammad says curtly, his large brown eyes filled with tears.

An eerie silence falls over the truck as it batters along, kicking up heavy dust that hangs low to the ground. We sit still as stones, bumping up and down, not knowing where we're going and what will happen to us when the truck is switched off.

A few hours before sunset, the brakes squeal, and the truck slows down and parks in front of an isolated barn. The driver whispers something to his friend and gets out. I hold my breath as he walks around the back to open the door for us.

"Get out and carry your suitcases with you. You'll sleep here tonight. Just stay in the barn, and someone will pick you up tomorrow morning."

Thank God the second guy remains in the truck with the guns.

"What are we going to eat?" Mammad asks. "We are extremely hungry, sir."

"Here is some bread and cheese." He hands Mammad a white square fabric tied with two knots on the top.

The thick layer of dirt under his long fingernails is enough for me to lose my appetite. Mammad grabs our dinner, and we head for the barn.

As I walk behind the boys, it dawns on me that our lives are now in the hands of complete strangers. They may decide not to show up tomorrow or the day after, though Baba has told us many times not to worry too much, since Omar's operation has helped many of his colleagues and their families to cross the border to Pakistan unharmed. What other choice do I have but to trust these men and hope that our journey, too, will end in triumph?

Jahan unlatches the gate, and the wooden door screeches and swings open. Inside, a dozen goats and a few sheep are busy chewing.

"James," Mammad asks Jahan with a brow raised, "do you think one of the goats is a human in disguise spying on us?"

We all burst into laughter.

"Could be," Jahan says, rubbing his chin.

A strong musty smell assaults my nose. "I can't sleep here. It stinks," I complain, plugging my nostrils with my fingers.

"Would you rather party with the friendly goats inside or the Big Bad Wolf outside?" Mammad asks as he stares at the contents inside the cloth wrap.

I peek over his shoulder. "We can't eat this cheese, Mammad. It's covered with mold."

"Great. Mammad and I can then eat your ration for tonight," Jahan says. "I'm so hungry, I could eat a cow."

Jahan and Mammad devour the small amounts of bread and cheese as I sit back and watch with disgust. After dinner, Mammad searches the barn and finds a lantern with a box of matches. He lights the lamp, and a warm orange glow instantly fills the space around us.

We stack some hay in one corner of the barn and lie down for the night. The ground feels rough and scratchy, making my tired limbs stiffer than they had been minutes earlier when I was standing.

As I stare at the light, Mamman's image appears before my eyes and quickly fades into a cloud of dust, just like it happened eight hours earlier. Longing for her tears at my heart and cuts so deeply that I want to scream to get it out of my chest. A part of me wishes that I had stayed with my parents in Tehran, but I am here now, and there is no turning back the clock.

ॶ   ॶ   ॶ

It's near dawn when I hear a car engine roaring outside. Like me, Mammad has been up the entire night and is now nervously pushing back his soft, light-brown hair away from his forehead. We exchange a quick glance and turn to look at Jahan. He's fast asleep, and his face is nearly covered by a swarm of buzzing flies.

Minutes later, a man wearing a long, loose cotton shirt over baggy pants staggers into sight, holding a small flashlight.

"We need to leave now. Get your bags. Let's go," he says, pointing the flashlight up and down while his front gold teeth glisten in the dark.

He searches the dark ground with his dim light, and we follow behind him. Once outside the barn, I see a silhouette of a second man standing next to a small gray car, his appearance somewhat faded in the glare of headlights. We approach the car, and the boys lay our two suitcases in the trunk.

The man on the passenger side rolls over the front seat. "Get in," he says, nodding to one side.

While boarding, I realize these are not the same men who drove us here in the white pickup truck, wondering where they are now. Headlights blaze against the barn as the car grinds, rattles vigorously, and slowly takes off.

We travel through the barren desert at a very high speed, making numerous emergency stops, for the boys have severe diarrhea. Every time they load in and out, I tell my brother, "Double-O-Seven, didn't I tell you not to eat that cheese?"

"Shut up, Azadeh," Jahan says each time as he bends over to climb in.

It feels good to have outsmarted him, but they both look so pale. I hope they feel better soon, for circumstances are not in their favor to see a doctor if they need one.

Once, after the boys crawl out in a hurry, I step outside, feeling a rush of heat traveling up through my blouse. I shade my eyes and look out into the distance. There is nothing ahead but sandy ground and blue skies meeting at the horizon far away from where we are. It's hard to understand why Omar keeps all the details of his human trafficking business a top secret, since there are no street names, traffic lights, or even landmarks for the Iranian police to set up traps and bust his operation. I bet the path we have traveled so far had not seen tire marks before and will likely never seem them again.

The miles click away for six long hours before the driver says, "Congratulations. We just crossed the border to Pakistan. You are now safe."

Safe sounds rather strange to my ears, but he's absolutely right. We're safer with a bunch of smugglers in the deserts of Pakistan than in our own living rooms in Tehran, bombed mercilessly by Iraqi planes night after night.

We travel for another hour before the dusty trail merges into a rugged road that runs parallel to a lake. The driver pulls over and stops near the water. One man tells us to get out and wait for them before climbing back in and speeding away.

I hope we don't have to stay here overnight; my lips are parched, my throat is dry, and my stomach is cramping nonstop. It's hard to believe they haven't offered us any food or drink in the past twenty-four hours.

The water in the lake looks fresh, but I'm too afraid to drink it. I tell the boys not to drink it, either, and this time, they take my advice. As the hours pass, the afternoon heat grows strong, beating hard on the ground with no shade in sight to seek refuge from the sun. My body is now unbearably hot, slicked in sweat and thirsty as hell.

Suddenly, Mammad springs to his feet and sighs. "I'm going in for a swim." He removes his shirt and trousers and walks into the lake. Jahan follows.

I wipe the sweat away from my forehead, roll up my pants, and wade in. The water, now up to my calves, washes pleasant cooling sensations over my body. Minutes later, I am floating next to Jahan and Mammad.

With clinging wet clothes, I step onto the shore. Mammad looks up and begins to hum the popular tune from the James Bond movies. I smile and ask him to cut it out, but in the midst of all this chaos, the James Bond humor is starting to grow on me some—a welcome distraction from the harsh realities of life, not knowing what will happen to us or our loved ones back home in Tehran.

The sun is low, and the sky is filled with red and purple streaks when the same two men who dropped us off earlier return in the same gray car. They give us some water and hard bread to eat. My stomach growls as I gobble down the bread and ask for more.

One man offers me his half-eaten piece and says, "There is no more after this."

I eat the second piece slowly as I watch the dust road spread dimly under the headlights, not thinking of anything at all, for my mind is too exhausted to think, to care, to analyze. Finally, I surrender to sleep after being up and alert for two straight days and one long night.

The next morning, I open my eyes to a bright, sunny day. My neck and limbs feel stiff from hours in the car. Occasionally, I see wild camels roaming the hot desert, but it's an assembly of nomads grazing their livestock in the stark beauty of a rare oasis that catches my eye. It's amazing how these people have survived for centuries living off this desolate, barren land. A few miles down from the oasis, a group of nomads on foot with camel caravans are marching on. As I watch them, I imagine myself dressed in ragged clothes walking among them: a nomad on the road with no place to call home.

After seventeen hours of driving, we arrive at New Candy, a primitive village with a short main street, narrow, unpaved dirt roads, and a few token trees. The scene reminds me of Najmieh's village in Shomal with one exception: her village was lush and lined with beautiful old trees. But the houses look almost the same: small, white-painted mud shacks with no foliage to soften their rough appeal.

The two men take our passports before they leave us in front of a small shack. I watch them drive away with our most important possession, but by now, I have come to fully trust these men. They always show up and take us somewhere else, somewhere that I believe is closer to our final *unknown* destination.

Jahan knocks on the door as a white donkey tied to a post brays and rattles the chain around its neck. A thin old man wearing tattered cotton shoes and a brown smock opens the doors and invites us in. His ear-to-ear smile reveals crooked yellow teeth, a testament to the hard life the people of this village live.

As we walk inside, the smell of smoke and unwashed humanity overwhelms me. My own body smells sweaty and gross, but not nearly as bad as the stale stench in this house. A tired-looking, grayed-haired woman with leathery skin hands each of us a pile of clothes, and the old man asks us to change. I sniff the clothes, and they too give off a foul odor, just like the house, the old man, and his wife.

I hold a sheet up for the boys to change and wait. The sight of Jahan and Mammad as imposters in white oversized turbans, cream-colored long shirts, and baggy pants makes me laugh so hard that my stomach hurts. Mammad returns the favor as I quickly change behind the manual curtain. My garment looks similar to the boys', but instead of a turban, I am wearing a long cotton checkered scarf that reveals only the triangle of my badly sunburned face. Now we fit in perfectly well, looking and smelling like any other inhabitant of this house.

The family has three older sons and a young daughter about three years of age. The little girl has striking sapphire eyes and matted strawberry-blonde hair. Her facial features don't resemble her parents or any of her siblings, making me wonder if she belongs to someone else, some other family who can't afford or doesn't want the burden of raising a little girl. That's probably how Najmieh lived her life before she came to live with us. I touch voojood and thank God for what's inside: a Polaroid of Najmieh posing with my family, the only thing I have left now to remember her, Mamman, Baba, and Afshan.

At night, the yellow glow of a lantern, hung from the low ceiling, illuminates the room as moths buzz and circle around the light. The zapping sound of tiny flesh cremating in front of my eyes makes me think of my own uncertain life. Like a moth on fire, I too could vanish into thin air in the vast deserts of Pakistan with no one ever knowing of my whereabouts. Tears pool in my eyes as I watch the old woman prepare dinner for her family and the three of us.

We all sit around a white plastic tablecloth spread on a scratchy, colorful tribal rug to have dinner. The smell of freshly steamed rice and curry makes my stomach growl. I glance at my black, dirty fingernails for a split second before rolling my fingers on the plate to make a rice ball and dip it into a steaming bowl of yellow potato stew.

Following dinner, the wife serves fresh, sweet tea from a large charcoal, bronze *samovar* that hisses every few minutes, emitting puffs of white clouds. We each drink a cup of buttery-tasting tea and eat a handful serving of sweetened, fried almonds. Everything, though not plentiful, tastes wonderful, especially after two nights of dry bread and rotten cheese. The savory meal replenishes my energy supply, giving me new hope that the worst is now behind us.

After I put down my teacup, the little girl drops herself on my lap. I stroke her matted hair, thinking of my little sister and the worried look on her face when she learned that I was leaving Iran. Meanwhile, the little girl seems quite content, giggling and kicking her legs until her mother gestures and calls her name. I wonder if she is ever going to find out about the world that exists outside the periphery of New Candy.

The room is pitch black when we wrap our tired bodies in dirty, goat-smelling blankets and sprawl side by side on the scratchy rug that we sat on earlier to have dinner with the family. Before long, snoring comes from every corner of the room. Slowly, I drift into sleep, dreaming of my family in a place that's foreign to me.

When I wake up, I realize it doesn't matter where that place was in my dream. I'll be happy anywhere as long as I'm with my family laughing, sharing, creating new memories.

§　§　§

The next day, two men, more new faces, appear just before noon to claim us.

Mammad asks about our passports, and one man replies, "I don't have your passports, boy. Don't worry. They are in good hands."

Whose hands? Omar's? Are we even going to see Omar, the mastermind of this operation, before our journey ends? All the mystery surrounding him reminds me of Charlie in *Charlie's Angels*, an American crime drama television series. Like Charlie, Omar pulls all the strings, but no one is allowed to see his face or question his authority.

Outside, two mopeds are parked next to the white braying donkey. One of the men hops on a moped and asks Jahan to sit behind him. A minute later, Jahan is sandwiched tightly between the first driver and me. Mammad sits behind the second driver, holding one small suitcase in each hand.

The moped Jahan and I are on tags behind the one Mammad is riding. At times, the mopeds rattle considerably as they struggle along, straining and lifting up dust, making our bodies bounce up and down on hard leather seats. My butt is starting to feel sore, and there isn't a thing I can do to stop it from getting worse.

After a few hours of passing through rough terrain, my suitcase unlatches.

"Oh no! Stop!" I cry out, watching my underwear and other clothing items flutter in the arid landscape.

The driver of the first moped makes a quick turn and stops,

and we park behind them. In spite of my pleas, the two men decide against chasing my belongings that are now blown away in different directions across the winding dirt road. We agree to leave the empty suitcase behind with the rest of the missing articles it once held inside. Now, only a few articles in voojood, a small dictionary, a few pictures, my reading glasses, a comb, and a toothbrush are all that I have of my past life.

Mammad securely tucks the only suitcase we have left between him and the driver. The mopeds once again begin to shake and bang over the dirt road. My butt and legs are now completely numb, and my head and face are so unbearably hot. I fear that my tired limbs may soon run out of energy and refuse to hold me up, forcing my body to crash into the ground. The thought of the boys debating with the drivers over what to do with my body sends shivers down my spine. I hope I am not left behind, like my suitcase, to turn into dust in the deserts of Pakistan.

In the early evening hours, we reach a mountain pass. The drivers park the mopeds, and we all get off.

"Pass this hill and a second one behind it. Someone will pick you up at the other end. If you don't see anyone there when you arrive, just wait, and someone will show up before dark."

"We're really hungry, sir. Do you have anything for us to eat?" Mammad asks.

"No. We don't have any food."

Hearing that there is no food fills my stomach with a sharp cramping pain.

"But you can drink some water," one man says, offering us his leather canteen.

We each take a few minutes to nourish our dried, scratchy mouths and stretch our cramped bodies. My butt is now so sore that I can't tell where my back ends and my butt starts anymore. Jahan grabs our suitcase, and we plod up the hill, trudging over the curving top of the first hill, descending and ascending again.

When we reach the valley of the second hill, no one is there to claim us. We take off our sweaty socks and shoes and wait, watching the sun slowly disappear behind the hills, turning dusk into darkness on its way.

I remember reading somewhere that leopards are native to the mountainous regions of Pakistan, though I don't recall them hunting in packs like lions do. So unless one is extremely hungry, as we are now, it likely won't leap out to challenge the three of us. I survey our surroundings for a pair of gleaming eyes, but it's dark, and I can't see the edge of the cliff hanging over us.

Slowly, stars begin to brighten the sky, some winking in patterns I recognize. The one twinkling with the most intensity now is the same star that Najmieh and I could pick out on most clear nights from our rooftop in Tehran. I close my eyes and imagine Najmieh sitting under the stars thinking of me, the same way I always think of her when I gaze up and lose myself in the endless black and sparkle of the sky.

Late into the night, rumbling noises approach from a distance. Soon after, two bearded men on motorcycles appear and stop near us. They're dressed in long cotton shirts over baggy pants, just like Jahan and Mammad. The taillights cast a reddish glow on our feet as we hop on. Seconds later, the bikes roar and streak away, churning up dust along the way. The bumpy ride makes my stomach lurch, leaving a taste of acid in the back of my throat. I'd better not vomit, or my starving body will lose whatever is left of that rice and stew I ate some twenty-eight hours earlier.

A rundown cottage in the middle of nowhere becomes our home for the night. For dinner, the men offer us bread with a greasy spread that resembles animal fat. Mammad and I just eat the bread, but Jahan eats the bread with the greasy topping.

As the night progresses, scampering noises grow louder around me, sending chills down my spine. Rats, some as large as cats, are everywhere, searching for bits of food here and there. To avoid contact with the wandering rodents, I sit alert on top of our small suitcase, watching the passage of night into dawn, thinking of Mamman,

Baba, and Afshan, hoping that they are safe and are not too worried about us.

§ § §

Before noon, a farm truck pulls over, and the driver, another new face, steps out.

"We must leave now. It's a long way to Karachi."

After almost six days of being kept in the dark, someone finally tells us where we are headed next, a place with a recognizable name.

I sit next to the driver in the front as Jahan and Mammad hop on the back. The old truck creaks along a narrow highway for hundreds of miles without the driver and I exchanging a single word; the only sounds heard are tires on the road and the occasional whiz of cars traveling on the opposite side. On the way, we pass many clusters of dun, mud-block homes that at times are hard to distinguish against the rustic background. We stop only at a few roadside restaurants to eat and use the bathroom. At night, the headlights come on, illuminating the long, narrow highway ahead. Scattered lights appear and disappear for two straight nights before we reach our final destination late in the morning of July 1, exactly six days after we left our home in Tehran.

"That's Karachi," the driver says as we approach a large, lively seaport city.

I feel moisture in the air and turn my head to glance at the boys in the back, wearing grimaces of misery after being exposed to the elements for two days and two nights. Jahan's full, curly hair looks almost white, filled with debris and dust.

We are now *so* far away from home. I wonder if Mamman and Baba know that we are alive, very tired and hungry, but unharmed.

The farm truck slows down and stops in a parking lot of a modern motel. The facility has many flats spread over a large area. We wait outside the car for the driver to return with the key to our room. My limbs crack and pop as I roll my neck and shoulders and stretch my thighs and calves. The boys are busy too, exercising their limbs. When the driver comes back, he gestures, and we follow.

He stops in front of a suite, hands Mammad the key, and says, "You'll stay here for a few days. Someone will drop by soon to give you your passports."

Then he leaves without saying good-bye, probably driving all the way back to pick up a few more tired souls and deliver them to this very spot. I feel pity for him, yet without men like him, I would be stuck in Iran, living a life that the ayatollah imposes on me, a life that at times felt like I was almost dead, muted, covered up, aimlessly wandering the streets.

Inside, the room is nice and clean with beds, a TV, and a full bathroom. The thought of sleeping on a bed tonight brings instant joy to my extremities. I win the race to the bathroom and start to wash up. The sight of a cool running faucet is tempting me to put my head under the fresh stream.

Water drips from my hair as I step out of the bathroom and stand under the ceiling fan running on full blast. The brush of cold air against my wet hair soothes my soul and rejuvenates my spirit, energizing my tired body with new hope and optimism.

I reach inside the zipper pocket of voojood and take out a crisp hundred-dollar bill. "I'm starving. I'm going out to buy some food from the market across the street."

"Wait up. I'll go with you," Mammad says, pacing toward me as I open the door.

We walk down the damp hallway toward the front office. Inside, I hand the receptionist a hundred-dollar bill and ask for rupees in exchange.

"*Ney* dollars."

Frustrated, I glare at him, but Mammad pulls me back. "He doesn't speak any Farsi, Azadeh. There is no point in arguing with him."

Back in the hallway, I collapse into tears. "Mammad, my stomach hurts so badly."

He cuddles me close to him. "I'm hungry too, Azadeh, very hungry. Just hang in there. We'll find a way to get some food soon."

When we enter our room, Jahan is chatting with a stranger dressed in a nice suit. Surprisingly, he is clean shaven and smells like Old Spice, the scent of Baba's aftershave. His appearance makes me wonder if he, instead of Omar, is the head of the smuggling operation.

The man gives us our stamped passports, fifteen large rupee bills, and our airline tickets. Jahan opens the airline package as I stuff the money inside the zipper pocket of voojood, feeling excited that we can buy us food with the rupees.

"Let me tell you what the plan is," the man says, his large agate-and-gold ring glistening in the light. "On July 4, just three days from now, you will leave Karachi for London, stay there overnight, and fly to Madrid the next morning."

"Who will take us to the airport?" Mammad asks.

"I will, but before I leave, I'll take the girl with me to the motel's office to call your folks."

"Can we all go to the office?" I ask.

"No. That will look too suspicious."

The chance of talking with my parents overtakes my fear of him, and I quickly agree to go. On the way, I cautiously walk behind him with my heart pounding, watching his every step to make sure he turns in the direction of the main office. When he reaches for the swinging door, a rush of relief escapes my body.

Inside, he talks to the receptionist and pays him some cash. He pockets the money, leads us to a small room behind the counter, and leaves us alone.

My eyes search the room and focus on a black rotary phone placed on top of a large wooden desk, crowded with stacks of paper and old newspapers. The prospect of hearing my mother's voice through that phone instantly soothes my painful cramps, as if the butterflies in my stomach have chased the hunger away.

The man walks over to the desk and gestures. "Girl, come over here and sit on this chair." His large frame looms above me as he begins to talk over my head. "Now, listen carefully to what I'm telling you, girl. Once we're connected, you have only two minutes to talk."

"Two minutes! That's not enough time. I need more time, sir."

"That's all you get: two minutes. It's for security reasons, and don't ask me any more questions."

"Okay, sir. I won't."

I panic and try to organize in my head what to tell my parents in two minutes time.

"What is your phone number, girl?"

I tell him the number as he picks up the receiver. As I hear *beep*, my mind goes blank, not recalling a single word that I just went over to tell my parents.

"Salaam, khanoom," the man says.

That has to be Mamman.

"Your children are now in Karachi, and everything went according to plan. They'll be in Madrid on July 5. Your daughter is right next to me. I'm going to put her on, and you have less than two minutes to talk."

"Azadeh, how are you?" Mamman asks in a choked voice.

"I'm fine," I say, my heart almost bursting out of my chest. "How are you?"

"I'm so relieved. I have been smoking nonstop since I came home. Are you okay?"

"Yes. We're all fine," I say, puzzling over why Mamman, who hates cigarettes, is now smoking. "Are you all coming soon?"

"We can't talk about that now. Do you still have your red toothbrush?"

"Yes. I have the blue one, as well."

The exchange regarding toothbrushes was Mamman's idea. If the smugglers had mistreated us, I would have told her that I had lost the blue toothbrush. Come to think of it, Mamman is the real James Bond, although she has never watched a single spy movie from the beginning to the end.

"Azadeh jan, Baba wants to talk to you."

"Azadeh, we miss you and Jahan already."

His voice instantly warms my heart. "I miss everyone too. I hope to see you all very soon."

I don't want to let go of the receiver, but the man is asking me to hang up.

"Is Mammad there?" Baba asks. "Your aunt wants to talk to him."

"No. He's in our motel room with Jahan. Baba, the man is asking me to hang up now. Love you all."

"Good-bye, my lovely daughter."

"Good-bye, Baba jan." I sniffle and hang up. Calmness takes over me as if I have just taken a bite of my favorite dessert: Aunt Gisela's strawberry-filled chocolate cake.

Before the man leaves our room, he tells us, "Be ready to leave at eight in the morning on July 4. You can wear your regular clothes to go to the airport, but until then, keep your Pakistani clothing on."

"They stink so bad," Jahan complains while lifting his shoulder and sniffing himself.

"Take off your clothes, and I'll send someone over to pick them up for laundry. Stay in the room until your clothes are back. Do I make myself clear?"

"Yes, sir," Jahan says, rolling his eyes.

"I have to go now. See you in two days."

"Since we can't go anywhere until our goddamn clothes are back," Jahan says, "I'm going to take a shower—a *long* one."

He goes in the bathroom and runs the water as Mammad and I lie down for a quick nap, waiting for our turn to freshen up.

A few hours later, we hear a knock on the door. Our camouflaged clothes are back, starched and cleaned, smelling strong, in a good way this time. It feels refreshing to put on a pair of clean underwear, even though they are the same ones that I have been wearing since I left home six days earlier.

We quickly dress and head out in search of food. In the open market across the street, carts heaped with colorful fruits, vegetables, bread, and sweets are on display, making my stomach growl, craving everything in sight. I flash a large rupee bill to pay for fruit, six loaves of large flatbread, a jar of cherry jam, and a dozen Coca-Cola bottles. While gobbling the bread, I shove the change inside voojood without counting it.

On the way back to our room, we each peel and eat a few bananas and drink a couple of sodas, only to drop off the groceries and leave for dinner.

The motel's restaurant is not crowded, so we seat ourselves near a large window facing the Arabian Sea, where the sun is glowing just above the water, immersed in a sea of fiery orange and golden streaks.

The waiter approaches and greets us with a big smile. Unfortunately, he doesn't speak a word of Farsi or English, so Jahan begins to flap his arms and make chicken noises. The waiter points to an item on the menu with his right index finger while kissing the tip of his left curled fingers a few times. We order three Coca-Colas and three servings of what we hope to be a chicken dish.

The sun is almost halfway down in the water when the waiter returns. He's carrying two large, thin metal silver trays in his arms and a third one balanced on his head. As he puts the trays down, delicious smells of fried onions, garlic, and curry waft from the steaming bowls of chicken stew. Next to each bowl, a mountain of fresh parsley and cilantro topped with a few cut radishes and raw onion slices garnish each tray. We stuff large pieces of flatbread with curried chicken and vegetables. The meat is spicy but extremely tender and tasty.

While paying for dinner, I say, "Food is not that expensive here. So far, we have spent only one large rupee bill and have fourteen more to spare in the next two days."

Without hesitation, Mammad gestures for the waiter. "This calls for a celebration. Jahan, please allow me to order this time."

Soon the waiter appears. My mouth drops as I watch Mammad place his palms flat on the table and roll his head, mooing like a cow.

The waiter giggles and points to another item on the menu while blowing kisses on the tips of his curled fingers. Mammad orders two servings of a beef dish, and I point to a dessert on the next table and then point to myself. The waiter nods and leaves, returning quickly with our orders plus three cups of creamy-looking tea. We didn't order any tea, but the wonderful smell of cardamom is hard to resist, so we decide to keep it. Unlike the boys, who are savoring the second course, I don't care much for my bland dessert, corn cakes with cream, but the buttery-tasting, sugary tea more than satisfies my need for something rich and sweet.

By the end of our meal, the sun has completely disappeared into the graying sea, leaving the coastline to shimmer in glowing lights for as far as my eyes can see. The scene reminds me of our many family vacations in Shomal, the northern part of Iran enclosed by the Caspian Sea, where Najmieh's family lived. Wherever Najmieh is, I hope she is as happy as can be.

We rush back to our room, quickly brush our teeth, and crash. With my stomach full, my mind at ease, and my parents' comforting voices ringing in my ears, I fall asleep in a flash.

The next day, I wake up refreshed, ready and excited to make breakfast for the boys and myself. When Jahan and Mammad get up, the side desk is set for breakfast with cherry jam sandwiches, cups of Coca-Cola, and fresh-cut fruits. We eat together, talk, and laugh, sharing memories of our recent past. At the end of our meal, we clink our Coca-Cola bottles, giving thanks to God with heavy hearts, since we know many young people in Iran aren't as fortunate as we are to buy their freedom and change their lives.

Compared to the excitement of the previous week, our few days in Karachi proceed at a slow pace, where we mainly watch live World Cup matches on TV in our room and dine at the motel's restaurant. I hope that Baba, too, is watching the games on TV, jumping up and down like Jahan and Mammad while shouting "*Goooooooooal!*" without breathing.

§ § §

As usual, the weather is overcast and sticky on July 4 when the man in the suit shows up at eight in the morning to drive us to the airport.

"Do you have any rupees left?" he asks.

"No," I blurt out. "We used almost all the money you gave us to buy food and drinks."

I hand him just a few coins, keeping the nine large rupee bills hidden inside voojood. I'm sure we need this money a lot more than this guy; his expensive gold-and-diamond watch and red agate ring probably worth more than all we have in cash.

"That was a lot of money to spend on food for three days," he says, his eyes narrowing with suspicion. "You were probably taken advantage of, girl. Get your bags. Let's go."

Surprisingly, the man in the suit is now carrying our camouflaged clothing in a plastic bag. It's unbelievable that for twenty-two thousand American dollars per head, this human trafficking operation can't provide each client with brand-new camouflage wear.

I glance at my reflection in the car window dressed in Mammad's short-sleeved white polo shirt and Jahan's khaki slacks. The first thing I'll do once in Madrid is to go clothes shopping; nothing fancy, just tight jeans, miniskirts, and tank tops. Most importantly, though, I will never again have to wear a long headscarf and can let my hair hang loose to breathe and shine under the sun.

With voojood crisscrossed around my shoulder, I shut the car door, feeling optimistic about leaving the Middle East for Europe or even America later if luck is on our side.

Shortly thereafter, the airport comes into full view, a large concrete building submerged in a sea of fog. Once inside the international terminal, the man in the suit says good-bye and turns away as we approach the airline attendant at the gate.

I hand him our tickets and smile.

He frowns with his eyes moving up and down my body.

Panic swells at the back of my throat. The next thing I know, my passport is being waved close to my face.

"This is *jaa-lee*," he equivocates, his eyes flickering around the terminal.

With a quick motion, he snatches Jahan's and Mammad's passports from their hands, waving them in their faces.

"These are all jaa-lee. Call the police. Call the police."

I can feel my face crumpling in terror like Jahan and Mammad's, since *jaa-lee* means fake in Farsi. The terminal starts to spin in my head as I lean against Mammad, trying to find my bearings.

"This is it. We're doomed," Jahan whispers, his face turning white. "They're going to arrest us. I hope what happened to that guy in *Midnight Express* doesn't become our reality in Pakistan."

Scenes from the movie *Midnight Express*—where a young American man was tortured for years in a Turkish prison—flash in my head, making me so dizzy that I almost faint. Amid all this commotion, the man in the suit who drove us to the airport approaches. He begins speaking to the attendant in Urdu and nodding. Then he turns in our direction.

"He wants one thousand American dollars to let you board the plane. If you have the money, pay him *now*. Hurry up. The police are almost here. I can hear them whistling. Hurry. Hurry up, girl."

Tears of outrage collect behind my eyes as I rummage through the small inside pocket of voojood and pull out ten one-hundred-dollar bills. The attendant's fury evaporates quickly as he pockets the money and shoves the passports back into my shaky hands.

"Thank you," I say, my legs quivering.

The police have now arrived, wandering the terminal. I look down and pray under my breath. *God, please let us get on that plane. Please.* My heart is beating so loudly that I can hear its ticktock. I take a deep breath and turn to look at Mammad, "I am about to pass out."

Mammad grabs my arm and helps me walk outside to climb the stairs and board the aircraft. The three of us sit near the end of the plane, Jahan in the middle between Mammad and me. I cautiously look around to see if the police are coming after us. A sigh of relief escapes my lips when the doors shut and the flight attendants, dressed in colorful tunics, pants, and headscarves, begin walking down the aisle to check seat belts.

"You are such an idiot, Mammad," I hear Jahan's voice as I turn my head away from the window. "You got barf all over you. Why did you slap that stupid bag? Disgusting," Jahan continues, leaning toward me.

I can now smell raw vomit. "Mammad, I can't believe what you just did," I say, holding my nose.

Mammad panics and stands up, heading for the bathroom while the plane is in takeoff. A stewardess motions him to sit down. The foul smell is starting to make me sick. When the seat belt sign turns off, Mammad rushes to the lavatory. Many seats in the plane are vacant, so Jahan and I quickly change our seats.

When Mammad returns, he mutters in disgust, "Do they ever service this damn Pakistani plane?"

I blow him a kiss and pout my lips to let him know I feel sorry for him. Not long after takeoff, I lean my head against the window and fall asleep. My body feels so fatigued from the unexpected scare at the terminal that I can barely keep my eyes open during the entire flight.

§ § §

Twelve hours later, we exit the plane in London. Two British officers immediately approach us and flash their badges.

"Pardon us, madam and gentlemen. We have orders to confiscate your passports."

Caught by yet another unexpected turn, I hand them our passports, fearing that it is all over for us. Our plan was to sleep at the airport tonight and catch our plane to Madrid early tomorrow morning.

The officers page through our passports and ask us to follow them. Outside, a police car is parked at the curbside. One officer asks us to please get in and sit in the back.

"Excuse me, sir," I say, struggling to swallow my fright just to get some answers. "Are you taking us to jail? Why? We're going to Madrid tomorrow. We have tickets, see?"

I offer them our airline tickets, but one officer turns and shoves them back into my hand. "No, no, no. Keep your tickets. We are not taking you to jail," he says, flashing a mouth full of crooked, crowded teeth.

The thought of the Iranian government executing our parents if we were to be deported makes my chest feel so tight that I can barely breathe. I have to find a way to let these officers know what the facts are before it's too late.

"You know Bee Gees? Nice singers," Jahan blurts out.

The police officers don't respond.

"Why don't you tell them about James Bond? He is British too. I bet you didn't know that?" Mammad tells Jahan in Farsi.

"Mammad, for someone who doesn't even know what's inside a barf bag, you certainly have a big mouth. These guys are probably telling each other that Iranian perfumes smell like vomit."

"Who gives a hoot about all this nonsense? Where the hell are they taking us?" I ask, peeking over Jahan's curly hair to look out the window.

The car stops at a parking lot facing a five-story motel. Overhead, I can hear planes roaring, so we must be very close to the airport. One officer tells us to exit the car and follow him.

Inside a small motel room, Jahan, Mammad, and I line up behind the officer as he takes his time to draw a clock with the hands pointed to six o'clock on the front page of the guest's notepad. He finishes his artwork by sketching a picture of a plane with a smiley face.

"Be ready to leave for the airport at six in the morning. Have a good rest," he says, looking as if he has done this before.

"So that's what this detour was all about," I whisper in Farsi, feeling relieved but also angry at the officer for not sharing this information with us at the airport.

Hours later, I peek through the eyehole and see the two officers sitting on folding chairs. I sigh and walk away, thinking that these officers are surely making Margaret Thatcher proud by watching us like a hawk so we don't disappear and become a burden on their lives. I hope and pray that Spanish people will see us in a different light.

A police car picks up the officers and the three of us early in the morning of July 5. The two officers stand next to us at the airport terminal, inviting unwanted stares and whispers in our direction. At this point, though, I'm too worn out to care about what anyone here thinks of me. Soon, I'll never see any of these faces again, so let them think I'm a troublemaker; I know I'm not, and that's all that counts.

When our flight is announced, the officers walk with us to the counter at the gate and wait for the airline attendant to check our passports and tickets. As we begin to preboard, they wish us good luck and turn, probably on their way to pick up more Iranian escapees who are disembarking a Pakistani plane.

Our flight from London to Madrid is booked on Iberia Airline. Since the war broke out between Iran and Iraq, Spain is the only European country that allows Iranians to enter without a visa, and as such, many Iranian families now reside in Spain, mainly waiting for visas to the United States.

Once we board the plane and settle comfortably in our seats, Mammad says, "If all women in Spain look like these flight attendants, we are going to heaven!"

"You are 100 percent right," Jahan replies. "I thought Spanish girls were all brunettes. I like the tall, thin angel with blonde curls and green eyes. She is sitting just two rows behind us."

Annoyed, I tune out, thinking instead of my family in Iran. Baba promised to take care of everything quickly so our family can reunite soon in Spain, but I can't help worrying about his safety. What if the government arrests him for smuggling Jahan out of Iran? Technically, Jahan should be in the battlefield now fighting the war with Iraq. Too many things can go wrong, things that I probably haven't even thought about.

I eat breakfast and sleep most of the way until the plane begins its descent. Now only God knows what may be awaiting us when we get off this plane.

We breeze through the customs and head for the airport exit. As we step onto a busy crosswalk, I hug tightly on voojood. We are now on our own.

Escapades in Madrid

Madrid, July 1982

The taxi driver throws his hands up in the air when I offer him rupees to pay for the cab fare.

"Pesetas, *señorita. Por favor.* Pesetas," he growls, handing me back the foreign currency and gesturing to a building across the street.

"Azadeh, get out. I think he's asking you to go over there and bring him back pesetas," Jahan says, pointing to a bank.

When I walk out of the bank with cash in hand, the boys are standing next to our small suitcase at the curbside. Tears pool in my eyes as I touch voojood and stare at the suitcase, the only two possessions that have followed us all the way from Iran. If these objects could talk, they would ask, "How could you leave our friend, your suitcase, behind to shrivel under the blaze of the hot desert sun?"

I spread the bills in my hand to pay for the fare. The taxi driver puffs his stinky cigar in my face as he grabs a large bill from my collection, mumbles in Spanish, and speeds away.

As we stand on the sidewalk to discuss what to do next, young men swarm around, hollering at one another, tossing soccer balls back and forth, drinking liquor, and waving miniature national flags—mostly of Spain but also England.

After observing the crowd for a few minutes, Jahan says, "I'm 100 percent sure Spain and England are facing off today."

I think Jahan is probably right. Spain is the host of the World Cup tournament this year, and before we left Karachi, Spain and England were still in the running.

"If there is a game tonight, I'm cheering for Spain." I sigh, hoping for a taste of sweet revenge. I'm still angry with the British for treating us badly at the airport.

"You know, if Iran weren't so screwed up, I could have been the Paolo Rossi of Iran," Jahan says.

Paolo Rossi, a member of the Italian national soccer team, is Jahan's current favorite player. Back home, the walls of his bedroom are plastered with large posters of the Italian and German national soccer teams. For a while, he's been saying that either Germany or Italy will win the year's World Cup. In a way, he's right, for if he had had the same opportunities as the athletes enjoy in Europe, he might have become a world-renowned soccer player. When I watch him and his friends play, he's by far the best.

Thinking of my own potential, I say, "Well, if Iran weren't so screwed up, I could have become the Marie Curie of Iran."

"Who is Marie Curie?" Mammad asks, raising a brow.

"She was a very famous chemist. The first woman to win a Nobel Prize."

"Azadeh, you do share something in common with Marie Curie," Jahan says, nodding.

"And what may that be?" I ask, thinking that he might be referring to our common love for chemistry.

"You are *curie* as a bat." He chuckles softly at his joke, using *curie* to mean blind.

"Very funny, Jahan."

"Can you two please stop bickering and get back to what really matters, like where the hell are we going to sleep tonight?" Mammad asks. "Most hotels are probably booked to accommodate all the crazed English noblemen in town."

We walk from one hotel to the next but are unable to reserve a room. After an hour of wandering the streets, Jahan comes up with a brilliant idea.

"Correct me if I'm wrong, but I bet *hostel* means *hotel* in Spanish. Let's go inside a hostel and find out."

Hostel Nuria, the fifth hostel that we try, has a number of vacancies. I leave a deposit for three nights' rent in cash with the clerk. She hands Mammad the key, and we head for the elevator.

Next to the elevator knob, a pair of ornate iron gates joined in the middle by an antique gold doorknob reveals a dark, empty space behind. Tight spaces usually don't bother me, but I'm starting to feel claustrophobic.

A loud skidding sound approaches the lobby. Mammad twists the gold doorknob, and we step over a hollow space into the elevator. It slowly wobbles up and stops abruptly, moving up or down, several inches each time, to adjust its height with the floor. Finally, the motion stops, a buzzer sounds, and off we skip over the hollow space into the third floor lobby. A sign in the hallway points to the direction of our room, which unfortunately happens to be right next door to the noisy elevator.

Mammad inserts the key in the lock and opens the door into a pitch-black room. He slides his hand along the wall and flicks the light switch. Right next to the door, on the left-hand side, is a half bath housing a small shower stall with a curtain but no sink or toilet.

"Um, I'm no real estate agent, but isn't a half bath usually a sink plus a toilet? You know, the bare essentials?" Mammad asks.

I wander out looking for a toilet. A single toilet and sink plus a few shower stalls are located at the end of the hall.

Our room has three twin beds and two dressers in between the beds, but no built-in closet space. The squeaky beds are furnished with lumpy mattresses, faded olive-colored bedcovers, and pillows wrapped in plastic. Hanging over the middle bed, the blackened blades of a ceiling fan slowly turn, chirping like a singing sparrow.

The room lacks a mirror, radio, TV and phone, but a clock sits on top of a dresser.

"How do we tell time and call home with a dead clock and no telephone in this room?" I ask, shaking my head.

"Let's not think about that now. I'm starving," Jahan says. "How about McDonald's?"

"Great choice," I say without hesitation, since my brother and I have had the pleasure of tasting McDonald's burgers and shakes during past European vacations.

After lunch, we wander the streets for hours, asking unsuspecting Spaniards for directions to a public telephone house, but no one seems to understand our English.

"Deus ex machina!" Jahan shouts, pointing up to a building ahead with a large sign that reads *Telefónica*.

"What the hell is deus ex machina?" Mammad asks, wrinkling his forehead.

"Oh my God, Mammad. Have you read a single book in your life? It means God popping out of a machine in Greek."

"So, what's that supposed to mean?"

"Never mind, Mammad. Let's go in."

"*Un momento*," says a friendly phone operator as we walk in and ask for help. He writes down a sequence of numbers on a piece of paper and hands it to me.

We jam inside a tiny phone booth and barely manage to close the folding door behind us. The cost is about four hundred pesetas, or roughly two American dollars per minute to call home. Sweat drips from my hands as I dial the numbers on a large black rotary phone with a rotating finger plate instead of a punch-hole platform. Mamman picks up after just one ring and starts to cry.

"Don't cry, Mamman, please. We found a great place to stay in Madrid and everything is fine. I hope you're not smoking anymore," I say, trying my best to hold back tears.

"No, I gave that up last week after you called from Karachi."

"I'm glad. Smoking doesn't really suit you."

I bet Mamman has been sitting on the sofa in the family room all week long awaiting this phone call.

"Can I speak to Jahan?" Mamman asks. "Is he with you this time?"

"Yes, he is here. Tell Baba that I miss him a lot."

I choke up and hand the receiver to Jahan. He speaks to Mamman for a few minutes and cracks a few jokes. When he hangs up with tears in his eyes, my heart aches to hug him, but my mind pulls me back, for our relationship has been strained for so long.

Mammad dials his phone number as Jahan and I sit uncomfortably together. "Lodging and food are quite cheap in Madrid, much cheaper than Iran," he tells his father. "Spanish hamburgers are extremely delicious. We can last in Madrid for months on four thousand dollars. Don't worry about us too much."

As we walk out of the telephone house, Mammad tells us, "My father said Ibrahim can wire us money if we're low on cash." Ibrahim is Mammad's eldest brother who lives in Maryland in America.

"What a relief to have another source of funds besides what's left inside voojood." I say with a sigh.

Next door to the telephone house is a department store, so we decide to go in and buy some clothes. Inside, groceries and furniture are also marked for sale. I separate from the boys, and we agree to meet later.

I ride the escalator up to women's apparel, determined to buy clothing that the ayatollah will certainly despise. Looking through the racks, I go for the most revealing items: miniskirts and bright, tight tank tops. With merchandise in hand, the boys are waiting for me at the bottom of the escalator, since I forgot to give them cash before we parted. Their baskets contain shorts, T-shirts, canvas shoes, and underwear. We also buy groceries, a package of razors, batteries for the dead clock on the dresser, and cotton pillowcases to replace the plastic covers in our room.

Jahan begs to buy a small TV to watch the World Cup games, but Mammad objects. "The money we have is not for luxury items, Jahan."

I agree with Mammad but keep my mouth shut.

Back in our hostel room, I step inside the tiny shower stall and close the curtain behind me, eager to clean up and put on my brand-new floral print nightgown. Within five minutes, I experience a broad range of water temperatures, from ice cold to boiling hot that show almost no correlation to the twisting of the knobs marked red and blue. I wash up quickly and get out, feeling too exhausted to go downstairs and complain about the faulty shower.

As night falls, I realize no one cares to sleep in Madrid. Every time my eyes feel heavy, I hear people laugh and holler as they crash bottles outside or chatter inside while riding the slow, noisy elevator to their floors, only to flush a few leaky toilets before diving into their squeaky beds. I'd do just about anything to have one night of peaceful rest in my own bed in Tehran.

Looking over at Jahan snoring takes me back to those warm, sleepless summer nights at Grandma's house. "A man is blessed with a mind that comes alive and goes dead with the rise and fall of the sun," Grandma used to tell me while Grandpa snored and Jahan slept quietly through the night. I wonder what has happened to my brother's nasal passages since then. It can't be puberty, since Mammad is silent as a rock.

The rays of morning light are about to shine as I drift off into a deep sleep, only to be awakened a few hours later; the boys are up, making their own chattering sounds. I put the pillow over my head to muffle the suffocating, noisy world around me, but I'm already up.

After waiting in line to use the only toilet and sink on our floor, we dress in our new clothes and colorful canvas shoes, all clean and ready for hostel breakfast.

When Mammad sees me in a short jean miniskirt and a tight orange tank top, he whistles and says, "*Wow*, literally unveiling Azadeh. You can easily be mistaken for a Spanish beauty in this town. What do you think, Jahan?"

Jahan barely graces me with a smile and says, "She looks okay, I suppose. Slightly better than she normally does."

Rankled memories of arguing with him over meaningless subjects fill my head. Instead of responding as I normally do, I turn to look at Mammad.

"Thank you, Mammad. You look very handsome yourself."

Outside, next to our room, the elevator is open, so we hop on and press for the lobby. Suddenly, Jahan screams as his new canvas shoes fly off his feet. A small bat crawls from inside one shoe and takes flight, hovering above our heads while shrieking and flashing its sharp teeth.

The three of us yell, "SOS! Help us, please!" and run around the small space to avoid contact with the flying monster. The elevator rattles vigorously, setting off the emergency buzzer. By the time we reach the lobby, the bat has disappeared, and we can't wait to jump out.

A hostel attendant, frowning and yelling in Spanish, opens the elevator door. He shoves us to one side and steps in to silence the loud buzzer.

Mammad tries to explain our saga in broken English, but even flapping his arms and squeaking like a bat is of no use. The clerk looks mad as hell, wagging his finger while rambling before walking away.

"Is this the house of Frankenstein or what?" Jahan asks, shaking his head. "Why the hell is he mad at us? We should be mad at him for running a bat-infested hostel."

"Forget it, Jahan," Mammad says. "Let's go and eat. I am *so* hungry."

Almost everyone in the small breakfast area smokes while eating. The thick air burns my eyes, and I can taste smoke at the back of my throat. The breakfast of coffee, milk, juice, pastries, sliced bread, and cold cuts could have been decent, but the food stinks like cigarette smoke. We each grab a few items and sit around a small table.

"I'm eating breakfast at McDonald's tomorrow," I say, and the boys nod.

Outside the hostel, garbage and broken glass are scattered everywhere. All the partying people who kept me up the night before have left their signature on this otherwise charming brick sidewalk.

We walk a few blocks and enter Plaza de España, a large square teeming with life—young people kissing, licking ice creams, and having a good time—simple pleasures that I've never had the pleasure of experiencing in Iran.

At the center of the square, a large monument of a bearded man sitting on a block with a book in his lap grabs my attention. He has to be an important Spaniard, not a king, for he isn't wearing a crown; but based on the elaborate collar around his neck, he is likely a famous philosopher from the Middle Ages. He resembles Galileo and is even dressed like him, but Galileo was Italian, so that can't possibly be him. Right in front of his feet, two horsemen are cast in bronze, although it appears one is riding a donkey or a weird-looking horse with large ears sticking up. *Where have I seen these horsemen?*

Mammad's voice interrupts my thought. "Azadeh, let's get some ice cream."

We sit at the edge of a large water fountain, licking ice cream and observing the crowd. I glance around in search of a face that looks like mine, an olive-skinned teenager with dark features and loneliness in her eyes, an escapee with a name I can easily pronounce.

ᔕ ᔕ ᔕ

During the next week, the boys spend most of their waking hours at a smoky Irish pub watching the World Cup games on TV, while I mostly sit on my creaky bed in Hostel Nuria, memorizing English words from a small Farsi-English dictionary.

A few days after the World Cup finals end, the boys are still hanging out a lot doing God knows what. One afternoon, as they walk in, I glance up at the clock. It's only four thirty, which is way too early to leave for dinner.

"Azadeh, we're so lucky you weren't tagging along today," Jahan says.

"Why? Did a cute girl check you out and ask for a date?"

"Pretty much, although cute is quite an understatement," Mammad says. "We are now officially taken."

My jaw drops. "Do these girls speak any English?"

"Well, their English is better that ours, but we mainly spoke the language of *amor* with the two *señoritas*, Yolanda and Marisol. I have already kissed Yolanda on the mouth."

"Many congratulations, Mammad. Let the sun shine and the bells ring for you and Jahan. This is such exciting news, but don't expect me to hand either of you any cash to waste on foolish love affairs. Really, we can't afford it, guys."

"We need to talk about all that, Azadeh," Jahan says, looking annoyed. "We prefer if each of us keeps one-third of the remaining cash and pays for one-third of common expenses."

His aloofness fuels my anger. "We can't do that without asking our parents first," I say in one breath. "I'm going to the telephone house soon to call Baba and tell him about Yolanda and the other girl, Mary something."

"You can't do that," Jahan says through gritted teeth.

I take the dictionary from my lap and stand up, putting my hands on my hips. "Why not, Jahan? I can, and I will. I don't care if you want to have a girlfriend, but Baba shouldn't pay for your romantic escapades in Madrid."

"For your information, the girls paid for our gelatos this afternoon, and we are taking them out to dinner tonight," Mammad says, anger growing in his voice.

I turn to face him. "I would say dinner for four, even at McDonald's, costs a lot more than four scoops of gelato. Wouldn't you agree, Mammad?"

Jahan's eyes widen, and his nostrils flare as he cries out, "That's enough! We were going to invite you to dinner, but not anymore. You are on your own tonight."

"We'll continue the money discussion tomorrow. Don't wait up for us," Mammad says. He jumps in the small shower stall and starts singing Iranian love songs.

A palpable tension hangs in the air as the boys get dressed, slap on lots of cheap cologne on their freshly shaved faces, and walk out

211

without saying good-bye. The sound of their sneakers swishing against the floor dies quickly, leaving me all alone.

How could they abandon me like this? I ask, feeling as if the walls are caving in on me. Up to now, we have had dinners together every single night. *What am I going to do without them in Madrid? Who's going to eat with me or talk to me from now on?*

That night, I go to bed hungry and cry myself to sleep.

§ § §

Weeks later, the boys walk in and find me crying in bed.

"What's wrong, Azadeh?" Mammad asks as he sits next to me on the bed.

"Nothing. I'm fine. I just miss home, that's all," I say and look up.

"Sorry for not paying much attention to you in the past few weeks. But I am happy to report that Yolanda and Marisol can't wait to meet the rest of our family," Mammad says, stroking my hair.

"I guess that would be me," I say, giving him a hug. "I would love to meet them too. I'm so tired of being alone."

I agree to meet the boys and their girlfriends at a popular Madrid discotheque later, not too far from Hostel Nuria. Thrilled, I get dressed quickly and leave, heading for a large department store.

I browse for an hour, looking for items on sale, but the mustard-yellow summer dress that I really want is not here. It's right across the street, displayed in a window of an expensive-looking boutique. *Should I buy it or not?*

Minutes later, I'm wearing the dress, and everything fits just right, from the V-neckline down to the soft, flowing bottom that drapes right above my knees. "This dress is made just for me," I whisper, glancing at the mirror behind me to see how it looks from the back. Unlike the boys, who often buy meals and gifts for their new flames, I haven't yet spent any fun money on myself. *What should I do with this pretty dress?*

I return to the hostel in my new dress, shoes, and costume jewelry, feeling guilty as hell. Plus, I also bought a blow dryer, makeup, and a desk mirror to get ready for tonight.

Standing naked inside the small shower stall, I wait and pray, but the water has no intention of warming up today. Perhaps that's God's way of punishing me for being wasteful with our funds. Finally, I give up, force my body under the dinky, cold shower spray, and wash up quickly, fully awakened to showcase my disco talent that has thus far been witnessed only by family and friends at private gatherings in Tehran.

Wrapped in towels, I blow dry my shoulder-length curly hair straight in front of the small desk mirror, apply some makeup, and put on my new outfit, just in time to leave the hostel.

The entrance line to the flashy discotheque seems endless. As I walk to take my place at the end of the line, I hear Mammad's voice.

"Azadeh, we are here. Right here."

The boys are smiling from ear to ear, holding hands with their Spanish sweethearts. Yolanda and Marisol are cute but not drop-dead gorgeous. The boys have obviously left out a few flaws. Yolanda, a thin blonde, has long straight hair and lively hazel eyes, but she shows too much teeth when she smiles. Marisol, a well-endowed petite brunette, has brown shoulder-length, curly hair and dark, shiny eyes but lots of freckles on her face and body. The pairing surprises me a bit, since Jahan prefers blondes and Mammad is into brunettes.

We hug, kiss, and exchange greetings. After the formalities are done with, the union feels slightly awkward, for unlike the boys, who speak the language of amor, I need a real language to communicate with the lovely señoritas.

The disco is throbbing with noise and activity when we walk in. Loud music echoes, "All the things you do to me—and everything you said—I just can't get enough—I just can't get enough …" as people boogie on stage with a zest that I haven't seen before. We order soft drinks and sit around a table. Soon after, the boys ask their girlfriends to dance. After a few numbers, Mammad and Yolanda dance toward our table and invite me to join them. I immediately accept. Seconds later, I'm dancing like a madwoman as if I can make up for all the oppression that I had endured in the past three years. The DJ plays and replays three popular songs: "Don't You Want Me" by Human League, "Just Can't Get Enough" by Depeche Mode, and "Tainted Love" by Soft Cell.

At exactly midnight, colorful neon lights zoom in on me from all different directions as the DJ makes an announcement in Spanish. I've been dancing for hours like a wild animal set free from a cage, sweating all over my pretty, newly purchased summer dress. With lights shining on my head, I worry about my hair and pat it a few times. To my dismay, the neat-sexy-straight hairdo I walked in with has now transformed into that all too familiar big-curly-frizzy mess.

Marisol runs to me and says, "You are the dancing queen. Great performance. You won."

Before I have a chance to respond, the club scene erupts, energized by the blasting sound of ABBA's popular song "Dancing Queen." People have now formed a circle around me, and it seems as if they're clapping for me to dance. With a puzzled look on my face, I continue to choreograph and execute a combination of belly- and disco-dancing moves while singing along with, "You can dance, you can jive, having the time of your life. Dancing queen, young and sweet, only seventeen."

ABBA might as well be singing to me, a seventeen-year-old teenager having the time of her life dancing.

After the song ends, strobe lights bring people in and out of focus like holograms, as the DJ approaches and hands me an envelope. He puts a crown on my head and kisses me hard on the mouth without giving me a chance to object. Then he raises my hand, just like a referee at the end of a boxing match. Never in a million years would I have guessed a funky-looking DJ in Madrid would be my first kiss.

"*Gracias, señor*," I say and turn to make my way back to our table with a tiara on my head, feeling like Cinderella, hoping that a prince might take notice and ask me to dance.

"What's going on?" I ask.

"Congratulations. You just won a dance contest," Mammad says.

"But I never entered one."

"Never mind. The envelope you are holding contains *diez* free tickets to the club," Mammad says, holding up all his fingers. "You are *numero úno* girl."

"I am impressed, Mammad. Thanks to Yolanda, your Spanish is much improved."

"You know, in Iran, you'd get ten lashes—actually, more like thirty or thirty-five—for dancing like that in public. Here, you get a prize for it. Not bad! Not bad at all! What a difference a continent can make," Jahan says, nodding.

🕉 🕉 🕉

The next evening, a tall, handsome young man approaches me in Plaza de España. I stare at his curly brown hair that stands upright about five inches above his head before staring into his glassy, emerald eyes. He's dressed in tight, dark leather pants, a black skintight T-shirt, and leather sandals—like John Travolta in *Saturday Night Fever*. He bends over and bellows in a thundering voice with his thumbs stuck on each side of a square, mammoth-sized silver buckle in his belt.

"Joo are the dancing queen. I saw joo last night. Joo are *muy bonita* … very pretty." He repeatedly mutters phrases in Spanish, followed by an English translation.

"*Nada* Spanish," I reply, thinking that he might well be the prince who was watching me the night before, but he's certainly not dressed or groomed like one.

"English is okay. Joo are so bonita … beautiful. Joo from Turkey?"

"Nada. From Iran." I say, trying to avoid his gaze.

"Girls from Iran are muy bonita. Joo like me?"

"I don't know. Maybe. Do you have a name?"

"Juan Carlos, the same as the king of Spain. Today, I'm the king, and joo're my queen," he says, puffing out his chest and rolling his shoulders back.

There we go—the prince and his Cinderella.

"Joo want to have dinner with me?" he asks, revealing a perfect white smile.

I can't say nada to a handsome Spaniard, so I say yes, and with that, our relationship begins.

That night, in our room at Hostel Nuria, I tell Jahan and Mammad, "I'm now officially taken. I have a handsome boyfriend, and his name is Juan Carlos. He saw me dancing last night, and tonight, he bought me dinner plus three scoops of gelato."

"Great move, Azadeh. That'll certainly bring our costs down," Jahan says.

"Be careful. Don't go anywhere with him alone, Azadeh," Mammad warns.

"I won't. I promise. You know what Juan Carlos told me about the monument of the bearded man in Plaza de España?"

"What?" Jahan asks, curious as I have been since the first day I saw it.

"That's the guy who wrote *Don Quixote*, and that's why he's holding a book. The two bronze horsemen in front of his feet are the main characters in the book, Don Quixote and his best friend. I forgot what the author's name is again, but Juan Carlos said he was the most famous author who ever lived."

"You're right! I thought I had seen those goofy-looking horsemen somewhere, but I had no idea the guy who wrote *Don Quixote* was Spanish."

"Me too. Good night, guys."

"Who is Don Quixote?" Mammad whispers into the dark.

"Dear God, Mammad. Ask Yolanda, *please*," Jahan says in a condescending voice.

I close my eyes and think of Juan Carlos, hoping that he'll show up for our date tomorrow.

The more I mull over what Juan Carlos said about *Don Quixote*, the more I disagree with him. That's not the best book ever written. *Oliver Twist* is ten times better than *Don Quixote*. Reluctantly, in this case, England has my vote. It's odd that I can't even think of one novel that's written by an Iranian author. I don't understand why our stories are always told in poetry and almost never in prose. I bet Grandma could have been a famous author if she were literate and could write her stories down.

I fall asleep dreaming of Grandma, not alive but molded into a large monument in the middle of a busy square in Tehran. She is sitting on a block with a book in her lap, just like the bearded man in Plaza de España. I open the book, and inside the pages, Grandma comes alive. She's twelve, frightened to death. Her mother is decorating her feet and hands with henna as her aunt plucks her eyebrows, preparing her for marriage to Grandpa, a handsome young man fourteen years her senior.

ဢ ဢ ဢ

During the following weeks, I spend all my waking hours with Juan Carlos. We often meet in the early afternoon at Gran Vía metro station. From there, we take a train and spend all day sightseeing, eating, flirting, and kissing a whole lot. Madrid reminds me so much of Tehran before the Islamic Revolution: the busy sidewalks, young men whistling and staring at pretty women passing by, cars honking and cutting pedestrians off as they try to cross busy intersections, and dark, crammed alleys that open into enormous, well-manicured squares.

Thanks to Juan Carlos, I can now imagine myself living in Madrid with my family, adjusting to the Spanish way of life. Unlike me, however, who can't wait to renounce my nationality, Juan Carlos takes tremendous pride in his heritage. He often exaggerates the importance of everything we see, from small sculptures in museums to large, ancient buildings. I wish I could take him sightseeing in Iran, especially the historical city of Isfahan. Once he sees the breathtaking turquoise-and-gold mosques of Isfahan, shimmering like jewels under the sun, he may change his mind about Madrid's rightful place in time. Contrary to what he says, Spain has never been the center of ancient art and civilization the way Persia, Greece, and Rome have been.

Most nights, Juan Carlos and I dance at discotheques until dawn. I'm now living the life of a happy-go-lucky teenager in Madrid, but sadly, our courtship is about to end. Juan Carlos has plans to leave the following week by train to Sweden. He's been telling me almost every day, "Joo should come with me to Sweden. We can work during the day and party all night long." I would love to go with him, but I can't, since I don't have a visa.

It breaks my heart to think of him gone and me again alone in Spain, wandering about. But for now, the present is what counts. Juan Carlos has planned a big surprise for me, and I'm not going to worry about what happens in three days when he's gone. Maybe I'll still be here when he gets back from Sweden, and we can pick up where we left off.

ဪ ဪ ဪ

Juan Carlos shows up at the Gran Vía metro station, looking even more peculiar than his idol, John Travolta. A large pair of binoculars is slung around his neck, and a white handkerchief is tied onto his large belt buckle.

"Why are you wearing these?" I ask, touching his binoculars.

"Joo'll see. It's a big surprise. Let's go."

He ties a white handkerchief onto my belt buckle, grabs my hand, and off we hop on a train bound for Las Ventas.

We exit the train and walk up the stairs to the street level, where I see a large, charming brick sports stadium ahead. *That's my big surprise?* I sigh. I'd rather go dancing than watch a sports event that can go on and on.

I look up and smile at him, and he smiles back. He flashes our tickets at the booth, and arm in arm, we stroll into the Las Ventas stadium. The hot and muggy air smells of sweat and cigar smoke. We walk down a set of steep, narrow steps and sit on concrete rows. Not far from our seats, enormous bulls with razor-sharp horns are held captive behind bars inside separate stalls.

"What's up with the bulls?" I ask, excited that this may not be a sporting event.

Juan Carlos smiles. "Be patient, my bonita Azadeh. Joo will soon find out."

I look up and see three flags flying high above our seats against a bright, cloudless blue sky. The middle one is the national flag of Spain.

I wonder if this could be a rodeo show like in Hollywood cowboy movies. If so, it might be fun to watch.

The stadium is nearly packed when loud horns begin to blare. The jubilant crowd rises, erupting in cheers and applause, and I do the same.

As we sit down, a door near us flies open with a bang. A massive bull charges out, roaming the ring while kicking up dirt and slamming its horns into concrete walls. On the opposite side of the arena, I see three men wearing magenta capes and matching socks pulled high up over their white tights march into the field.

"Look, the banderilleros are in the ring, Azadeh!" Juan Carlos exclaims as they stomp their feet and jerk their capes.

Suddenly, the bull turns and charges toward the banderilleros. To my horror, they quickly work in unison to plunge sharp yellow-and-red darts into the bull's neck and shoulders.

How stupid of me. This is a bullfight. I sigh, remembering reading something about the event in one of Hemingway's novels. The bull will be tormented and killed at the end, and I don't want to see any of it up close.

"Juan Carlos, I feel very sick. Can we leave now and do something else, *please?*"

Annoyed, he whispers above my ears. "What? What are joo saying? Joo don't like this? We can't leave. This is exciting. Joo have to see it."

When I glance up, a new character is riding a white blindfolded horse with heavy, colorful pads draping alongside its midsection.

He sits erect in the middle of the saddle wearing a tan-and-gold embroidered jacket, matching pants, long socks, and a Spanish hat. His hands are clasped around the hilt of a giant lance.

"Here comes the picador," Juan Carlos announces, gleefully rubbing his hands together.

The picador roams the stadium once and stops near the sideline, peering at the banderilleros who are still busy provoking the bull.

Suddenly, the bull charges toward the horse. Juan Carlos rises and screams as the bull thrusts its horn into the padded belly of the horse, and the picador wedges his sharp lance deep inside the bull's shoulder. Red blood pours down its neck and back. The banderilleros insert more darts into its neck, and more blood, thick and maroon, pours over its sides.

My head throbs in pain as I look up and see yet another cartoonish character wearing an elaborate red-and-gold embroidered suit, making his grand entrance as the picador leaves the arena.

"Look over there, Azadeh. That's the matador. Get up," Juan Carlos orders. He stands up, clapping his hands and stomping his feet.

The matador moves slowly, taking wide steps with grace and confidence. He prances around the ring, puffs out his chest, and throws his Mickey Mouse cap onto the ground.

While the matador is excited and ready to showcase his talent, the poor bull is injured and tired, but not yet defeated, still twisting, panting, and bucking his head.

The matador yells, stomps his feet, and shakes his red cape.

The bull charges at him and sails under the matador's cape as he swiftly swivels his hips to the side.

The crowd cheers and screams, "*Olé!*"

The matador continues to tango across the ring, occasionally turning his back and strutting away with macho confidence, leaving the bull in a desperate search of his cape.

Suddenly, the matador stops the show by hiding his cape behind him. He thoughtfully observes the bull while walking slowly toward the sideline.

The next time I look up, the matador is standing at the center of the arena with a long lance in his hand. He holds his cape off to the side and raises the lance straight out—parallel to the ground—in front of him, facing the bull wobbling on its feet.

The bull looks up and charges at him.

Just before they collide, the matador plunges the lance deep into the bull's neck and releases his hand. The lance stands upright at first but quickly bends over on the bull's back. The poor animal is still standing up, confused and in pain.

I wonder if anyone else in this arena feels like I do, hoping for the bull to turn around and gore the arrogant matador with its sharp horns before it dies. But that can't possibly happen, since the unsightly comical banderilleros are back on the scene, waving their purple capes wildly, befuddling the bull until it collapses onto the ground. Blood squirts from its nose, mouth, neck, and back as its body heaves before the angels arrive on the scene to claim its tortured soul.

I look down and hold my head in my hands, wondering if there is a place left on this earth where I belong—a place where crazy things that go on in Iran and Spain are outlawed.

The crowd is now standing up, waving white handkerchiefs in the air while screaming, "Olé!"

"Get up, Azadeh. Joo have to see this," Juan Carlos says, his binoculars zoomed on the kill.

"Nada," I reply in a firm voice. I wish I could just get up and leave, but I can't. I don't have any cash on me, and my metro tickets are tucked deep inside his tight leather pants pocket. Never again will I go somewhere without carrying money in my purse.

Cheers and applause fill the air as the matador parades around the ring holding his Mickey Mouse cap out in front of him. In the background, a group of men and horses enter the arena, tie up the bull, and drag its lifeless body out by its neck.

Minutes later, it starts all over again with a fresh bull. How foolish of me to think that the fall of the Roman Empire had closed the chapter on gladiators and coliseum-style executions. I close my eyes and rub my temples to soothe the throbbing pain on both sides of my head. At this very moment, the ayatollah seems like an angel compared to the crazed people in this arena who can't wait for the second bull to be tortured to its death in front of their cheerful eyes.

Each time Juan Carlos rises and cheers, my feelings for him subside into angry sensations, anguish, and confusion. I can no longer think of him as a gentleman who listens intently and speaks softly, bringing some level of normalcy and security into my otherwise uncertain life in this foreign land.

The crowd's bloodthirsty appetite is finally sated after eight bulls are brutally murdered, and the pandemonium ends in standing ovation. Outside the stadium, butchers in white bloody aprons are selling meat. Beads of sweat bubble on their foreheads as they cut into the flesh of the hanging corpses.

The strong stench of blood fills my stomach with pain and grief, reminding me of the revolution days when blood was all that I saw and smelled on the streets.

A large chattering crowd has now formed a long line to purchase a piece of bull delicacy. Juan Carlos approaches the end of the line and asks, "Would joo like some fresh bull to cook and eat at my house? Papa is not home tonight."

"Nada. I feel *very* sick. I must go home *now*," I say, thinking that he must be absolutely clueless.

He looks the other way and starts to walk ahead of me toward the metro station.

"See joo tomorrow at eight. Good-bye," he says nonchalantly, handing me my metro ticket without kissing or hugging me.

I take a seat, close my eyes, and inhale, relieved that crazed Juan Carlos isn't sitting next to me reminiscing about the afternoon's events. The sky darkens with each passing of the train as it threads in and out of tunnels. It's after nine when I exit the Gran Vía station. As I walk back to Hostel Nuria, memories of home wash over me. I wish to be there now, gossiping with my girlfriends, taking my little sister out for a treat, talking to Mamman, and going to amusement parks and movies with Baba. I want them all back in my life. This place is not my home. I don't relate to anyone, I don't enjoy what people do here for fun, and I don't believe they care for me at all.

§ § §

The next day, I meet Juan Carlos at the Gran Vía discotheque, the same place where he had watched me dance my way up to the coveted title of dancing queen. I feel awkward standing next to him, not knowing how to act or what to say. Thank God Yolanda, Marisol, and the boys are about to join us shortly.

When our party assembles, Juan Carlos hugs the girls and flatters them the same way he boosted my ego three weeks earlier. By the end of the night, though, Juan Carlos and Yolanda are glued together on the stage, slow dancing, her head pressed tightly against his broad chest, his tongue in her ear nibbling away.

Suddenly, Mammad kicks the table and turns in my direction. "This is all your fault for introducing this gigolo to my girlfriend!"

"She isn't an innocent bystander, Mammad. Obviously, she doesn't love you," I say, feeling a pang of jealously myself. I pick up my soda and swallow a few sips, imaging myself out there kicking Yolanda in the shin.

"You're probably right, Azadeh," Mammad says, letting out a heavy sigh. "We were going to break up soon, anyway. She's going to Sweden in a few days."

The news of Yolanda's departure to Sweden makes me almost choke on my drink. "You're kidding, Mammad. What a coincidence! Juan Carlos is also going to Sweden."

"Well, then, that explains why they're so into each other. I'm *so* tired of this place and its disloyal citizens. Can they at least not do it in front of us?"

"Forget about them, Mammad. I hope we can get our visas to go to America. I can't wait to meet Mr. Banki later this week."

Mr. Banki is my father's good friend from college. He lives in Los

Angeles, and Baba has finally convinced him to fly to Madrid with his twenty-four-year-old American girlfriend, Sharon, to accompany us to the American embassy. We're meeting them on Thursday in the Gran Vía Grand Hotel in Madrid.

"Don't get your hopes up, Azadeh. I have heard the American embassy hasn't issued a single visa to an Iranian for months now. If our passports are graced with a rejection stamp, we can't even go back to the embassy for another six months."

The thought of spending six long months in Spain terrifies me to the core. I close my eyes and pray to God for a different outcome in our case.

After that night, I never see Juan Carlos again. I can only imagine that by now he and Yolanda are together somewhere in a picturesque Swedish village, milking cows during the day and making love all night long. A part of me no longer blames him for cheering during a bullfight, because like anyone else, he is a product of his past. Likewise, it scares me to think that the next generation of kids in Iran will likely feel completely content living a religious life because, unlike me, they have no memory of how things were before their time.

ৡ   ৡ   ৡ

A few days after the disco disaster, we meet Mr. Banki and Sharon in the lobby of Gran Vía Grand Hotel.

Sharon's eyes are hazel, large, and lively, accentuated by long eyelashes covered in thick mascara. Her long hair is brown and wavy, and she's wearing a white, see-through shirt with shoulder pads over a long jean skirt. Poor Mr. Banki, a balding, potbellied, middle-aged man, looks more like her father than her boyfriend.

Sharon greets me in a warm, friendly voice. "Hello, dear. Are you all ready to come to the United States of America? I'm here to help you get your visas, and let me tell you all that we're going to get them tomorrow."

She then proceeds to give each of us a bear hug. My heart swells at the thought of leaving Spain for the United States with Sharon sitting next to me on the plane. While giggling like a schoolgirl, Sharon invites us to lunch, but Mr. Banki quickly interrupts.

"Sharon, we have other plans for today," he says curtly and turns to look at us.

"Kids, we'll see you tomorrow at the American embassy early in the morning. You can take a taxi to get there."

On the way back to Hostel Nuria, Mammad says, "Mr. Banki seemed kind of rude. I bet he couldn't wait for us to leave."

"He's always been like that," I say, remembering the many times I had seen him at our house in Tehran, never cracking a smile, always cold and serious.

"Why is Sharon going out with him? She's so much better looking than he is," Jahan asks, shooting up a brow.

"Well, that's certainly good news for you, Jahan," I say, smiling.

"Why?"

"Because that means American girls are not that picky, so you may get lucky if we get there."

The next morning, we meet Sharon and Mr. Banki in front of the American embassy at four o'clock. Already, a bustling crowd of mostly Iranians is lined up behind the closed gate.

By noon, not a single Iranian has walked out of the embassy victorious, smiling, showing off his or her approval visa stamp. But Sharon keeps insisting, "Everything is fine. Trust me; you'll get your visas in no time. Don't worry."

My only hope is that no other Iranian is standing alongside a persistent, attractive American chaperone.

We're next in line when a middle-aged black man in a full suit and tie flags us over to his booth. We approach and present him with our passports.

"I am very sorry, kids. I can't grant visas to Iranians."

His throaty voice echoes in my ears as I swallow and watch his hand reach for that infamous rejection stamp. The thought of spending even one more day in Madrid brings tears to the back of my eyes.

"Just wait. Wait a second. Hold on, please," Sharon interrupts, and the man stops reaching for the stamp. "Come on now. I know these kids. They're good kids, and they'll be staying with me. All they want to do is to come to the United States for a few months to learn English. That's all. I have signed them up to take ESL classes at a community college in Los Angeles." She continues to talk as she hands him college registration forms.

He examines the papers, takes off his thick, black-framed glasses, leans forward on his chair, and stabs his desk with a pencil a few times. Then he glances up as I look down and collapse into tears.

"Young lady, why are you crying?" he asks, staring at me as though he can read the thoughts of despair imprinted on my forehead.

"I don't want to live in Madrid. I don't speak any Spanish. I don't know how to go back to Iran. We have friends in America, but we have no one in Madrid." I choke up and shed more tears.

"Well," he says with a sigh, rubbing his forehead. "In that case, I will grant you a six-month student visa, but you have to promise me to leave the United States before your visas expire."

"I'll promise you, I mean, we—my brother, my cousin, and I— we all promise you. Thank you, sir," I say quickly, my heart almost bursting out of my chest.

"You're most welcome," he says, opening each passport and punching in the approval stamp. "Now, go on, young lady. Pack your bags. Good luck to you, your brother, and your cousin."

I look at him and smile. He sticks his thumb up in the air, and I do the same while laughing in my head: that gesture in my culture is equivalent to giving an American the middle finger.

Outside the embassy, Sharon hugs me tightly as I cry on her shoulder. "This is unbelievable, just unbelievable. I'm so happy for you all. We have to celebrate tonight," Sharon says, her light hazel eyes sparkling like jewels in the bright sunlight.

"We can't, Sharon. We have other plans," Mr. Banki objects like he did last time, and we part shortly thereafter.

That night, I go to the telephone house to call home. The phone rings a few times before Baba picks up, and we exchange jubilant greetings.

"Baba, today is the *best* day of my life. Thank you for sending me with Jahan."

"I have no regrets, Azadeh. You were right, and I was wrong. Have a nice journey to America. Our thoughts are with you. Good-bye, my lovely daughter."

"Good-bye, Baba jan." I hang up, feeling a rush of relief to have finally won Baba's approval.

§   §   §

We show our passports and tickets to board a United Airlines flight to Los Angeles.

A middle-aged stewardess in a navy-blue suit and high heels guides me to my seat and hands me a pillow and blanket. Jahan is seated a few rows back, since we purchased our tickets late, and only a few scattered seats were available by then. Mammad left a few hours earlier on a different flight to Baltimore to stay with his brother in Maryland.

An old lady sitting next to me asks, "What's your name, sweetie?"

"Azadeh," I say, smiling.

"Zaita, what an interesting name. Where are you from, Zaita?" she asks as she fastens her seat belt.

"E-run," I say, humored by the odd pronunciation of my name.

"You mean *I-ran*, good heavens. How old are you?"

"Seventeen." I say, puzzled by the odd pronunciation of my country's name.

"My granddaughter Emily is also seventeen …"

The old lady's tiny posture, sweet smile, and friendly voice remind me so much of Grandma. Her granddaughter is so lucky to still have her in her life.

I fasten my seat belt and lean my head against the seat as I watch the old lady fall asleep. Before long, my head fills with images of me laughing and flirting with handsome men in college, the same way I saw it happen in so many movies. I bet if cranky Mr. Banki can find himself an attractive American partner like Sharon, so can I.

Frequent food service often wakes up the old lady, giving me a rare opportunity to ask how to pronounce the highlighted words in my small dictionary. She's a retired elementary school teacher, which explains why she's so patient with me, enunciating words over and over until I say them just right.

After twelve hours, the plane begins to descend toward Los Angeles International Airport. As we get closer, I feel a shiver climb up my spine. I crane my neck to look down on the magnificent HOLLYWOOD sign, imprinted in large white letters across a hillside, an image I had seen before on a postcard. At this moment, for the first time, I feel completely at peace with my decision to leave Iran, a decision that has made space for an unknown future to enrich my life with new challenges and surprises yet to unfold.

Soon I'll find out if America *is* the land of the free, where you can become who you were born to be.

❧ The Sky Detective

Stanford, December 2004

The phone rings in my office at Stanford University. I have a feeling that's Baba calling me.

"Azadeh, I see you!" Baba screams into the phone.

I hold the receiver back, smiling. "See me where?"

"It's you in *Time*, this beautiful picture of you floating in clouds."

In the photograph, I'm resting my arms on a deck of dark, reddish clouds looking down on the earth as my reflection glances up at the sky. A golden key and colored text identify me as THE SKY DETECTIVE: LOOKING FOR CLUES, ABOVE AND BELOW.

"I know, Baba. I've been working with *Time* on this article for a while."

"Why didn't you tell us?" He sighs.

"I wanted to surprise you, Baba. I know you read *Time* from cover to cover."

I have received a number of prestigious accolades before, but this one I treasure the most, for I know it means the world to Baba.

"Surprise me!" He sighs again. "I almost had a heart attack when I turned the page. I'm so proud of you, Azadeh. What have you done this time?"

"Nothing. Just the usual—ozone, volcanoes, clouds, atmosphere ..."

To my dismay, Baba is probably running out to buy thirty copies of *Time*, or that's what he told me before we hung up. I pleaded with him not to, and as always, he agreed, but I'm sure I'll be receiving a flood of congratulatory phone calls from his colleagues and friends later tonight.

I reach for the copy of *Time* on my desk to look at the picture inside. The reddish glow of the clouds takes me back to my adolescent years when I struggled hard to figure out what was in the sky that made it shimmer just before sundown. Today, I know all there is to know about the sky—the sunset glows, the clouds, the rainbows, and a whole suite of interesting phenomena undetectable to the naked eye. Now when I look up and see a rainbow, I don't ask how and why it forms; its existence can be explained by the way sunlight interacts with air and water drops and the medium between the two. Instead, in the beauty of the colors, I often see Grandma's warm brown eyes smiling on me.

I once asked her, "What makes a rainbow in the sky?"

"A rainbow is the God's bow of promise," she said. "A token that a bridge exists between heaven and earth."

I stared at the sparkling rainbow in front of us that arched over the entire Caspian Sea and wondered what was really above the rainbow: more blues skies or heavens? That was when I was eight, and Grandma was alive and healthy. Eight years later, after a revolution and a short battle with cancer, she passed on. The look in her dying eyes, sunken holes filled with so much pain, haunts me even more now that I am a mother myself. She never got a chance to kiss her son good-bye, for the Revolutionary Guards were after Uncle Muhammad, like they were after so many people who publicly opposed the ayatollah.

As I read the *Time* article, memories of thumbing through doctored copies of *Time* with my next-door neighbor during the shah's reign flash in my head—entire pages torn out, articles blackened in ink, and warning messages in Farsi stamped on the sides of the black markings. I wonder what the government of Iran will do with this article, a story about a successful Iranian woman working with *the* enemy in their eyes. Are they going to tear all the pages out or mask my unveiled head and the unflattering statements about the ayatollah in black ink? I hope they refrain, for unlike the times of the shah, the truth is only a mouse click away.

Weeks after the *Time* article was published, I receive a postcard from Germany written in Uncle Mahmood's messy handwriting: *Remember what I told you when you were eight? Improvise, child. That's what makes you become a leader later in life. Liked your "voodoo" picture in* Time!

I was expecting this postcard, as that's the way Uncle Mahmood keeps in touch with his family in America. Uncle considering me to be a leader now, although I don't view myself as one, would likely mean that I am on the right track to make a difference in the world.

I once asked Uncle, "Why don't you sign your name on your postcards?"

"Don't you already know it's me?" he replied, rubbing his chin.

"I guess so," I said, laughing. "You always have a logical answer for what you do. Uncle, I have a question for you."

"Shoot."

"Why did you stop practicing geology?"

"Don't you already know why?"

He was right. I did know. Uncle had spent the last four decades helping refugees in Germany and writing books and articles about the dire political situation in Iran.

That night, after I finish reviewing a science proposal, I jot down a few childhood memories, hoping to gain a better insight into my past—what it all meant, how to make it count, and ways to make amends with the people I left behind.

This is all for you, Najmieh. It's to let the world know that you existed and that your life had a purpose—that I write this book. In the end, your life, my life, or any person's life, rich or poor, is just a story that dies with you if not told. I recently learned that your name means star in Farsi. I hope someday I'll be able to tell you that you have been and will always be the guiding star of my life. Sadly, the revolution that promised to change the way of life for you and people like you turned out to be a sham. I'm afraid Iran will never be free so long as ruthless shahs and unholy ayatollahs have their eyes on it.

Acknowledgments

Thank you, Dr. Linda Joy Myers, Dr. Jacqueline Doyle, Dr. Adina Paytan, Laurie McLean, Karen Gentzler, Mahnaz Fashandi, Eren Goknar, Kara Levine, Lilah Fox, Jerry Alexander, Maura Sutter, Jill Goodfriend, Kathy Pagan, Mandana Biegi, Narsis Tabazadeh, Janneke Jobis-Brown, Debbie Kantorik, Nicole Moore, Byddi Lee, Catherine Thrush, Martha Kendall, Martha Engber, Doug Stillinger, John Duel, and Jordan Rosenfeld, for helping me turn my manuscript into a published book.

Thank you, Dr. Brian Toon, Dr. Richard Turco, Dr. Howard Reiss, Dr. Jack Kaye, Dr. Susan Solomon, and Estelle Condon, for encouraging and mentoring me in science.

Thank you, Uncle Mahmood, for introducing me to chemistry when I was young.

Thank you, Mamman, Baba, Afshan, Afshin, and my dear friend Lili Haghighi, for assisting me with personal and historical facts described in this memoir.

Thank you, Dionna, Daniel, and Jessica, for brightening my life beyond my expectations.

And thank you, Dave Peterson and the members of the Menlo Church, for teaching me to experience God in a fresh and a meaningful way.

MAR 0 9 2016

CPSIA information can be obtained
at www.ICGtesting.com
Printed in the USA
LVOW04s1432030216
473522LV00019B/737/P